C(

Intercultural Philosophy

Philosophy and the Global Context
Series Editor: Michael Krausz, Bryn Mawr College

This new series addresses a range of emerging global concerns. It situates philosophical efforts in their global and cultural contexts, and it offers works from thinkers whose cultures are challenged by globalizing movements. Comparative and intercultural studies address such social and political issues as the environment, poverty, consumerism, civil society, tolerance, colonialism, global ethics, and community in cyberspace. They also address related methodological issues of translation and cross-cultural understanding.

Intellectual Property: Moral, Legal, and International Dilemmas (1997) by Adam D. Moore

Ethics of Consumption: The Good Life, Justice, and Global Stewardship (1998) edited by David A. Crocker and Toby Linden

Alternative Visions: Paths in the Global Village (1998) by Fred Dallmayr

Philosophical Reflections on the Changes in Eastern Europe (1998) by William L. McBride

Intercultural Philosophy (2000) by Ram Adhar Mall

Formal Transgression (2000) by Eddy M. Souffrant

Intercultural Philosophy

Ram Adhar Mall

ROWMAN & LITTLEFIELD PUBLISHERS, INC.
Lanham • Boulder • New York • Oxford

ROWMAN & LITTLEFIELD PUBLISHERS, INC.

Published in the United States of America
by Rowman & Littlefield Publishers, Inc.
4720 Boston Way, Lanham, Maryland 20706
http://www.rowmanlittlefield.com

12 Hid's Copse Road
Cumnor Hill, Oxford OX2 9JJ, England

British Library Cataloguing in Publication Information Available

Library of Congress Cataloging-in-Publication Data

Mall, Ram Adhar, 1937–
    Intercultural philosophy / Ram Adhar Mall.
        p.   cm. — (Philosophy and the global context)
    Includes bibliographical references and index.
    ISBN 0–8476–9278–7 (alk. paper). — ISBN 0-8476-9279-5 (pbk. :
alk. paper)
    1. Philosophy, Comparative.   2. Philosophy and civilization.
I. Title.   II. Series.
B59.M35   2000
100—dc21   99-37921
                                                              CIP

Printed in the United States of America

⊖™ The paper used in this publication meets the minimum requirements of
American National Standard for Information Sciences—Permanence of Paper for
Printed Library Materials, ANSI/NISO Z39.48–1992.

Contents

Preface   ix

Introduction   xi

Chapter 1   Intercultural Philosophy—A Conceptual Clarification   1

Preliminary Remarks   1
The Hermeneutic Situation Today   2
Culture and Philosophy   4
The Concept of Intercultural Philosophy   5
Cultural Encounters   7
Interculturality Before Multiculturality   8
Philosophy and Interculturality   9
Notes   11

Chapter 2   Toward a Theory of an Analogous Hermeneutics   13

Preliminary Remarks   13
The Concept of Interculturality   14
The Concept of an Analogous Intercultural Hermeneutics   15
Toward an Ethos of Interculturality   17
Asia Versus Europe or Universism Versus Universalism   19
Notes   23

Chapter 3   Hermeneutics of the One Under Different Names   25

Universality and Particularity   25
Original Context   26
The Import of the Vedic Dictum Today   27
The Idea of "Religio Perennis"   28
The Vedic Dictum and the Idea of "Philosophia Perennis"   29
Toward a Metonymic Theory of One Truth Under
    Different Names   31
Notes   32

Chapter 4   Intercultural Philosophy and Postmodernity   35

The De Facto Hermeneutic Situation   35
The Concept of Interculturality   36

The Concept of Postmodernity   38
Interculturality and Postmodernity   41
Modernity, Postmodernity, Interculturality, and Beyond   42
Notes   43

Chapter 5   An Intercultural Philosophy of Unity Without Uniformity   45

Preliminary Remarks   45
The Principle of Unity   46
A Critical Examination of Hegel's Philosophy of Unity   49
Toward a Concept of a Nonreductive, Open, and Normative
   Hermeneutics   52

Chapter 6   Two Metaphors of Time-Arrow and Time-Cycle   59

The Thesis Defended   59
An Empirico-Phenomenological Approach   60
Time-Arrow and Time-Cycle   61
A Critical Comparison   62
Three Factors in Time Consciousness   64
An Intercultural Perspective   65
Temporality and Historicity   65
Concluding Remarks   66
Notes   67

Chapter 7   Metonymic Reflections on Shamkara's Concept of Brahman
            and Plato's Seventh Epistle   69

Preliminary Remarks   69
Shamkara's Concept of the Nondual, the Nirguna Brahman   70
Plato's Concept of the One and the Good (Hen and Agathon) and
   His Epistle VII   74
Shamkara and Plato Compared and Contrasted   77
Concluding Remarks   78
Notes   80

Chapter 8   The God of Phenomenology in Comparative Contrast to Those
            of Philosophy and Theology   83

Husserl's Religious Leanings   83
Husserl's Concept of Teleology   84
Two Paths to God: The Historical and the Philosophical   85
The Program of Phenomenology in Relation to Teleology
   and Theology   85
Phenomenology of Religion   87
Hume, Husserl, and Hegel   89
Husserl and Scheler   90
Husserl's Phenomenology and the Problem of God's Transcendence
   and Immanence   91
Husserl, the Phenomenologist, and Husserl, the Believer   92
Notes   93

Chapter 9   The Concept of the Absolute—An Intercultural Perspective   99

Preliminary Remarks   99
Toward the Concept of an Overlapping Absolute   100
An Interreligious Hermeneutics   101
Philosophy of Values and the Absolute in Indian Thought   102
An Intercultural Concept of Tolerance   104
Notes   107

Chapter 10   Europe in the Mirror of World Cultures—On the Myth of the
Europeanization of Humanity: A Non-European Discovery
of Europe   109

Historical Remarks   109
On the Myth "Europe"   111
"European" as an Adjective to the Name Philosophy   112
On European Reason   112
European Culture   113
On the Idea of European Unity   116
Helping to Give the Adjective Its Right   117
On the Place of Eurocentric Difference   119
Europe and the Term *History*   120
Notes   122

Bibliography   125

Index   145

About the Author   155

Preface

Various papers presented and published during the last few years have been considered in the process of writing this book. Chapter 1 is mainly a revised and expanded version of two papers presented (in German) and discussed first at the international conference "The Structure of the Intercultural World" held in Kyoto in 1995 and published in the International Institute for Advanced Studies, Kyoto, reports the same year. The expanded version of the paper was also delivered as the keynote address at the international conference of the Society of Intercultural Philosophy held at Bremen in 1995 and was published in volume 5 of the Studies in Intercultural Philosophy series.

Chapter 2 is a revised version of a paper presented at the international conference "China and the West in Dialogue" held at the University of Trier in Germany in 1997.

Chapter 3 is an expanded version of an article published in *Relativism, Suffering and Beyond: Essays in Honour of Bimal Krishna Matilal.*

Chapter 4 was written for this volume except for a portion based on a paper read and discussed at the international conference "Postmodernity and the Uprise of Cultural Studies" held in Maastricht in 1997.

Chapter 5 is a revised and condensed version of a paper presented at an international conference in Durban in 1985 and published in *Focus on Quality.*

Chapter 6 is an expanded version of a paper presented at the international conference "Time and Temporality in Intercultural Perspective," held at Rotterdam in 1995 and published in volume 4 of the series Studies in Intercultural Philosophy in 1996.

Chapter 7 is a revised version of an article published in the *Journal of the Indian Council of Philosophical Research* in 1992. This article was a revised version of a paper originally presented and discussed at the International Congress of Vendanta, held in Oxford, Ohio, in 1990.

Chapter 8 is a revised version of an article published in *Husserl Studies* 8 (1991).

Chapter 9 has been rewritten for this volume and was first presented as a paper at the international conference in Tunis in 1994 and published in *Valeurs et Absolu* in Tunis 1995.

Chapter 10 was written for this volume.

I am grateful to my colleagues, students, and friends who gave me the opportunity to present and discuss my ideas. I also acknowledge my debt to the members of my "seminar privatissime," Udo Classen, Morteza Ghasempur, Dieter Lohmar,

Hermann-Josef Scheidgen, and Notker Schneider, with whom I have been discussing important philosophical topics in intercultural perspectives for the last twenty-five years. This private circle has been and still is one of the main sources for the development of my thought.

The idea to collect some of my papers and to write a few more for this volume was born during a discussion with my colleague and friend Michael Krausz in Kyoto in 1997. He suggested I make some of my ideas regarding intercultural philosophy available to English readers.

For the unfailing help I have received from my wife, Renate Mall, for all these years, I can hardly find words to adequately express my gratitude. She prepared the word-processed manuscript of this volume with the assistance of Michael Hubig and Gita Mall, who also deserve thanks.

Introduction

In my attempt to answer the question, "What is intercultural philosophy?" I find myself caught up in a paradox that I can neither avoid nor resolve fully, for I am simultaneously an insider and an outsider. To think from within more than one tradition is both a disturbing experience and quite difficult to achieve. It has been my experience that belonging to different cultures does not make one unfit to do philosophy interculturally; rather, intercultural belonging favors this type of philosophy. All ways of doing philosophy are committed to the universal unity of one philosophia perennis; however, this unit is not already fixed but a regulative idea toward which to ceaselessly strive.

This paradoxical situation is also promising because the phenomenon of interculturality is not just an intellectual and aesthetic category for me. It is also an existential and experiential one. My Indian cultural background and education along with my study of and training in European philosophy for the past forty years provide me with the opportunity to do philosophy in an intercultural perspective and to view one perspective from the point of view of the other. All of the essays in this book contribute to a theory and a practice of intercultural thinking that has been one of the central areas of my teaching and research, particularly in Germany, for the past ten years.

The term philosophy is defined in multiple ways, not only intraculturally but also interculturally. There are two methodological moves to learn what philosophy is about: first, by concentrating on the questions, and second, by concentrating on the answers. The first move is more promising than the second one, for philosophical questions not only outnumber philosophical answers but also are more persisting and lasting. There is, in other words, a primacy of questions over answers in human life; the discipline called philosophy is no exception to this rule. Thus, one of the best ways to know what philosophy is about is to ask the question, "What do we do when we do philosophy?" There is some form of Wittgensteinean "family resemblance" to be found, although more with regard to the philosophical questions than to that of the answers.

Intercultural philosophical thinking rejects the idea of the total purity of a culture as a myth or a fiction. This rejection applies even to philosophy, which is one of the finest products of the human mind and culture. In this context, it is necessary to raise one general question: "How do European, Chinese, Indian, African, and Latin American philosophies justify their being European, Chinese, Indian, African, and Latin American while simultaneously sharing in the universal applicability of the term philosophy?" Any answer to this question must consider the cross-cultural elements that shape all philosophical traditions to various degrees.

It is wrong to think that intercultural philosophy is just a trendy expression in the wake of postmodern thinking and necessitated by today's global context. Despite the liberal pluralism common to both intercultural philosophy and postmodern thinking, the phenomenon of intercultural thinking, far from being an outcome of postmodernity, exists in its own right beyond mere temporality, historicity, and contextuality.

Intercultural philosophical thinking thus rejects any absolutistic and exclusive claim of philosophical tradition—whether European or non-European—to be in sole possession of the one philosophical truth. Such absolutistic claims lead to a narrow culturalism contrary to the open and tolerant spirit of intercultural thinking.

The general term philosophy possesses both cultural and cross-cultural aspects. The very phrase *European philosophy,* for example, testifies to this fact, for it underlies the universal applicability of the general term philosophy along with the legitimate use of the adjective *European.* The same analysis applies to other phrases, such as *Chinese philosophy* or *Indian philosophy.*

To the question of whether intercultural philosophy is a new philosophical discipline added to the existing branches of philosophy, such as ontology, epistemology, ethics, and so on, the answer is *no.* Intercultural philosophy is first and foremost the name of a philosophical attitude, a philosophical conviction that no one philosophy is the philosophy for the whole of humankind. This attitude applies mutatis mutandis to culture and religion, too. Intercultural philosophy is, in other words, the name of a new orientation in and of philosophy, and it accompanies all of the different concrete philosophical traditions and forbids them to put themselves in an absolute, monolithic position.

There is a widespread, though unfounded, fear among certain philosophical circles that philosophy hereby loses its identity, is deconstructed, and becomes fully relativistic. The fact is that the deconstructivist aspect of this new orientation of intercultural philosophy does not relativize the universal applicability as such, but does so only to the absolutistic use made of this term by certain philosophical traditions that define philosophy and their traditions reciprocally. Indian philosophy, for example, is philosophy and in this sense overlaps with other philosophical traditions. It is however, also Indian and therefore different from other orientations and shows its cultural embeddedness. The adjectival differences are illuminating: they may be complementary, but they never deny or even undermine the universal unity of philosophical thinking.

Thus, intercultural philosophy stands for a process of emancipation from all types of centrisms, whether European or non-European. Intercultural philosophy allows for preferential and differentiating treatment of philosophical traditions, but it is neither discriminatory nor monolithic. Rather, it enables us to view critically and sympathetically one philosophical tradition from the point of view of another and vice versa.

The essays in this book are diverse, but they all deal with the theme of intercultural philosophy. The first chapter provides a conceptual clarification of the term *intercultural philosophy* and works out a theoretical foundation for it. In the second chapter, a new concept of an "analogous hermeneutics" is introduced after a critical denial of the hermeneutics of total identity and of radical difference. An application of this hermeneutics is undertaken in the third chapter. The central thesis here is that the one philosophical Truth is available to various philosophical traditions. Chapter 4 dismisses the idea of the sole dependence of interculturality on postmodernity; intercultural philosophical thinking is an independent phenomenon in its own right, although it is supported by the spirit of postmodernity. A theory of unity without uniformity is worked out in chapter 5, whereby unity and diversity are regarded as equally original phenomena. An intercultural perspective is brought to bear on the phenomenon of time in chapter 6. In chapter 7, the works of Shamkara and Plato are compared and contrasted regarding the one Truth, which is, undoubtedly, always in need of expression, but, nevertheless, defies total expressibility. In chapter 8, a phenomenological theory of God is worked out by comparing and contrasting it with the God of metaphysics and theology. Chapter 9 thematizes the philosophically very pertinent question of the absolute and locates it, in the spirit of a nonessentialistic but descriptive phenomenology, in the felt absence of its presence. The absolute is an unfulfilled noematic correlate.

1

Intercultural Philosophy—
A Conceptual Clarification

Preliminary Remarks

The meeting of different cultures, philosophies, and religions—which we have less aspired to than have had happen to us in the wake of modernity, with all its global technological formations—calls for an intensive and reciprocal dialogue involving all concerned. The general concept of philosophy possesses a universal connotation over and above its particular, adjectival qualifications, such as Chinese, Indian, European, and so on. This connotation gives us the right to speak of interculturality. Every philosophy must tie on to another and form part of a larger whole, making every philosophy a cross-cultural phenomenon. We do accept and recognize more than one genuine Gestalt of philosophy, but still missing is a conceptual clarification and a theory of a philosophical foundation of interculturality.[1]

Philosophy is one of the most refined products of the human mind and culture. Because the idea of a totally pure culture is a fiction—a myth, rather—there is almost no philosophy that can claim to be fully free from influence. Different cultures and philosophies influence one other and maintain their idiosyncratic features, which enables us to apply different adjectives to the nouns *philosophy* and *culture*. One may go even further and maintain some sort of tautology in the phrase *intercultural philosophy,* for philosophy is by nature intercultural.

Philosophy is a general concept with individual instances. To know wherein the overlapping general character lies, let us consider the question, "Under what conditions are we entitled to say that two things, A and B, are first just different and second radically different?" If two things—for example, two cultures or philosophies—are just different, then they are two different instances of the general concept. If we take them to be radically different, then we are not entitled to use the same general concept for both of them, for they are different as cultures and philosophies. In such a case, we cannot even articulate this radical difference, for the very general concept loses its applicability. Thus, the concepts of culture and philosophy within which we are obliged to operate must be of an analogous character. No culture—Chinese, European, Indian, or any other—is monolithic and monadic. Any attempt to examine cultures as closed systems is philosophically and methodologically unsound and even politically dangerous because it may lead to the idealogy of "culturalism," which ascribes to certain cultures absolute values and treats others as a means to an end. Even if there were one "truth," no philosophy, no culture, no religion, and no political thought could claim to possess it exclusively.

We may trace the origin of culture and philosophy even deeper in the past until the continuous thread is lost in the abysmal depth of the past. We generally speak of three birthplaces of philosophy: China, India, and Greece. Jaspers's widely known axle hypothesis argues for such a view. Philosophy—that is, the activity in which we engage when we do philosophy—is first a cross-cultural universal and then Greek, Indian, Chinese, and so on, and not the other way round. I have always wondered how the Greco-Eurocentric concept of philosophy succeeded in exclusively absolutizing itself, and I came to the conclusion that major factors were of an extraphilosophical nature, such as imperial, colonialistic, and political forces.[2]

Modern Europe's sciences and technology are credited with the cultural encounters that occur in a global context today. The universalistic bent of the European mind seems to be disillusioned in part because it is now forced to realize that the days when Europe alone was destined to make and influence history are gone. This change has defined the present world context that in turn contextualizes globally important themes, such as culture, philosophy, religion, ethics, arts, literature, politics, and ecology. The demand for universal validity and acceptance has become paradoxical, and the need for a binding pluralism becomes incumbent on us. The transculturality of the conceptual and categorical apparatus of the natural and formal sciences is, of course, different from the normative demand put on the attitude of interculturality in the fields of the humanities.

According to Mircea Eliade, Western philosophy cannot move within its own tradition without becoming provincial.[3] Today, more than ever, Eliade as words apply mutatis mutandis to all cultures, philosophies, and religions in the global context.

In his programmatic lecture "Man in the Age of Adjustment," Max Scheler developed a cosmopolitan vision of the future of humankind and spoke about the fateful need for an adjustment between Asia and Europe. It is interesting to note that Scheler uses the phrase *world age* (Weltalter) and does not simply speak of an age. What he means is the global network of almost all events in the modern-world context.[4]

The Hermeneutic Situation Today

The way the continents address one other today is of a different quality and takes place in a philosophical, religious, cultural, and political atmosphere of inevitable reciprocity. The de facto hermeneutic situation is characterized by the fact that for the last few decades non-Europeans have also thought and written about Europe, explaining it and judging it. This was hardly the case during the time of Alexander the Great's invasion of India or Columbus's discovery of the United States. This new hermeneutic situation also bears the label of a four-fold hermeneutic dialectic. First is the way in which Europeans understand themselves. Second is the European understanding of non-Europeans. Third is the way in which non-Europeans understand themselves, and fourth is the way non-Europeans draw a picture of Europeans. The fact that Europe itself is now an object of interpretation is quite astonishing, primarily, of course, for the European mind. The phenomenon of understanding is a very complex process, be it self-understanding or understanding of the other. It is very self-complacent to believe that one's understanding of the other is better than his or her self-understanding, but nearly all of the different branches of orientalism have followed such a line of thinking.

Because encounters among today's cultures (in spite of the dominance of European culture) do not take place on a one-way road, there is mutual exchange among all of the cultures involved in the process. (For example, in the field of medicine, Chinese acupuncture and Indian ayurvedic medicine have been brought to Europe.) With intercultural understanding as a goal, we cannot just insist on resolving problems of mutual understanding regarding the truth or the falsity of a specific culture, religion, or philosophy in a metaphysical vein before undertaking steps toward concrete mutual understanding. Any a priori, metaphysical, or ideological decision precludes the possibility of genuine understanding.

Today, we must take into account that there are multiple perspectives that philosophers, theologians, and ethnologists can take, which means they can turn to themselves and make their own cultures an object of study. It is better to be diffident in one's claim to Truth. Philosophers may discuss the question of true knowledge in the best epistemological way, but ultimately our preference for a particular set of arguments will prevail. All discourses deal with arguments for or against these preferences. Toward the goal of an intercultural understanding, we expect all cultures to argue and to let others argue, which is the aim of epistemologically oriented hermeneutics. Those who talk about the radical "other" claim the Truth for themselves and underrate the importance and virtue of relativism and pluralism.[5] The foreignness of the other is a phenomenon we are confronted with in our own home cultures. The question of making sense of a foreign culture possesses a constitutive reciprocity. There is a generic similarity between intra- and intercultural understandings and misunderstandings.

The alien, or the other, is given to us before our attempt at understanding the other. A hermeneutics that reduces and absorbs the other destroys the spirit of interculturality. In our search for an adequate hermeneutics of intercultural philosophy, there is only one hermeneutics that does justice to an understanding of the other. This hermeneutics is analogous, meaning that, where there is an inaccessibility of the other with regard to contents, all that we can rely on are the analogous structural patterns that make understanding possible beyond all centrisms. Analogous hermeneutics does not demand identity of views for understanding.

Culture and Philosophy

Culture in complementary polarity to nature stands for all sorts of performances, achievements, and products of the human mind, starting from the simplest agricultural equipments and extending to sciences, arts, religion, and philosophy. The term *culture* acquires a different meaning depending on the context in which it is used. These contexts may be philosophical, sociological, religious, biological, anthropological, historical, and so on. A. Kroeber and C. Kluckhohn have worked out as many as 150 definitions of *culture*.[6] The case does not seem to be much different in the field of philosophy.

Philosophy lives in and through the tension caused by the temporal and the nontemporal, the particular and the universal, and the historical and the nonhistorical. Philosophy is undoubtedly born in particular cultures and thus is local in character, but it is not exhausted in any one of its manifold local manifestations. The myriad adjectives—Chinese, European, Indian, African, Latin American— verify this fact. Philosophies are fundamentally similar in their universal attempt to explain and understand the world of things and beings around us, but they also illuminate differences among themselves. There is no doubt about the cultural embeddedness of philosophy, but this embeddedness does not mean the loss of the universalistic application of the generic concept of philosophy. In other words, the extremes of both a radical relativism and an exclusive essentialism must be abandoned.

There is no denying that the phenomenon of interculturality shows itself in nearly all walks of life. The result is three main types of reaction. First, individuals stick to their own culture more and more when confronted with foreign cultures. In many countries today, we witness this reaction in terms of multicultural problems. Second, one neglects the foreign culture and becomes fully indifferent. In such a situation, different cultures are simply juxtaposed in a multicultural society. Third, individuals try to view the whole matter impartially, pleading for the theory and the practice of a pluralistic norm of live and let live, read and let read, and believe and let believe. The third reaction, which is really the intercultural philosophical attitude, defines the spirit of intercultural philosophy.

The process of reciprocal understanding and rapprochement is jeopardized by a fundamentalistic tendency that may appear in different masks. Serving the cause of intercultural philosophy is an attitude of diffidence with regard to our claims to truth. One who takes intercultural philosophy seriously allows for a change of perspective, which, of course, does not necessarily mean a change of stance. The change of perspective helps us to cultivate the virtue of tolerance. It is wrong to confuse intercultural thinking with a reaction or a shift made in the face of the pluralistic situation of philosophical positions and traditions in today's global world context of philosophy. It is also wrong to romanticize the attitude of intercultural philosophy and mistake it to be just an aesthetic category. We do philosophy as a moral commitment. As a result, intercultural philosophy should not be equated with the exotic and amateurish interest in all that is non-European. In other words, interculturality is not a trendy expression. The de facto hermeneutic situation of intercultural meetings and confrontations is far too sensitive and has far-reaching consequences, and the task of mutual understanding cannot be left solely to politicians, economists, and the mass media. A Viennese journal reported on international tourism as a cross-cultural phenomenon. In the summer of 1984, a group of Kenyans decided to test the worth of tourism as an intercultural meeting ground. Carrying cameras and tips with them, they approached a group of German tourists, persuaded them to take a group photo for their Kenyan family members at home, and even promised to give them tips. The German tourists were annoyed and found this behavior unpardonable. They asked for a tourist guide and even the police.[7] Even the idea of reciprocal exotic feeling was too much for the German group. This example may be inappropriate and not very philosophical, but it nevertheless makes one thing clear: what matters is not what is done but who does it.

The European historiography of philosophy has wrongly, but successfully, neglected the proper introduction of non-European philosophies and cultures. There may be a few exceptions to this Eurocentric practice, which has its origin not in the Greek logos qua logos but rather in extraphilosophical factors, such as colonialism, imperialism, missionarism, and so on. It is ironic that Hegel, who devoted many pages to non-European philosophies, cultures, and religions in his history of world philosophy, is one of the main philosophers who refused the title of philosophy for non-European cultures.[8]

The Concept of Intercultural Philosophy

Interculturality is a multifaceted phenomenon. In a metalinguistic discussion, it functions as a construct. In the field of purely formal disciplines, it stands for the internationalism of scientific and formal categories. It enables physicists and mathematicians from all over the world to communicate with little difficulty. In one of its facets, interculturality is also used for world trade, following market laws and other socioeconomic interests.

The concept of interculturality, as thematized here, stands for a mental and a moral category. It is not to be identified with the culturality of a particular culture, and it is also not an eclecticism of a manifold of cultures. It is also not to be equated with a mere abstraction. We cannot fix the nature of intercultural philosophy just per definition. Likewise, as stated previously, it is also wrong to misread intercultural philosophy as simply a reaction or a shift made in the face of today's de facto pluralistic philosophical traditions. Intercultural philosophy is also not a matter of aesthetitization. It must not be confused with cultural romanticism or exoticism, which is why a word of caution is needed against the long-lived romantic, exotic, and mostly amateurish interest in all that is non-European.

In its positive import, intercultural philosophy is the name of a philosophical conviction, attitude, and insight. No philosophy is *the* philosophy, and no culture is *the* culture. Such an insight accompanies all of the different philosophies and cultures and prevents them from absolutizing themselves. Interculturality of philosophy thus resides in different cultures, but it also transcends their narrow limits.

Intercultural philosophy, therefore, proceeds methodologically as follows: it does not unnecessarily give privileged treatment to any philosophy, culture, or religion. It also rejects the idea of a mere hierarchical gradation of cultures and philosophies. It takes seriously the idea of cultural plurality and deems it valuable. Any study of philosophy from an intercultural perspective situates itself beyond all centrisms—be it Asian, European, or Chinese, to name just a few. Philosophy in cultural comparison subscribes to a hermeneutic model of reciprocity that does not take the other to be just an echo of itself. In our attempt to understand others, we cannot fully avoid the hermeneutic circle. We must, however, take care not to dogmatize it either. Those who take the hermeneutic circle to be our philosophical fate fail to avoid a repetition of self-understanding in the name of understanding the other. For this reason, intercultural philosophy rejects the idea of a hermeneutics of identity that is intolerant of difference. In our attempt to understand others, we meet to differ and differ to meet. The other is also experienced by us through its resistance to our attempt to assimilate it fully. The other also makes itself known to us through the aesthetic feeling it arouses in us.

The intercultural hermeneutics pleaded for here and that underlies our concept of intercultural philosophy is a nonreductive, open, creative, and tolerant hermeneutics. It approves of overlapping centers, searches for them, finds them, and cultivates them. These overlapping structures are the common factors that make communication possible and allow philosophies and cultures to retain their individual characters. The modern–postmodern debate thus loses its sting when put in this context of overlapping and abiding structures.

Intercultural philosophy has a four-fold perspective: philosophical, theological, political, and pedagogical. The phenomenon of interculturality under philosophical optics means that the one philosophia perennis is no one's possession alone. There is a metonymic relation between the name and the named. The one philosophical truth is no doubt in need of language, but it also resists total linguisticality. There is, therefore, more than one place from which philosophy originated.[9] It is a prejudice to think that philosophy has a preference for a special language, tradition, or culture. From the theological perspective, interculturality is interreligiosity—based on the firm conviction that the one religio perennis (sanâtana dharma) is also no one's possession. The highest religious truth is in need of expression, but it also resists total expressibility. We find aphorisms in all religious traditions, thereby testifying to this fact. Under political optics, interculturality is another name for a pluralistic democratic attitude with the conviction that political wisdom does not belong only to one group, party, or ideology. All philosophies of history with the absolutistic claim of possessing the only true, real message are politically fundamentalistic and practically dangerous. The pedagogical perspective is the most important one, for it prepares the way for the practical implementation of the inner culture of interculturality.

The epistemological modesty of interculturality in philosophy, religious tolerance in theology, and a moral commitment to a pluralistic-democratic attitude in politics are the standards and values that are the prerequisites of an interculturally oriented society. These values also represent the goals to be achieved in society.

This perspective is the most feasible way to achieve cooperation and communication in a multicultural society that is always in danger of being merely juxtaposed.

Cultural Encounters

When we follow, for example, the cultural and the religious encounters of the Indian subcontinent in the past, we find different patterns of encounter. When the Aryans came from central Asia to India, they met the old culture of the Dravidian people. They suppressed the original Indian culture, but they did not extinguish it. The caste system can be traced back to this encounter. The Hindu culture as such is a mixture of Aryan and non-Aryan elements. In spite of many difficulties, India has always experimented with multiculturalism guided by the rigvedic dictum of one Truth under different names.

After the victory of Alexander the Great, there was a short but intense encounter between the Indian and the Greek cultures. This encounter is exemplified by the well-known kingdom of Menandros in northern India. We have many reports of this time, and the debate of King Milinda is famous in world literature. In this encounter, we find a very paradigmatic philosophical, intercultural, political, and religious pattern of discourse between the king, who was very interested in philosophy and religion, and the Buddhist monk-philosopher Nagasena:

> Then the king said, "Venerable sir, will you discuss with me again."
> "If your majesty will discuss as a scholar, yes; but if you will discuss as a king, no."
> "How is it then that scholars discuss?"
> "When scholars discuss there is summing up, unravelling; one or other is shown to be in error and he admits his mistake and yet is not thereby angered."
> "And how is it that kings discuss?"
> "When a king discusses a matter and he advances a point of view, if anyone differs from him on that point he is apt to punish him."
> "Very well then, it is as a scholar that I will discuss. Let your reverence talk without fear."[10]

Nagasena here lays down the conditions for the possibility of an honest discourse, which, of course, demands not only intellectual honesty but also the cultivation of ethical and moral qualities that turn philosophical, religious, and political discourse as a way of life over and above its being a way of thought. The ideal of "unforced discourse" (Habermas's herrschaftsfreie Diskussion) is enriched. The ethos on which such a discourse is based aims at an inner transformation.

At the end of the first millennium after Christ, Muslims began their invasion of India. Mahmud Gazni was one of them. Over time, these invaders succeeded in establishing foreign rule in India that lasted until it was replaced by British rule. In spite of the religious troubles facing India today, Hindus and Muslims have lived together in an interculturally and interreligiously oriented multicultual and multireligious society. Sufism is one of the best examples of this living together, as are cases of reciprocal influences in the arts, music, and architecture.

European colonization of non-European countries was more radical and aimed at the europeanization of the whole world. It is true that India has westernized herself to a great extent, but it is not true that India has europeanized herself totally. Europeanization stands for the software of Western culture and religion, whereas westernization represents its hardware. The cultural encounter in India led to a renewal of Indian tradition from within, leading to its most powerful aspect—the political activities of Mahatma Gandhi.

There have been, in contrast, cultural encounters in human history that were quite pernicious. Examples are the encounter of the Arab–Islamic culture with that of ancient Iran and the encounter between European culture and those of the cultures of the American continents.

Historical events are polyperspectival. A single event can be characterized as fortunate or unfortunate depending on the optics of the victor or the vanquished. The discovery of America was good luck for the Europeans but bad for the Native Americans. Georg Lichtenberg has written, "The particular American who first discovered Columbus made a bad discovery."[11]

It is undoubtedly true that nearly all cultural encounters show signs of tension and violence, but the legitimate question is, "Why do certain encounters end in the total destruction of one or more cultures?" The reason might be found in the very nature of the cultures encountering one other. One of the main reasons for the destructive character of cultural and religious (and even political) encounters must lie in the claims of exclusive truth made by certain cultures. Absolutistic claims are, by nature, violent. A portion of what Donald Davidson calls the principle of charity could have saved many cultural encounters from disastrous consequences. This principle requires us to make as much sense of, and find a great deal of truth in, the system and behavior of others.[12]

When cultures meet in the spirit of tolerance and interculturality, they further the cause of cooperation and communication among cultures and religions. In spite of the tensions between Taoism, Confucianism, and Buddhism in China, these three Weltanschauungen succeeded in living together. The spirit of the Chinese saying, "three teachings, one family," must have been of great help. The overlapping sense of the idea of one family allows us to recognize the three different teachings and yet denies that they are radically different. Radically different is something that cannot even be articulated.

Interculturality Before Multiculturality

Undoubtedly, we are justified in speaking of the home culture, but such locations possess their legitimacy within limits because none of these cultures is a monolithic structure. In all societies, there is a culture of the majority as well as one of the minority. For the past few years, we have tried to avoid the apparently discriminating term *minority* and used the term *multiculturality*. In spite of the differences among cultures, our point of departure must be their equal ranking.

I am convinced that an intercultural society led by the regulative idea of an overlapping unity without uniformity is to be preferred over a merely multicultural one. This preference is because a mulitcultural society tends toward an illusionary purity of the different cultures believing in a static identity that does not exist. Those who overrate identity cannot avoid becoming formalistic, exclusivistic, or even fundamentalistic. Theodor Adorno rightly brands identity as the prototype of ideology.[13] Mere information, in whatever quantity, is not enough for a respectful, reciprocal understanding between cultures. Europeans were well informed about other cultures and even opened departments such as orientalism at the university level, but they still practiced Eurocentrism in their diverse contacts with the world outside of Europe. The precondition for the possibility of mutual understanding is the deep-seated conviction that the one philosophia and religio perennis is nobody's exclusive possession alone. In the absence of this software of intercultural understanding, the hardware of widespread global information is of little value.

The term *interculturality* stands for an attitude, for the conviction that no culture is *the* culture for the whole of humankind. We do not thereby deconstruct philosophy, culture, or religion but only the extremely relativistic and absolutistic use of them made in the past and even today in certain circles. This attitude, this culture of interculturality, accompanies all cultures like a shadow and hinders them from absolutizing themselves; this attitude is the very condition needed for the possibility of a genuine comparative philosophy. This attitude also leads to cooperation and communication among different cultures. Intercultural philosophy also stands for a process of emancipation from the narrow Eurocentric outlook and allows the spirit of philosophy to reign wherever it deems fit. The spirit of interculturalism approves of pluralism as a value without undermining a personal commitment to one's own position. It is not monolithic and discriminatory, although it is preferential and discriminating.

The concept of intercultural philosophy is an attempt to answer the question that has continually been asked—whether and how the cultural manifold can be brought into line with a general and universal concept of truth. The deadly logic of either–or is, of course, of no help here, for it accords a privileged treatment to one side or the other. A satisfactory solution may be found beyond the two fictions of total identity and radical difference in overlapping structures among cultures, philosophies, and religions.

Philosophy and Interculturality

Intercultural philosophy as an open, tolerant, and pluralistic attitude consists of the philosophical conviction that the one philosophia perennis is the possession of no single culture or philosophical tradition. Such an attitude is in a position to change cultural encounters into cultural contacts.

In certain quarters, there is fear that an interculturally oriented philosophical attitude might destroy the very ideas of truth, philosophy, and culture. This fear is misguided. What is destroyed through deconstruction is not so much the idea of philosophy or truth but rather the radically relativistic and extremely absolutistic use made of these concepts in certain philosophical traditions. The one perennial philosophy knows no prejudices and does not give a privileged treatment to any one tradition or culture. It does not have one mother tongue; it is polylingual. Thus, the adjective *intercultural* is not just an appendage to philosophy; it may sometimes be more important than the noun it qualifies. Different cultures have their own philosophical traditions as complementary expressions of the human mind.

Intercultural philosophy is also an indication of a conflict combined with a demand. It indicates a conflict because non-European philosophies, cultures, and religions rightly reject European arrogance and ignorance. Thus, it stands for a demand to let the spirit of philosophy reign wherever it deems fit, and it leads further toward an emancipatory aspect of intercultural philosophy, which is quite different from the inner European emancipation from absolutism in politics and religion in the age of enlightenment. The intercultural emancipation in today's hermeneutic world context of philosophy is the emancipation of non-European philosophical thought from Eurocentrism. In other words, it aims at a historiography of philosophy to be written in the spirit of intercultural orientation.

The famous Latin American philosopher Leopoldo Zea rightly criticizes the self-centeredness of Europe and tries to show a genuine alternative to it. He does this through his pioneering interpretation of the Greek word *logos*. The concept of logos stands for two things: (1) the human capacity of reason and understanding and (2) the ability to make use of words and language to communicate with others. It is true that the word *logos* is of Greek origin, but it is not true to say that the idea of logos is exclusively Greek or European.[14] To make sense of the term *art*, we do not ask only about the etymology; rather, we ask the question, "What do we do when we engage ourselves in artistic activities?" Similarly, to know what philosophy is, we should not ask where the word comes from, but rather what we do when we do philosophy. In some way, famous philosophers such as Hegel, Heidegger, and Husserl succumbed to the view that doing philosophy is the exclusive property of the Greek or the European mind. Such an attitude has led to a very restrictive definition of philosophy.

The idea of intercultural philosophy envisaged here aims at a philosophy that enables us to feel the presence of a generic concept of philosophical truth in its omnipresence in different philosophical traditions. It also leads us to dismiss the tendency to absolutize one's own pattern of thought. Our interculturally oriented concept of philosophy warns us not to confuse one's own way of doing philosophy with the only possible way of doing philosophy.

The theory and practice of intercultural philosophy as conceived in this book imply a need for a fundamental change in our attitude in teaching and research in the field of philosophy. It leads to the conception of a new historiography of philosophy. Intercultural philosophy is an imperative today, and we are philosophically, morally, and politically committed to it. As a basically new orientation, it aims at the cultivation of a philosophical attitude that teaches us to be diffident not only with regard to our certainties but also with regard to philosophical doubts.

Notes

1. F. Wimmer, *Interkulturelle Philosophie: Geschichte und Theorie* (Vol. I, Vienna 1990); R. A. Mall and H. Hülsmann, *Die drei Geburtsorte der Philosophie: China, Indien, Europa* (Bonn 1989); H. Kimmerle, *Die Dimension des Interkulturellen* (Amsterdam 1994); F. C. Copleston, *Philosophies and Cultures* (Oxford 1980); K. Jaspers, *Weltgeschichte der Philosophie* (Munich 1982).

2. Copleston, *Philosophies and Cultures;* Mall and Hülsmann, *Die drei Geburtsorte der Philosophie.*

3. M. Eliade, *Die Sehnsucht nach dem Ursprung* (Vienna 1973), 84; Copleston, *Philosophies and Cultures.*

4. M. Scheler, *Philosophische Weltanschauung* (Munich 1968), 89, 118.

5. J. Kekes, *The Morality of Pluralism* (Princeton 1993).

6. A. Kroeber and C. Kluckhohn, *Culture: A Critical Review of Concepts and Definitions* (New York 1952).

7. M. Baiculescu, "Freiheit mit Reiseleiter," *Der Falter,* no. 8 (1985): 13.

8. R. A. Mall, "Interkulturelle Philosophie und die Historiographie," in *Ethnozentrismus,* ed. M. Brocker and H. Nau (Darmstadt 1997).

9. Mall and Hülsmann, *Die drei Geburtsorte der Philosophie.*

10. B. Pesala, *The Debate of King Milinda* (Delhi 1991), 4–5.

11. In *FAZ* 13, no. 3 (1992).

12. D. Davidson, *Inquiries in Truth and Interpretations* (Oxford 1984), 152.

13. T. W. Adorno, *Negative Dialektik* (Frankfurt 1973), 151.

14. L. Zea, *Signale aus dem Abseits—Eine lateinamerikanische Philosophie der Geschichte* (Munich 1989), 32.

2

Toward a Theory of an Analogous Hermeneutics

Preliminary Remarks

Today's global intercultural context has made one thing abundantly clear: the de facto intercultural hermeneutic situation has outgrown the Greco-European and Judaic-Christian interpretations of culture, philosophy, and religion. This situation calls for deconstruction of the exclusive relation between truth and tradition. Truth *of* the tradition and truth *in* the tradition are two different things and must not be confused.

It is true, although one-sided, that much of what we do in the name of intercultural studies is oriented from the perspective of Western thought and shows signs of the West's asymmetry and hegemony. This one-sidedness is the result of a historical contingency that made European thought the main paradigm of reference. Added to this paradigm is the prejudice of the early orientalists, who viewed philosophy, culture, and religion as Western achievements. I have been trying to overcome this contingency, this asymmetry, and hoping to contribute to a common, global discourse and conversation of humankind that extends beyond the narrow limits of the East–West dichotomy. In the spirit of intercultural philosophy, European and non-European cultures and philosophies may be viewed reciprocally.

Chauvinism, whether religious, cultural, philosophical, national, or geographical, must be given up for the sake of, as well as to realize, intercultural understanding. Western philosophy, according Mircea Eliade, cannot move within its own tradition without becoming provincial. Today, more than ever before, Eliade's words apply mutatis mutandis to all philosophical, cultural, and religious traditions. Intercultural networks make it necessary to abstain from absolutization.

In my attempt to address the conditions, possibilities, and limits of intercultural understanding, I find myself caught up in a paradox that I can neither avoid nor fully resolve, for I am simultaneously an insider and an outsider. This chapter is thus an impressionistic account of my continual efforts to translate philosophies, religions, and cultures. I am thereby guided by the conviction that the two fictions of total translatability and commensurability and of radical untranslatability and incommensurability among cultures must be abandoned in favor of a metonymic thesis of dynamically overlapping structures. No culture is a windowless monad, so all cultures possess to varying degrees intercultural overlappings.

The metonymic figure of speech in its intuitive import emphasizes our indubitable consciousness of the difference between the name and the named. Because no philosophical reflection can fully overtake the reflected-upon, there is always the possibility of multiple expressions. This fact is the bedrock for our practice of translating one culture into another. A closer look at the history of ideas from an intercultural perspective shows clearly that the practice of translation does not succeed; rather, it precedes the question regarding the possibility. Regarding the problem of translating cultures, Paul Ricoeur says that there is no absolute alienation and that there is always a genuine possibility of translation. One can understand without repeating, imagine without experiencing, and transform oneself into the other and still remain the self one is.[1]

Regardless of the merits and demerits of modern globalization, we cannot equate European history with world history as it used to be the case in the eighteenth and nineteenth centuries. Europe today is one major center, but it is not the only one. According to Derrida, Europeans often talk of crisis when their universality is in danger.[2] After reading Huntington's book on the clash of civilizations, I cannot avoid the impression that he does lament the lost universality of the European culture, although he rightly pleads for mutual understanding across cultures. Samuel P. Huntington is realist enough not to go no further than lamenting. He advises European people to regain their cultural identity so they are in a position to meet the challenges of other cultures.[3] Huntington is neither merely a pessimist nor entirely an optimist; he oscillates between the two poles. His general contextualization does not favor universalism, and he pleads for a binding pluralism. The discovery of non-European cultures is mainly a European achievement leading to the unintended irony of relativizing European culture itself. Many missionaries, for example, left Europe to convert others, but some of them were themselves converted.

The Concept of Interculturality

The term *interculturality* as used in this book is neither a trendy expression nor a romantic idea in this age of global technological formation and world tourism. It must not be taken as compensation by non-European cultures born out an inferiority complex. Interculturality is also not just a shift made while facing the de facto encounters of today's world cultures.

Interculturality is far from being just a construct, an abstraction, or a syncretic idea; the concept of interculturality stands for the conviction and the insight that no culture is the one culture for the whole of humankind. The fear that we may thereby deconstruct the general applicability of terms such as *philosophy, truth, culture, religion,* and so on, is unfounded. The concept of interculturality does, however, deconstruct the monolithic, absolutistic, and exclusivistic uses of these terms. Intercultural thinking thus stands for an emancipatory process from all kinds of centrisms, be it Euro-, Sino-, or Afrocentrism. The spirit of interculturality approves of pluralism, diversity, and difference as values and does not take them as privations of unity and uniformity. An acceptance of diversity follows from the spirit of interculturality. It is wrong to view diversity as Aristotelian accidents. An intercultural horizon can very well envisage the "compossibility" (a Leibnizian term) of diverse cultural patterns, striking a new note between total alterity and universality. The concept of order that intercultural thinking implies is an order in, through, and with differences, thereby making room for a polyphony of different voices.

The general concept of unity must always to be viewed in the context of diversity. Intercultural philosophy subscribes to the idea of universal applicability cross-culturally of the term *philosophy,* but it takes seriously the challenge of cultural relativism in that it denies the monolithic conviction that pretends to possess an absolute "Archimedian standpoint" over and above the bounds of cultures and historical contexts. Intercultural philosophy aims at genuine recognition among different philosophical traditions and maintains that this difference may itself be the freedom that must be reciprocally recognized.

The Concept of an Analogous Intercultural Hermeneutics

The word *hermeneutics* is indubitably Greek and Western, but the idea and the practice are anthropological constants. Indian thought, for example, possesses a very rich hermeneutic tradition. The science of hermeneutics as an art of interpretation and understanding undergoes a fundamental change in today's global context of interculturality, and it experiences an unprecedented widening of its horizons that does not necessarily go hand in hand with a real fusing of the horizons (Gadamer's Horizontverschmelzung). Every hermeneutics, therefore, has its own culturally sedimented roots and cannot claim universal and unconditional acceptance. Any dialogue—most important, of course, is the intercultural one—has to take this insight as its point of departure.

In the history of Greco-Christian-European philosophy, the term *analogy* is used to solve the very perplexing problem arising from holy scripture and helenistic philosophy because of two paradoxical messages: the incommensurability of God with His creation and the possibility of a comparison between the creator and the created. Because God and His creation do not belong to the same species, analogy in both theology and speculative metaphysics has always suffered from a tension between univocality and equivocation. My use of the term *analogy* in this volume relates to things and beings belonging to the same species, and we can use the means of analogy as a valid cause for the cognition of similarity. In the field of intercultural understanding, analogy stands for, first, a consciousness of nonidentity; second, a consciousness of difference; third, a consciousness of not total difference; and, fourth, a consciousness of not total identity. Analogy is defined here as a likeness of relation among unlike things.

The concept of "analogous hermeneutics," which does justice to the present de facto hermeneutic situation, is neither the hermeneutics of total identity, which reduces the other to an echo of itself and repeats its self-understanding in the name of understanding the other, nor that of radical difference, which makes the understanding of the other impossible. It does not put any one culture in an absolute position of generality and reduce all of the others to some form of it. There is no one universal hermeneutic subject over and above the sedimented cultural, historical subject; it is, rather, a reflexive-meditative attitude accompanying the different subjects with a warning not to reduce. Such a hermeneutic attitude helps us to overcome the feeling of being hopelessly involved in the hermeneutic circle. It further frees us from our tendency to define truth in terms of a particular tradition and this tradition in terms of truth. An excessive commitment to tradition and prejudices (Gadamer) endangers intercultural understanding. Here, Habermas is rightly critical of Gadamer's hermeneutics and its universalistic claim.

In the face of alternate traditions, cultures, and ethical pluralism, it is wrong to maintain that we are condemned only to our own tradition and can, at most, try to interpret and understand it. My moral intuition tells me that I can belong to my culture and can be, in some measure, a critic of it.

In the field of intercultural understanding, it is wrong to reduce a theory of meaning to a theory of truth and the latter to translatability. Donald Davidson tends toward the thesis of a mutual untranslatability and speaks of radically different frameworks.[4] However, cultures may be and are meaningful if we abstain from claiming the best intuition of truth only for ourselves. Understanding cultures is a complex matter, and I assume the common-sense view, that there are degrees of understanding and degrees of misunderstanding both in cases of self-understanding and understanding of the other.

It is in vain to try to resolve the problem of intercultural understanding in a metaphysical way. Concrete steps at mutual understanding must be taken. Any a priori, metaphysical, or ideological decision precludes the possibility of genuine understanding. Despite the great difficulties we face in our attempt to understand other cultures, intercultural understanding is both theoretically and practically possible. Of course, we must not exclude intercultural understanding per definition by saying, for example, that only a Buddhist can understand Buddhism, a Muslim Islam, a Christian Christianity, a Hegelian Hegel, a Taoist Taoism, and so on. To do so would be understanding by identification.

Even conceptual frameworks partly bear the signs of being embedded in philosophical, cultural, and religious tradition. To put a particular framework in an absolute position is methodologically wrong. Intercultural philosophy favors an analogous hermeneutics of overlapping structures beyond the two fictions of total identity (commensurability) and radical difference (incommensurability).

Such a hermeneutics also leads to a healthy concept of comparative philosophy,[5] which does not absolutize a particular philosophical convention. It rejects not only the idea of an absolute text but also that of an absolute interpretation. Comparative philosophy, worthy of its name, presupposes an intercultural orientation in philosophy.

The overlapping structures among cultures, philosophies, and religions, emphasized by our analogous hermeneutics, may have sources in the biological, anthropological, cultural, and social arrangement of human nature. There is, of course, a limit to every understanding if to understand means just to duplicate one's own way of understanding. An analogical apprehension of the other, as obtained between forms of understanding, may even be contrary. For this reason, we do concede that an antithesis is also a thesis. The concept of understanding characteristic of our analogous hermeneutics is more than simply a way of knowing. It implies moral commitment.

Toward an Ethos of Interculturality

The true spirit of interculturality proclaims as its motto that the desire to understand and the desire to be understood go hand in hand and are two sides of the same interculturally oriented hermeneutic coin. The desire to understand may turn out to be empty, and the desire only to be understood may become blind. In the long period of colonization, whether in culture, religion, or politics, the desire to be understood was most powerful on the part of the colonizers. It is not always wrong to maintain that orientalists, missionaries, and ethnologists played a conspiratorial role for a long time. They took great pains to learn foreign languages, such as Sanskrit and Chinese, not so much to understand others but to be understood by them.

Eliade uses the term *second renaissance,* referring to the discovery of Buddhism, the Upanishads, and the Sanskrit language in eighteenth- and nineteenth-century Europe. Although the hopes and promises of European discovery of Asia were very high, it really was a failure.[6] The reason for this failure, as opposed to the grand success of the first renaissance, lies in the fact that it primarily remained a philologically oriented field of work and research for the indologists and was not taken at all seriously by philosophers, theologians, and historians. Even an indologist like Max Müller, to whom India owes so much, could not avoid his bias regarding the superiority of Western philosophy and Christian religion. He wrote, "People do not yet see the full importance of the Veda in an historical study of religion. The bridge of thoughts . . . that spans the whole history of the Aryan world has the first arch in the Veda, its last in Kant's Critique. While in the Veda we may study the childhood, we may study in Kant's *Critique of Pure Reason* the perfect manhood of Aryan mind."[7] These words remind us of Hegel, who so often used the metaphor of childhood, young age, and manhood.

Indology, with its academic institutionalization at universities, is really a curious European invention. It is true that indologists deserve our praise for solid philological-cum-grammatical-cum-textual scholarship. Their main deficiency lies in their blindness to philosophical, historical, and religious content in the text and also in their prejudice against returning to the original text without taking the help of the rich hermeneutic tradition. In this case, Gadamer is perfectly right in denying the legitimacy of such a hermeneutic move, for one cannot reach the original text, the original intuition, unless one goes through interpretive history. It is a myth to believe in an absolute text and in an absolute interpretation.

If, today, in the wake of the global technological formation, we are on the verge of a third renaissance (and it seems we are), then we are all committed to leading it to success. This success is possible only when we give up all centrisms and claims to absolutistic truth. No culture and no religion is only an exporter or an importer. There is a give-and-take ethos at work in every reciprocal understanding.

An interculturally oriented philosopher is sometimes needed to face a dilemma. He or she cannot do good intercultural philosophy with centrism and can do no philosophy without a center. I have considered this paradox and have the following suggestion: to have a center does not necessarily mean to be centristic. We must differentiate between two types of centrism: centrism in a strong and in a weak sense. We must avoid the strong sense, for it is exclusive and discriminatory; but a weak sense of centrism allows us to have a center without putting our own center in an absolute position. This centrism asks us to be very sensitive to the problem of tolerance and advises us to tolerate the tolerant and to fight the different forms of intolerance, which, if unchallenged, lead to fundamentalistic practices.

The study of cultures and religions from an intercultural perspective shows fundamental similarities and illuminating differences. This complex pattern of similarities and dissimilarities forms an important basis for intercultural dialogue. Interreligiosity, for example, is the name of an ethos connecting all religions as their overlapping center. In the absence of such an ethos, all interreligious dialogues are of no real value. Methodologically and also from the point of view of conviction, it belongs to the very essence of such an interreligious ethos that there are various ways to the same religious truth. The claim to absolute truth is not necessarily bad if it is just for a person or a group, but the moment it demands universal following it becomes absolutistic in a fundamentalistic sense.[8]

If the hermeneutic dilemma exists in the seemingly paradoxical situation that we cannot understand without having certain prejudices and that we fail to understand if we have only prejudices, then the task of finding an escape is incumbent on us. To say that we are caught in this hermeneutic circle is of little help. The way out seems to lie in the intercultural conviction of one Truth under different names. Our concept of an analogous hermeneutics is guided by this conviction and bears ample resemblance to Wittgenstein's deepest insight into family resemblance, which must not be taken to be an identity. If we reject the identity thesis because it makes no room for diversities, then we also reject radical relativism because it heavily depends on a radical difference and leaves no room for overlapping features among cultures.[9]

Relativism, in the sense of emphasizing cultural differences, may very well result in open-mindedness and willingness to accept foreign virtues. But relativism that overrates the importance of difference and puts one particular difference in an absolute position may lead to an ethnocentric absolutism or to a supremacist view. Egalitarian universalism that acknowledges different cultures and philosophies as equal in the ability to think, to express, to ask questions, and to propose answers should be preferred over an ethnocentric universalism.

Asia Versus Europe or Universism Versus Universalism

It was the Dutch sinologist J. J. M. de Groot who first coined the word *universism* in 1918 for the Eastern (Chinese) view that humans and nature form a *continua* and do not stand in a dichotomic relation but in a relation of reciprocal complementarity. That which sustains the great cosmic nature is more fundamental, more pervasive, more powerful, and more binding than that which supports human history. Concepts, such as impartiality, justice, order, and so on, embedded in the view of universism pose a challenge to the Western Weltanschauung, which seems to believe that all of creation is exclusively for the sake of humans.

From the Greek historian Herodotus to Heidegger, there persists thinking that dichotomizes Asia and Europe far too much. Such dichotomizing and ontologizing may take a conspiratorial form and lead to some type of self-fulfilling prophecy. In his lecture "Europe and the German Philosophy," given in Rome in 1936, Heidegger spoke of the "protection of European peoples from all that is Asian" (Bewahrung der europäischen Völker vor dem Asiatischen).[10] Heidegger also maintained that the phrase *European philosophy* is a tautology because philosophy is only and can only be European. Karl Jaspers, the former friend and later opponent of Heidegger, warns us against hypostatizing the Asian–European contrast.[11] Karl Löwith has rightly taken Heidegger to task for the latter's conviction that the question of being (Seinsfrage) favors the occidental mind.[12] The hermeneutic philosophy of latter Gadamer comes nearer the truth, for it seems to concede that the other could also be right.

We have thus far discussed human encounters as cultural and religious and pleaded for the discovery and the cultivation of the virtue of an overlapping consensus[13] that would enable us to live and let live, to believe and let believe, and to interpret and let interpret. There has always been a human encounter with nature, but the human encounter with nature in our postindustrial society of global pervasiveness is something qualitatively new because it is heavily destructive and only partly reconstructive and globally fateful. Human encounter with nature mirrors the type of attitude adopted in our relation to nature. It is generally recognized that the Asian attitude toward nature is less anthropocentric than that of the European. This attitude applies despite the fact that in practice, and for all practical purposes, the ecological situation in Asian countries is in no way better than that in Western countries.

European anthropologists, in their search for an answer to the question regarding the special place of human beings in the cosmic household, tend to place humans against nature by assigning human beings either a godly descendence or special faculties called reason, language, and knowledge. Even if we hesitatingly accept this assignment and say, "So far, so good," it is unjust to deduce the right of humans to control nature recklessly. The monotheistic bias of the revealed religions in combination with their anthropocentric and theocentic prejudices hardly allows us to develop a positive feeling of an essential relationship toward nature at large. Chuang Tzu helps us to enlarge our concept of analogous hermeneutics to nature at large, beyond the narrow limits of mainly anthropocentrically oriented hermeneutics. Here, I quote a very witty, wise, and intriguing conversation between two Chinese philosophers, Chuang Tzu and his rival Hui Tzu. The central problem is not so much *whether* we understand but *how* we understand what we think we understand.

> Chuang Tzu and Hui Tzu were taking a lazy walk along the bank of the Hao River. Chuang Tzu said, "The white fish are swimming at ease. This is the happiness of the fish."
> "You are not fish," said Hui Tzu. "How do you know its happiness?"
> "You are not I," said Chuang Tzu. "How do you know that I do not know the happiness of the fish?"
> Hui Tzu said, "Of course I do not know since I am not you. But you are not the fish, and it is perfectly clear that you do not know the happiness of the fish."
> "Let us get at the bottom of the message," said Chuang Tzu. "When you asked how I knew the happiness of the fish, you already knew that I knew the happiness of the fish but asked how. I knew it along the river."[14]

This is a masterpiece even from a very theoretical and epistemological point of view. The rule is as follows: the light knows the light holds true not only in the case of human beings but also in the case of all beings of the universe at large. Some sort of an analogical apprehension is at work between the world of human beings and things in the cosmic nature. It is true that the difference between men and fish is great, but the difference between Chuang Tzu and Hui Tzu is also not just negligible, for one is not the other. Not to be able to know the happiness of the fish as a fish does is not radically different from Hui Tzu's inability to know that which Chuang Tzu knows. Analogous structures give us the opportunity for interpretations, leading to an understanding across the gaps of languages, cultures, religions, and even species. The conviction of universism, which is at work here, is different from the abstract universality of an anthropocentric rationality. Chuang Tzu wants us to realize the cognitive and the moral value of what he says about the happiness of the fish. Over and above the epistemological and moral lesson from Chuang Tzu, we are also led to a theory and a practice of a cosmic ecology with a give-and-take relation between human beings and nature at large.

The spirit of intercultural thinking is also alive in the formal sciences, such as logic. Consider the case of Indian logic in contrast to the Aristotelian. Indian syllogism, for example, has five members whereas there are three in Aristotelian logic. The typical example of an Indian syllogism is as follows:

1. The hill has fire (pratijñâ).
2. Because it has smoke (hetu).
3. Whatever has smoke has fire—for example, an oven (udâharana).
4. This hill has smoke, which is invariably associated with fire (upanaya).
5. Therefore, this hill has fire (nigamana).

This example shows that Indian logic keeps in touch with the empirical elements and does not totally formalize itself.[15] The concept of pure possibility is not favored by Indian logicians as is the case in Western logic. It is for this reason that Indian theory of inference does not admit a syllogism in which the premises and the conclusion are materially false but formally valid. The tendency of the Asian mind not to separate completely logic from psychology may be a healthy check on an excessive formalization that is a mixed pleasure in a technologically changed world. There is a need felt today for a rapprochement between logic and epistemology, for the price we pay for an excessive formalization seems to be out of proportion.

It is true that the law of contradiction is accepted by Buddhists and Aristotle, but the reason given for its validity may differ. According to Aristotle, A cannot be A and non-A because it would then lose its identity; according to Buddhists, A cannot be A and non-A because there is no identical A. Jaina logicians, in contrast, maintain that even the law of contradiction is not unconditionally true, for we do start from presuppositions (e.g., at the same time, place, and in the identical sense). The multivalued logic thus does not disturb the Indian mind so much. Neither in logic nor in metaphysics and religion do we need to be only two valued: true and false, right and wrong.

There is more than one logic—not in the sense of radical difference, which does not permit the use of the general concept of logic for all, but in the sense of the manifold ways of rational justification for the common fact of inference. Marcel Granet describes the Chinese way of bypassing the law of contradiction by invoking the law of harmony (ho). For the Chinese mind, it may be more natural and logical that I will die not because all men are mortal but because wise men like Confucius and Lao-Tzu died.[16]

Humans and nature are a two-way road. This piece of knowledge is undoubtedly human, but the important insight is a joint product of humans in their relation to nature. Being against the anthropocentric universalistic tendency of declaring human beings the summum bonum of all there is and degrading nature as just a means to an end and leaving nature totally to the mercy of self-centered human nature, it is high time to have second thoughts about our relationship with nature and to learn from Asian, especially Chinese, wisdom of universism.[17] This comprehensive attitude of universism is convinced of a necessarily mutual complementarity between humans and nature, assigns human beings a particular place in the cosmic scheme of things, and treats everything in this scheme equally.

Being against the theocentric and the anthropocentric models for human values, the ethos of universism pleads for the conviction of our embeddedness in the all-encompassing household of cosmic nature. This conviction means that we should strive for a humanity within nature and not outside of or without it. There is much to learn from the impartiality that reigns supreme in nature. It is an irony of human history and culture that the so-called animistic Weltanschauungen, which were decried as primitive by the so-called enlightened cultures and revered religions, are today best suited to serve the cause of an ecological peace of which world peace in its various aspects is a part. Asian religiosity pleads for positive attitude and essentially religious emotion not only toward human beings but also toward all living creatures, nature, and even inanimate things. Chuang Tzu's famous discourse on the happiness of the fish substantiates the thesis of universism beyond doubt. Here, too, some form of analogical apprehension is maintained between the world of human beings and cosmic nature at large.

The problem of ethics in its various ramifications—from the religious through the political to the ecological—is of central and global importance today. The love of and for nature is on everyone's lips, but one has the bad feeling that this love is really an expression of an excessively self-centered anthropocentric ethos of humans. It is humans who worry about the future. We love nature and want to reconstruct it not so much because we love nature as such and in her own right but because we love ourselves most. In the real spirit of an axiological deliberation, we must reorient ourselves and recognize the essentially interdependent relationship between humans and nature, leaving behind the classical models of anthropocentric and theocentric ethics.

The largest value system of which we human beings form a part demands from us not only our commitment to our fellow human beings but also to the whole ecosystem. Humans are cosmomorphic creatures (Scheler), and nothing entitles us to a singularily privileged rank in the democracy of all things in the organic cosmic nature. Oriental and occidental forms of ethos (over-)emphasizing nature and humans, respectively, are badly in need of a double-faceted adjustment: humans in their relation to society and humans in their relation to nature.

The concept of an analogous intercultural hermeneutics in close contact with that of interculturality leads to a fundamental change in our theoretical and practical attitude in teaching and research. It also implies a change in the ethnocentricity of historiography in all of the disciplines in the humanities. Furthermore, it is very critical of the deep-rooted tendency of modernity to subsumption and to various forms of appropriation.

In the name of understanding and overcoming the other, European thought from Hegel to Gadamer has been practicing some form of appropriation of the other. This appropriation was made easy by many extraphilosophical factors, such as colonialism, missionarism, imperialism, and so on.

Whoever thinks a universal logos, reason, culture, philosophy, and religion are to be fully and exclusively realized in one particular tradition—whether European or non-European—does not accept the independent reality of the other and jeopardizes a cross-cultural understanding. Truth is nobody's possession alone, and it does not favor any one particular Weltanschauung exclusively. The availability and nonavailability of one ultimate Truth, if there is one, go hand in hand and teach us to be diffident in our claim of possessing the Truth alone.

Notes

1. P. Ricoeur, *Geschichte und Wahrheit* (Munich 1974), 290–91.
2. R. A. Mall, *Philosophie im Vergleich der Kulturen: Interkulturelle Philosophie—eine neue Orientierung* (Darmstadt 1995), 41–42.
3. S. P. Huntington, *The Clash of Civilizations*, IV, 8 (New York 1996).
4. D. Davidson, "On the Very Idea of Conceptual Scheme," *Proceedings of the American Philosophical Association*, no. 17 (1973–74): 5–20.
5. R. A. Mall, "Metonymic Reflections on Shamkara's Concept of Brahman and Plato's Seventh Epistle," *Journal of Indian Council of Philosophical Research* 9, no. 2 (1992): 89–102.
6. M. Eliade, *Die Sehnsucht nach dem Ursprung* (Vienna 1973), 75–76.
7. K. Roy, *Hermeneutics: East and West* (Calcutta 1993), 67.
8. R. A. Mall, "Der Absolutheitsanspruch: Eine religionsphilosophische Meditation," *Loccumer Protokolle*, no. 7 (1991): 39–53.
9. R. Harré and M. Krausz, *Varieties of Relativism* (Oxford 1996).
10. H.-H. Gander (ed.) *Europa und die Philosophie* (Frankfurt 1993), 31.
11. K. Jaspers, *Vom Ursprung und Ziel der Geschichte* (Munich 1983), 97.
12. K. Löwith, *Geschichtliche Abhandlungen: Zur Kritik der geschichtlichen Existenz* (Stuttgart 1960), 175.
13. J. Rawls, *A Theory of Justice* (Cambridge 1971), 388.
14. W.-T. Chan, *A Source Book in Chinese Philosophy* (Princeton 1969), 209–10.
15. J. N. Mohanty, *Reason and Tradition in Indian Thought: An Essay on the Nature of Indian Philosophical Thinking* (Oxford 1992); B. K. Matilal, *Logic, Language and Reality* (Delhi 1990).
16. M. Granet, *Das chinesische Denken* (Frankfurt 1985), 254–55.
17. J. Needham, *History and Human Value: A Chinese Perspective for World Science and Technology* (Cambridge 1961); K.-K. Cho, "Restauration of Universism: Toward an Ethics of Accord Beyond Human Society," in *The World Community in Post-Industrial Society*, no. 5 (Seoul 1988): 2–19.

3

Hermeneutics of the One Under Different Names

Universality and Particularity

That human beings think, judge, feel, and act differently is a general observation amply verified empirically. The difference is not, however, total and fully exclusive, for we cannot even articulate such total difference. That human beings meet to differ and differ to meet seems to point to a deep-rooted, anthropological similarity as the basis for the possibility of understanding and communication among philosophies, cultures, and religions. A universality coexists with particularity. In this respect, there is a reason for talking about some form of a transcendental hermeneutic anthropology.

The idea of a common humanity may be considered a fact of empirical experience. It can also be given the status of a postulative norm that stands first for a methodological beginning and second for a regulative idea to be realized in the discourses of philosophies, religions, and cultures. The universality just hinted at must not be taken in a strong sense. It really makes its appearance in and through the overlapping centers that are present for different reasons.[1] The ekam sad of the rigvedic discovery transcends local, cultural, philosophical, and religious differences and yet helps us to comprehend them.

Mutual understanding among different cultures, philosophies, and religions is possible only when we avoid the two fictions of total identity and complete difference. Whereas total identity makes understanding redundant, total difference makes it impossible. Some taste, aptitude, and a certain mindset come before a preference for a particular religion and philosophy. So, the overlapping center for mutual communication must be located in a sentiment that stands for a mentality over and above particular conventions.

The hermeneutics we are badly in need of today and that can alone do justice to the de facto, existing, worldwide hermeneutic situation takes seriously the two elements of understanding others and being understood by them. Thus, the desire to understand and the desire to be understood go hand in hand, and the vedic dictum in terms of a living transcendental attitude makes such mutual communication possible. The term *transcendental attitude* refers not only to a methodological and formally logical possibility but also, and in our present context even more so, to a higher level of reflection and intuition accompanying our own particular philosophical conventions, cultures, and religions.

Either–or logic—that is, logic in terms of the principle of contradiction—is less suited to solve the problems facing interculturality and interreligiosity today, for such logic fails to understand the complexity of the subject at hand. Doubly valued logic has led more to demarcation than to cooperation. The ideal of negation of contradiction may be useful as a formalistic goal to be pursued; but, in the field of humanities (Geisteswissenschaften), where local and cultural patterns are of central importance, contradictions (at least in their less severe forms) are what we must learn to mitigate and to live with. Monistic patterns appear in different masks in religion, philosophy, culture, and politics, and they are always more or less intolerant, for they necessarily tend to negate what is not like what they are. The vedic dictum is an antidote for such a monistic way of thinking. It pleads for unity in terms of ekam sad, but it does not stand for uniformity. It is against a universal reading of reality and allows for a plurality of interpretations.

Original Context

The rigvedic dictum, that which is one Supreme Reality, the idea that only wise men name it differently, is, no doubt, cryptic, aphoristic, and enigmatic. Nevertheless, it represents a reservoir for further religious and philosophical interpretations and speculations. This is true not only within the context of Indian tradition but also in today's world context.

This vedic seems to be an answer to a question that the vedic seers must have put to themselves to determine the real nature of the one Truth that is intuited and realized in a spiritual, mystic experience. The vedic seers feel the primacy of questions over answers despite their mystic experience. It must have been this tension between critical thinking and reflection (manan) and spiritual, mystic experience (nididhyâsan) that led them to formulate this dictum, which stands for some form of monistic pluralism or pluralistic monism. I do not wish to introduce some type of neologism. This phrase stands only for the inner, unshakable intuitive experience and conviction that there is one Supreme Reality that appears under different names. It is the conviction that there are different ways to the same goal. It may also stand for a postulate, a regulative idea with which we should start whenever we come in contact with other philosophies, cultures, and religions. That which unites us is nearer the truth than that which separates us. The different names are verbal and sometimes even trivial if they claim to be exclusively in possession of the One Truth.

The context in which this vedic sentence originally occurs begins with documentation of the result of self-introspection. The vedic writer describes the beauty and grandeur of the sun and the moon. He says that he is ignorant and aspires for knowledge. He asks about the First Born (ko dadars prathamam jâyamâna).[2] In addition to the desire to know the unborn One, the vedic seer also displays some doubt and skepticism in his attitude, which is characteristic of philosophic thought, whether in the East or in the West.[3]

There is much controversy about whether this vedic saying is just anthropomorphic. The one Supreme Truth, which was there from eternity, is beyond names, for words and names came into being after human beings. That one (tadekam)[4] is beyond all analogies known to the human mind. The vedic seers thus may truly be interpreted as having formulated a metaphysical and a religious intuition with wide possibilities for application in different fields of human activities transcending the narrow historico-temporal contexts in which the One Truth under different names is expressed and exemplified.

The Import of the Vedic Dictum Today

It is undoubtedly true that nothing happens without a context, which may be of various natures. Because the different contexts are not simply watertight compartments comparable to windowless monads, the philosophical and religious interpretations take place both intra- and interculturally and intra- and interreligiously. The vedic dictum put to such a test fares quite well.

Western scholars as well as some Indian scholars also tend to interpret the vedic dictum in an anthropomorphic and polytheistic sense. Because they are convinced of a progressive, linear development from polytheism to monotheism and monism, they fail to see the well-grounded possibility of interpreting the vedic dictum as the deep-rooted conviction of the vedic sages that different gods are just different manifestations of the one supreme God. F. Max Müeller painfully constructed a term for such a position, which, according to his reading of the vedic dictum, is neither just a blunt polytheism nor a full-fledged monotheism. *Henotheism* is the term Max Müeller invented, and he meant a transitional stage from polytheism to monotheism. Seen from the Christian theological framework, such a reading might be eligible, but it hardly does justice to the Indian religious and philosophical framework that, although not radically different, believes in the real possibility of one God under different names. The richness and fullness of one God in no way suffer from being called by different names. It is the greed of narrow human thinking that claims the One exclusively. The Indian religious tradition, in contrast to that of Christianity, underlines the fact that the one God remains the same even after being worshipped under different names. Any tradition that disapproves of such a possibility tends to be monistic, leading to a very narrow hermeneutics that defines understanding in terms of self-understanding. The ekam sad of the vedic dictum is, of course, in need of language, but it also defies language in the sense of not being exhausted by its names. "Neither polytheism nor henotheism nor even monotheism," writes C. Sharma, "can be taken as the key-note of the early vedic philosophy."[5]

A pertinent question regarding the philosophical and theological import of this vedic dictum relates to the problem of whether the One is more than the sum total of the many names given to it or whether the many names make and exhaust the One. If we accept the latter, then it may lead to some form of uniformitarian thinking in philosophy and religion if the many names individually and exclusively claim the One. The first reading is more liberal and leaves room for transcendence with the additional quality of being comprehensive, tolerant, and adaptable. The Hindu-Trinity of the three gods in One Supreme God does not exhaust the One. The One is, no doubt, available to all three, but it is fully available to none of them exclusively. Exchanging names for the same thing includes some underlying metonymic relation. Any theory of philosophical and theological hermeneutics today must be more pervasive, tolerant, and open-minded, reading the philosophical and religious utterances of the past in the spirit of the vedic dictum. The above-quoted vedic dictum depicts the religio-philosophical framework of the Hindu mind for which the religious and philosophical truth presents itself in manifold ways. The vedic dictum, thus, allows us to read the Christian saying of there being many mansions in God's house as well as many paths leading to God's house. Such a reading paves the way for a better mutual understanding among religions, philosophies, and cultures. Implied is the concept of an "analogous hermeneutics" that allows the One to be called by different names. An analogous hermeneutics abstains from a hermeneutics for which the relation of identity is of paramount importance. It also rejects a hermeneutics that takes the differences radically. Monistic patterns are, therefore, less tolerant, for they plead for a hermeneutics that aims at either converting or neglecting the other. Recorded human history is full of examples substantiating this thesis. An analogous hermeneutics has as its departure overlapping centers among philosophies, cultures, and religions and tries to enlarge and deepen them for ever better understanding.

The Idea of "Religio Perennis"

The idea of religio perennis is that all of the truths in other fields of human life are derived from only one principle, which is called God. This idea points to the ultimate theological anchorage, which is amply testified to by the theological realism of Thomas Aquinas and by the claim of Catholic metaphysics to be the true form of philosophia perennis. Such one-sided and exclusive claims are not absent in Indian tradition. The term that shows some overlapping with the idea of a religio perennis in the Indian religious framework is "sanâtana dharma," the one eternal truth or religion.

It is, of course, true that in some of its historical forms Hinduism itself claims to be this eternal religion. This claim is not legitimate. Such a claim became dominant during the nineteenth and twentieth centuries, when Hinduism came in contact with Christianity. Tilak, Gandhi, Tagore, Ram Mohan Roy, and Dayananda subscribed more or less to such a reading of sanâtana dharma.

Sanâtana, or Shâshvatadharma, is not itself a dharma in the sense of being a positive religion with its own cult and other religious practices. Sanâtana dharma is like the transcendental ego that also is not something existing over and above the empirical and yet given to us at a higher level of consciousness. One who ascribes to such a reading of sanâtana dharma is committed to no one particular religion as the only true religion. Its neutrality is its strength, which must not be confused with disinterestedness.

To be true to the spirit of the vedic dictum it is not required to identify the "tadekam" with the positive religion of Hinduism. To do so would really mean committing the mistake of pars pro toto. The richness and tolerance of Hinduism lie in its conviction that the different religions, including Hinduism itself, are different expressions of the one eternal dharma. Hinduism may claim as its own original contribution to the philosophy of comparative religion only its insight to see the religio perennis as the eternal religious wisdom lying at the back of all positive religions.[6] This additional insight itself is not a positive religion to which one may truly belong. It is, rather, the ethos of an interreligiosity allowing us to believe firmly and let others believe. Nobody can call it exclusively his or her own. This insight is like a shadow that accompanies or should accompany all of the positive religions, reminding them all the time of the vedic dictum of ekam sad. It is also the very core of a religiously tolerant hermeneutics that alone is in the position to further the cause of a dialogue among religions. Sanâtana dharma can, thus, be interpreted in the real spirit of the vedic dictum as a regulative, basic religiosity, which is the very cornerstone of interreligiosity. It may also function as a guiding principle on the methodological level.[7]

The Vedic Dictum and the Idea of "Philosophia Perennis"

I have hinted at the religious overlapping between the sanâtana dharma and the religio perennis. A similar overlapping and conceptual concordance may be worked out between the ekam sad and the notion of a philosophia perennis. "Every one," Jaspers writes, "possesses philosophy only in his historical form, and this is of course, so far as it is true, an expression of philosophia perennis, which no one possesses as such."[8] The term *philosophia perennis* was first introduced by Augustinus Steuchus in 1540 to refer to the fundamental truths that are believed to exist in all races and cultures beyond the limitations of time and space.[9] In spite of this liberal attitude, philosophers have not stopped claiming to have located philosophia perennis in a particular race, culture, or philosophical convention.[10]

As there is no one positive religion that can and should be identified with the all-encompassing, universal, eternal religion, so also there is no one philosophical tradition in either the West or the East that can and should exclusively claim to possess the one philosophia perennis as such. The claim to possess philosophia perennis has been explicitly or implicitly made in nearly all traditions. Among the modern Western philosophers, there are three, Hegel, Husserl, and Heidegger, who in opposition to Schopenhauer, Deussen, Scheler, and Jaspers identify the very idea of philosophy with European philosophy. Heidegger even goes so far as to deny the application of the predicate philosophy to any other tradition. He writes, "The often heard expression the occidental-european philosophy is in truth a tautology."[11] The reason for this tautology is, according to Heidegger's rather a priori, nonempirical, linguistic, and ethnocentric claims, the further conviction that philosophy is just of Greek origin. The adjective *European* in the phrase *European philosophy* gets privileged treatment by Heidegger.[12] Such one-sidedness is also found on the Indian side, which claims that philosophy is essentially spiritual and Indian.[13]

Aldous Huxley uses the term *perennial philosophy* more in its cultural and historical aspects than Steuchus and aims at an integral thesis that uses the one philosophia perennis to express itself in various cultural and historical garbs. Huxley particularly emphasizes the converging elements.[14]

The vedic dictum of one Truth under different names rightly seems to plead for a liberal attitude that the one philosophia perennis is the exclusive possession of no one. It further makes clear that translations are rightly made. The thesis of the impossibility of translation is thus groundless, despite the fact that there are numerous difficulties in translating from one language and culture into another. The meeting of different philosophies, cultures, and religions today is badly in need of such an attitude. We require such an attitude not only interculturally but also intraculturally. Such an intercultural and interphilosophical attitude methodologically takes into consideration the new global hermeneutic situation and supports a renewal of philosophical dialogue. The philosophical conviction, characteristic of such an attitude, pleads for the thesis of philosophy having different places of origin. Philosophy qua philosophy is not totally culture bound, although it needs the soil of a culture to take root and grow. The one philosophia perennis, which is rightly said to be universal, cannot have any prejudice for or against a particular philosophical tradition. The vedic dictum might be taken to be a testimony to this fact. The ekam sad has no mother tongue.

Another characteristic feature of the vedic dictum can be seen in its philosophical modesty, for it does not overrate the importance of a logocentric orientation. Such modesty may lead to an epistemological attitude of abstaining from claiming total understanding of all that may be understood. It also prevents us from hypostatizing one eternal idea of philosophy and philosophical truth.

There is a tendency in certain philosophical conventions to define philosophical truth in terms of a particular tradition and that particular tradition in terms of philosophical truth. This strategy is not only circular but also vacuous and merely nominalistic. Philosophia perennis as the overlapping center is the sine qua non for philosophical understanding beyond the narrow limits of one's own tradition and within the broader context of world philosophy. "It is the philosophia perennis," Jaspers writes, "which provides the common ground where most distant persons are related with each other, the Chinese with the Westerners, the thinkers before 2500 years with those of the present."[15]

No philosophical convention can empty the endless reservoir of the philosophia perennis. It has been the dream of many metaphysicians and theologians to possess the one eternal Truth in its entirety and in all concreteness. This greedy illusion has led to an endless misunderstanding among different philosophical "Weltanschauungen." In the spirit of the phenomenological method, one may rightly view the philosophia perennis and the ekam sad of the vedic dictum as the ideal noematic correlate of the noetic acts of human beings belonging to different races, cultures, religions, and so on. Such a phenomenological deconstruction of philosophia perennis does not fully reject the idea of the universality of the philosophia perennis; rather, it puts it in an overall context of the universality of the noetico-noematic correlation.

The syâdvâda logic of the Jaina philosophy supplies an effective tool of liberal deconstruction of every point of view that places itself in an absolute status and claims to be exclusively in possession of the one Truth. Nothing is given to us in the absence of perspectives. The logic of syâdvâda, of course, must remain satisfied with the different perspectives taken without any further claim to an absolute reconciliation of different perspectives in one grand perspective. The Jainas might have taken their own Weltanschauung as an all-encompassing view, but that is, strictly speaking, no philosophy; it is rather a matter of personal decision and liking. It is also a lesson we should draw from the vedic dictum of ekam sad.

Toward a Metonymic Theory of One Truth Under Different Names

No two philosophies, cultures, or religions are totally commensurable or fully incommensurable. This is true interculturally as well as intraculturally. If the one Supreme Truth is to be found exclusively in one philosophical or religious tradition, then the phrase *diversity of cultures and religions* loses all meaning. Such an understanding of philosophia perennis and religio perennis also hampers mutual understanding among cultures, philosophies, and religions. The hermeneutics that is at work here is that of identity, which, strongly put, asserts that to understand Shamkara is to be a Samkarite, to understand Plato is to be a Platonic, and so on. A hermeneutics of identity has the further disadvantage that it relegates other philosophies, cultures, and religions more or less to some primitive forms on the way of the progressive march to the telos of one philosophy, culture, and religion. Hegel is a fitting example.

In opposition to the hermeneutics of identity, there is one of total difference, which posits radical differences among cultures, religions, and philosophies to the extent that even the general terms *culture, religion,* and *philosophy* are not applicable to other cultures, religions, and philosophies. One wonders whether such total difference can even be articulated. The hermeneutics of total difference nips in the bud the very possibility of mutual understanding. On closer analysis, we find both types of hermeneutics (one of total identity and the other of total difference) as two sides of the same coin, for they both establish their way of understanding as the most paradigmatic.

The vedic dictum of one Truth under different names tries to steer between these two extreme and fictional positions and allows us to accept and respect both similarities and differences, making room for the common expression of the one Supreme Truth in different philosophies, religions, and cultures. The one ultimate reality is undoubtedly in need of linguistic expression, but, at the same time, it resists every attempt at total expressibility.[16] The science of metonymy deals with the fact of using different names for associated things. It uses one word for another, expecting the different names to suggest one and the same thing. It thus points to the indubitable consciousness of difference between the name and the named, between concept and reality. The thing named is always in need of being named, although it is not totally taken up with its names. The metonymic figure of speech, in its ultimately metaphysical and religious aspect, stresses the fact that the one Supreme Reality, although in need of expression, is not totally available to language and expression. This must have been the deep-rooted conviction of the vedic seers when they put it in their famous words, "ekam sad viprâ bahudhâ vadanti."

In the spirit of vedic dictum, we are better suited to overcome the naive, mundane dogmatism that easily forgets that every point of view expresses a limited perspective.[17] No authentic philosopher or genuine believer can generate a dialogue among philosophies, cultures, and religions unless he or she is personally convinced of the truth that the One Truth is nobody's possession alone. The discovery of one Truth that the wise call by different names is one of the greatest contributions of Indian thought to the world.

The vedic dictum can even be extended to political, social, and ethical fields. All that we need is the cultivation of an interculturally oriented attitude that allows us to read and let read, to interpret and let interpret, to believe and let believe, and so on. To discover and possess this culture of interculturality and interreligiosity on the edge between critical reflection (manan) and meditation (nididhyâsan) is what we are badly in need of today, for much hope rests on the philosophy that it be not only a way of thought but also a way of life.[18]

The vedic dictum formulates a religious and philosophical conviction (one may as well call it insight, intellectual intuition, or a mystic experience) that is beyond mere historicism and relativism. It does accept the truth of relativism, but it is a relativism that makes the different names relative to the one Supreme Truth and not the names among themselves. It, thus, provides us with an overarching frame of reference.

Notes

1. R. A. Mall, *Philosophie im Vergleich der Kulturen: Interkulturelle Philosophie—eine neue Orientierung* (Darmstadt 1995).
2. *Rigveda*, I, 164 4.
3. *Rigveda*, X, 6, 7.
4. *Rigveda*, X, 129, 2.
5. C. Sharma, *A Critical Survey of Indian Philosophy* (Delhi 1976), 15.
6. P. A. Schilpp (ed.) *The Philosophy of Sarvepalli Radhakrishnan* (New York 1952), 80.
7. W. Halbfas, *India and Europe* (New York 1990).

8. "Jeder Mensch besitzt Philosophie nur in seiner geschichtlichen Gestalt, diese ist doch, sofern sie wahr ist, ein Ausdruck der philosophia perennis, die als solche niemand besitzt." K. Jaspers, *Weltgeschichte der Philosophie* (Munich 1982), 20–21 (my translation).

9. A. Steuchus, *De perenni philosophia* (London 1974).

10. R. A. Mall and H. Hülsmann, *Die drei Geburtsorte der Philosophie: China, Indien, Europa* (Bonn 1989), R. A. Mall, "Die orthaft ortlose philosophia perennis und die interkulturelle Philosophie," in *Das Begehren des Fremden*, ed. L. J. von Bonny Duala-M'bedy (Essen 1992).

11. M. Heidegger, *Was ist das—die Philosophie?* (Pfullingen 1963), 13 (my translation).

12. R. A. Mall, "Meditationen zum Adjektiv 'europäisch' aus interkultureller Sicht," in *Der technologische Imperativ: Heinz Hülsmann zum 75 Geburtstag*, ed. W. von Blumberger (Munich/Vienna 1992).

13. J. N. Mohanty, *Reason and Tradition in Indian Thought: An Essay on the Nature of Indian Philosophical Thinking* (Oxford 1992), 290.

14. A. Huxley, *The Perennial Philosophy* (London 1990).

15. "Es ist die philosophia perennis, welche die Gemeinsamkeit schafft, in der die Fernsten miteinander verbunden sind, die Chinesen mit den Abendländorn, die Denker vor 2500 Jahren mit der Gegon wart." Jaspers, *Weltgeschichte der Philosophie*, 56 (my translation).

16. R. A. Mall, "Metonymic Reflections on Shamkara's Concept of Brahman and Plato's Seventh Epistle," *Journal of Indian Council of Philosophical Research* 10, no. 3 (1993).

17. F. C. Copleston, *Philosophies and Cultures* (Oxford 1980), 2–5.

18. R. A. Mall, "Philosophie als Denk- und Lebensweg," in *Probleme philosophischer Mystik*, ed. E. von Jain and R. Margreiter (St. Augustine 1991).

4

Intercultural Philosophy and Postmodernity

The De Facto Hermeneutic Situation

Although interculturality does not necessarily originate from postmodernity, it is, nevertheless, supported by it. Interculturality is, thus, within as well as outside of postmodernity. Furthermore, interculturality and postmodernity share a common framework approving of the value of plurality in culture, philosophy, religion, and politics. They go hand in hand in their emancipatory protest against monistic tendencies. They do, however, recognize the tension lying at the back of the simultanaeity of contradictory processes, namely of globalization and fragmentation.

As for later Wittgenstein, world language is not the name of a single phenomenon called *world language* but rather the name of the class of an unlimited number of language games bound by the family resemblance beyond mere identity and difference among languages. Such is also the case with the intercultural philosophy that represents an attitude, an orientation, rather than a single fact or a single philosophical discipline.

Cultures have always come in contact with one other, whether in the form of a peaceful meeting (which has, unfortunately, been rare) or in a clash of cultures (which has occurred far too often). The total purity of culture is a myth. Cultures motivated by this myth have done more harm than good in and to the history of humankind because they have normally led to some form of racism.

Different factors have been working in the background of cultural encounters since the days of Alexander the Great in Persia and India, the discovery of America by Columbus, and the colonization of Asia and Africa by the Europeans. In all of these cases, there were many extratheoretical, extraphilosophical, and religious forces at work that helped these cultures to suppress, to rule, and even to destroy other cultures. The history of colonialism, imperialism, and missionarism testify to this fact.

For the past few decades, mainly after World War II, a fundamental change has taken place in the way different cultures meet and address one other. This change has brought a new quality to our global cultural context, which occurs in an inevitable reciprocity. The result has been a new, de facto hermeneutic situation characterized by the fact that, for the past few decades, non-European cultures have had a voice of their own that they use in their thinking and writing not only about themselves but also about others.

The Concept of Interculturality

I prefer the term *interculturality* over *transculturality* for the simple reason that all of our points of view are bound up in a culture and do not exist in vacuo. The prefix *inter-*, in comparison to *trans-*, points to an experiential core of existence. If there is any universal worthy of the name, beyond either being postulated or just defined, it is the intercultural one. The prefix *trans-* seems to point to something beyond and makes us believe in a transition.

Cultural encounters in today's global context reject the idea of a "concrete universal" (Hegel) if this concreteness is equated with a local gestalt of one particular philosophical convention. There is, thus, a renewed call for deconstruction of an exclusive relation, not only among cultures but, most important, between truth and tradition. The one Truth does not favor a particular tradition. If a tradition is believed to have a privileged position, then it confuses truth and tradition. Such confusion, resulting from the centristic claim of defining truth and tradition reciprocally, has reigned supreme in many cultural encounters in the past. Monoculturalism, one of the main characteristics of modernity, has been the essence of colonialism and of all other types of exclusivistic thinking.

One of the main trademarks of modernity is the idea of a unified subject. The concept of an all-encompassing and binding reason is a distinguishing feature of the project of modernity. Whoever puts one particular, sedimented gestalt of philosophy in an absolute position either does so in a purely formalistic way or violently overrates its importance. The tendency to absolutize oneself exclusively ultimately leads to deadlock, for different absolute positions, when confronted with one other, automatically relativize themselves.[1]

Much of what is done today in the name of comparative studies is mainly from the Western point of view and shows signs of the West's asymmetry and hegemony. That this asymmetry between the East and the West is the result of a historical contingency is evident from the steps that European history has taken during the past few hundred years. This asymmetry has made European thought the main paradigm of reference. Furthermore, there is still the deep-rooted prejudice of the academically institutionalized orientalistic studies, namely the prejudice that philosophy, culture, and religion worthy of their names are mainly, if not exclusively, Western achievements. The spirit of interculturality tries to overcome this asymmetry to foster conditions for the possibility of a common global discourse and conversation of humankind beyond the narrow limits of the East–West dichotomy.

There is, of course, no denying the fact that there is, to recall an expression of Husserl, a Westernization of the world. This Europeanization follows in the footsteps of modern European technological formation. Whether this very secular and outward form of Europeanization is lamentable is a very large and complicated question, and I am not going to address it here. Nevertheless, I want to emphasize that we are called on to differentiate between Europeanization and Westernization. It is mainly the hardware of Europeanization, not the software, that has become global. That is why it is not far from the point to maintain that Europeanization is an ideology, a dream, whereas Westernization is a fact. From Hegel to Husserl, Europeanization stands for the total acceptance of European culture, philosophy, and religion. Karl Jaspers is one of the very few modern philosophers who plead for the thesis that Europe is one of the centers of culture, philosophy, and religion and not the only one.

To overcome the above-mentioned asymmetry between the East and the West, we must abandon the habit of examining our own tradition, culture, philosophy, and religion—in this case, my own Indian one—from only the Western point of view. The ingenuity and the independent character of Indian thought, for example, also have the right to examine the European philosophical tradition from the Indian standpoint. Comparative philosophy is not a one-way road, and Indian philosophy can very well view European philosophy as a "purvapaksha"—that is, as a position to be discussed and criticized. The parameters of intercultural discourse must be defined anew, which means that we must start from the conviction that there are basic similarities and illuminating differences between the questions that different cultural and philosophical traditions ask and the answers that they give. We should abstain from overemphasizing the one at the expense of the other. The concept of interculturality sees the truth we discuss, debate, and engage in as situated somewhere between the two extreme positions of total identity and radical difference. The truth, if it is committed to intercultural communication and understanding, as it should be, is an overlapping concept about which philosophers from the East and the West can converse, trying to understand one other's ideas and arguments. They may thus meet to differ and differ to meet in the intercultural spirit of a binding pluralism.

The concept of "intercultural philosophy" as understood here is not an additional branch of philosophy. It is also not the name of a particular philosophical tradition, whether Western or non-Western. It is wrong to view it as an eclecticism of different philosophical traditions, an abstraction, or merely a formal construct. Intercultural philosophy is also not to be misunderstood as a reaction or a shift made in the face of the de facto situation of philosophy in a global context. Far from being a romanticization, an aesthetization, or just a trendy expression, intercultural philosophy is the name of an attitude for the deep philosophical conviction that the one philosophia perennis is the exclusive possession of no one particular philosophical tradition, be it Western or non-Western.

The Concept of Postmodernity

The idea of perfection, of final fulfillment and completion, has been a trademark of European thought, at least since the Christian, Hegelian, and Marxist philosophies of the history and destiny of humankind. These philosophies claim to have deciphered the only possible true meaning of history, and they always think in terms of projects to be completed. In contrast, there is no denying the fact that a plurality of culture has defied the claim of total uniformity. Any singular and all-binding reading of human history is doomed to failure. If such a universal reading were to come to power, then it would be dangerous.

The sensitive constellation of hermeneutics and interculturality defines the framework of philosophical arguments today. The child baptized as postmodernity seems to have multiple parentage, stretching from art and architecture to literature, philosophy, and religion. Views differ, and will continue to differ, regarding the real origin and nature of this epoch-making concept. It was, of course, Rudolf Pannwitz who, following Nietzsche, used this term in the cultural crisis around World War I.[2] My use of the term refers mainly to Arnold Toynbee, who used this term in 1947 or even before to describe and define an epoch of Western culture during the transition between a global interaction and merely Eurocentric discourse. What Toynbee wanted to emphasize was the challenge that the monolithic Western culture was forced to face and to accept—that no culture is the one culture for all of humankind.[3]

There is a tendency to narrow the basically international and world-encompassing horizon of the concept of postmodernity and to limit it to a discourse between modernity and postmodernity within the boundaries of a Western dialogue. Such a move is not only unjust but also shortsighted.[4]

One of the most important defining features of postmodernity is the perennial idea of protest against any exclusively absolutistic Weltanschauung. Postmodernity rejects the misuse of unity as uniformity and asks us to be very cautious and diffident in our use of the prefix *mono-*. The experiment that has been underway for many hundreds of years as the world-unifying concept of modernity can be accurately characterized by a lack of coherence between theory and practice. Western culture has promulgated and practiced the high ideals of democracy, freedom, liberalism, and human rights at least somewhat at home, but it has engaged in colonialism, imperialism, missionarism, and other forms of appropriation of the other. It seems that the masculine force of modernity, like imperialism, rationality, and universality, showed its superiority over feminine, virgin territories to be conquered by the Western adventurous spirit. It was Mahatma Gandhi who proved the strength of the so-called feminine force, such as nonviolence, "satyagraha," and so on.[5]

In answering the question, "What is postmodern?" which Lyotard asks, he speaks of different tendencies in and of our time and says, while alluding to Habermas, that he recently read a work by a well-respected author who defended against the neoconservatives the project of modernity that is not yet fully realized.[6] Habermas, of course, pleads for the project of modernity in the sense of realizing the unity of experience by accepting the thesis of the unity of one reason in the multiplicity of its voices (die Einheit der Vernunft in der Vielheit ihrer Stimmen). Habermas works out a very complex, intriguing, and rather idealized version of a binding theory of communication to support his thesis.[7]

I cannot discuss the theoretical soundness and feasibility of Habermas's theory here, but I would like to remark that, in the face of a pluralism of principles, it is hardly possible to defend a very strong version of consensualism. An obsessive desire for uniformity and universality may mislead us to absolutize exclusively a local, culture-bound concept of philosophy, reason, religion, and so on, and tempt us to practice bare assimilation and appropriation of the other in the name of cross-cultural understanding and communication. According to Habermas, agreement among subjects is to be induced only by the force of better argument. To ensure that this agreement happens by the force of a better argument, a symmetrical distribution of chances must be guaranteed. The question is whether it is possible to have pure communication devoid of all cultural influences. Habermas's communication model makes itself immune to all of the different social and manipulative factors by constructing an ideal speech situation. Such a model lacks empirical support and cannot be established inductively. Even if a communicative model, with its structures of communicative action, pertains to a particular culture, then it is still not possible to defend the universality of these structures. I suspect that such a tendency lies at the back of Hegel's philosophical endeavor, which bestows on every culture, philosophy, and religion a place in the hierarchy of Hegel's one all-encompassing model and culminates in the speculative philosophy of the absolute spirit and the revealed religion of Christianity.

The concept of postmodernity does not take diversity as a disvalue, a privation of the value of unity. It pleads for diversity as a value to be respected in the name of, and for the sake of, intercultural peace. The positive attitude of interculturality toward plurality and diversity does not result from our inability to dispose of plurality in culture, religion, and philosophy. Postmodern conviction in support of the intercultural attitude affirms plurality, but it does not make a cult of pluralism. Too much of anything, even pluralism, is bad.

The concept of postmodernity may be summarily characterized as follows:

1. In the field of theoretical philosophy, it rejects the thesis of a transcultural, transethnic universal subject of knowledge, which also means the rejection of all forms of methodological monism.
2. It is also suspicious of the concept of a universal rationality that claims to reign supreme in all walks of life. Reason and passion are co-sharers in and of our life. Any anthropology that reduces the one to the other is a cryptoanthropology.
3. The idea of total primacy of reason over passion and the concept of reason-guided and reason-governed history are one-sided and reductive in character.

Against the modernist view of reason, postmodernism denies the excessively logocentric prejudice of an inborn special access of reason to meaning and truth.[8]

Cultures are the embodiment of meanings and not just guardians of truth and reason. Lyotard is right when he argues that we more often think analogically and metaphorically than logically.[9] The postmodern attitude also entails a new conception of a postmodern theology that takes the presence of a plurality of religions as something to be accepted and respected rather than to fear. It seems to be God's wish that there be many religions as different paths to salvation. Polytheism, rightly interpreted and understood, is more tolerant than monotheism.

Postmodernity is neither a concept of temporality preceded by modernity or succeeding it nor merely a historically situated phenomenon. Postmodernity rejects the radical dichotomy of thesis and antithesis and does not mistake heterothesis for antithesis. The plural is at least co-original with the singular. It is wrong to identify postmodernity with bare aesthetization of everything leaving discourse and communication to the mercy of chance and good luck. Such an impression may arise when we find some postmodern thinkers occasionally going a bit too far in overrating the importance of plurality.

Our characterization of postmodernity allows us rightly to differentiate between two versions of it—a strong and a weak version. A strong version of postmodernity overrates the importance of, and the role played by, plurality; neglects the legitimate role played by unity; and underrates the importance of overlappings among cultures, philosophies, and religions. It makes rather too much of the undeniable factor of power in human discourse. Such a strong version is in places too suspicious of a consensus brought about peacefully and just by the persuasiveness of better arguments. Critics sometimes attribute this strong version of postmodernism to anarchism. In this regard, talk of the end of history, which certain postmodern thinkers profess, is rather short-sighted. It may be the expression of human experience overloaded with negativities.[10]

Opposing a strong version of postmodernity is the weak version of it, which is favored by the spirit of interculturality and accepts as well as respects diversity as a value; this version tries to work out overlappings among diverse cultures, philosophies, and religions without, of course, denying, reducing, or explaining away the presence of diversity. This conception of postmodernity removes the fear of many protagonists of modernity. They fear that to accept postmodernity is to land in relativism, nihilism, solipsism, and deconstructivism. But, to say that even the most powerful concepts of philosophy (e.g., reason, truth, knowledge, value) are relative is only to maintain that there are different ways of asking and answering philosophical questions and that there is more than one way of finding meaning in and for the world. If this is relativism, then I wonder how one cannot be a relativist.

Today, intercultural context is an additional richness of the ever-present intracultural variations. Those who find the above-mentioned characterization of relativism unacceptable seem to betray their absolutistic conviction that there is only one true culture, philosophy, and religion for the whole of humankind. Such a claim, so long as it remains a theoretical conviction, is not very harmful; it is, rather, ridiculous, particularly in the face of the global intercultural context of world philosophy. However, the moment such a claim obtains political power, it may become dangerous. Moreover, such an absolutistic claim is made by more than one culture, philosophy, and religion; and, where there is a plurality of absolutistic claims, they automatically relativize themselves.[11] It is wrong to wish to monopolize the activities called *philosophy, religion,* and *culture.*

Intercultural philosophy does not deny the universal connotation of the term *philosophy;* it only makes clear that its general applicability is not a concrete universal but is on the line of the Wittgensteinean idea of a world language that is not the name of a particular language but the name of the class of all language games. The concept of philosophy does not lose its universality if we allow the spirit of philosophy to be present in more than one philosophical tradition.[12] Whoever denies the universal presence of philosophy as mentioned above claims to possess the philosophical Truth alone. Such a claim is mistaken even intraculturally as well as in the intercultural context. There are cultures, religions, and philosophies that claim to possess the absolute Truth all alone, and Europe is the foremost example. Derrida seems to be right when he maintains that Europe often talks of crisis when its own universality of being accepted globally is in danger. There is no local universality; it is a contradiction in terms.

Interculturality and Postmodernity

Based on the discussion above, it follows that an intercultural philosophy pleading different but not radically different ways of doing philosophy cannot allow any tradition to possess the one philosophia perennis in toto. Intercultural philosophy as understood here does not arise from, but is strongly supported by, the spirit of postmodernity. The question of whether intercultural philosophy is to be placed within or outside of postmodernity can be answered both positively and negatively. It is outside of postmodernity, for it is a perennial protest against uniformities. It is, nonetheless, within postmodernity because it gets fresh support from within the framework of postmodernity. Intercultural philosophical and postmodern orientations join together in their common protest against the prefix *mono-* and question not unity or diversity but unity in the face of diversity.

If we emphasize the nonchronological, nonhistorical, and nonprogressive version of postmodernity and lay greater emphasis on its systematic and problematic orientation, then there seems to be a point in viewing interculturality and postmodernity as two sides of the same coin. Both strike a new note and plead for a polyphony of voices. Both go hand in hand not so much in the sense of erecting a philosophical project to be accepted by all (for that would not be philosophical at all) or in the sense of a universalistic philosophical theory (for that would be too monolithic to be acceptable) but in the sense of a common and cross-cultural discourse in which all of the different cultural traditions can participate equally and make their specific contribution toward the formation of world philosophy and global conversation beyond the narrow limits of the East or the West. Intercultural philosophy and postmodern thinking also lay bare the hollowness of cultural chauvinism in philosophy and discover in the claim of European philosophy to be the only philosophy proper an ethnocentrism that was universalized.

Intercultural and postmodern orientations in philosophy prepare the very ground on which comparative philosophy can be fruitfully done if the latter is not going to be a juxtaposition and tagging on of theories and -isms. Whoever compares under the presupposition of providing the only possible parameter for comparison from within his or her own philosophical tradition is not in a position to enter into an open discourse. Any comparative philosophy worthy of the name must cut across the East–West dichotomy to furnish an interculturally oriented philosophical endeavor with needed comprehensiveness, creativity, and openness. This is possible only when comparative studies are preceded and accompanied by an intercultural orientation in different branches of the humanities.

   Intercultural philosophy and postmodernity join hands in their protest against modernity that is overloaded with monolithic tendencies. Both plead for and defend a pluralistic stance that approves of provisionality and relativity without sinking into totally radical relativism. Intercultural philosophy warns us not to absolutize ourselves and advises us to be diffident not only with regard to our doubts but also with regard to our certainties.

Modernity, Postmodernity, Interculturality, and Beyond

Real intercultural understanding and communication failed to occur during the long period of Western modernity in its contact with non-Western cultures, religions, and philosophies not because of lack of information (for orientalists, ethnologists, and missionaries did furnish Europe with much information) but mainly because of unjustified claims to superiority, rationality, and universality. The dry, rational systems produced by the grand master narratives to appropriate the other were theoretically and practically violent and completely disembodied. Backed by powerful extraphilosophical factors, the West succeeded in neglecting and appropriating other cultures, religions, and philosophies. The life-worlds of others were not taken into consideration at all. Unity as uniformity reigned supreme, and the difference was something to be overcome.

   The concept of the well-known and much-talked-about "hermeneutic circle," overcultivated in certain versions of modern hermeneutics, makes us believe that cultures and traditions are just like monads, and they are condemned to move within themselves. They may cross the limits of the hermeneutic circle only at the expense of being untrue to their own history, culture, and tradition. Even philosophers of such high ranks as Hegel and Husserl were not free from such Eurocentric thinking. Husserl maintained that all non-European cultures were nearly duty bound to Europeanize themselves. The universal entelechie inherent in European culture does not need such a transformation.

   Postmodern thinkers start from the facticity of the plurality of cultures, denies the myth of total identity and the fiction of radical difference, takes difference (Derrida) seriously, sees the sedimented character of all cultures and traditions, and thus overcomes the narrow limits of the hermeneutic circle without transforming themselves into others or being untrue to their own cultures. The multilayered intercultural life-world is in need of a hermeneutics that steers clear between the two extremes of the hermeneutics of total identity and that of total difference. In places, there may be a postmodern celebration of plurality without much care for even a minimum of overlapping among cultures, philosophies, and religions. Such a move is too much of an aesthetization, leaving discourse to the mercy of chance and luck, which really amounts to neglecting the role that philosophical arguments play in our discourse. To be genuinely intercultural, any postmodern discourse must open up its deconstructivist model to an ever-widening horizon of cultural encounters, meetings, and communication.

Any just celebration of plurality must become part of an interculturally oriented vision for the realization of an intercultural attitude that does not allow the one Truth to be exclusively the possession of one particular culture alone. To cultivate such an attitude, one must view philosophy not only as a way of thought but also as a way of life. Intercultural philosophy and anthropology interact with each other and transform the person engaged in global, intercultural discourse and communication.

The desire to understand the other and the desire to be understood by the other—the hallmark of the hermeneutics of interculturality—is beyond both modernity and postmodernity, for this fundamental reciprocity constitutes an overlapping even in the absence of agreement or consensus. Where no consensus can be reached despite the good will of all of the parties engaged in the discourse, it is acquiescence that aids us. It is this feature of an interculturally oriented hermeneutics that mitigates the tension between modernity and postmodernity. Intercultural philosophy ties the concept of truth more to communication than to consensus. It is here that Jaspers, who was very interested in achieving the goal of communication, differs from the consensus theorists, who sometimes overrate the importance of consensus.

The main objective of intercultural philosophy is thus to cultivate insight into the epistemological, methodological, ethical, moral, cultural, and religious modesty of one's own approach to the one regulative ideal of ever-better understanding and communication among multiple cultures. Our multiple points of view are relative not so much to one another but rather to the intended goal of reaching the one Truth. The different views are complementary and not contrary.

I close my discussion by quoting the words of the Indian poet-philosopher Rabindra Nath Tagore who pointedly brings out the very sense of the beyond of interculturality in its relationship to modernity and postmodernity. He writes, "If humanity ever happens to be overwhelmed with the universal flood of a bigoted exclusiveness, then God will have to make provision for another Noah's Ark to save His creatures from the catastrophe of spiritual desolation."[13]

Notes

1. R. A. Mall, "Zur interkulturellen Theorie der Vernunft: Ein Paradigmenwechsel," in *Vernunftbegriffe in der Moderne*, ed. H. F. von Fulda and R.-P. Horstmann (Stuttgart 1994), 750–74.

2. R. Pannwitz, *Die Krisis der europäischen Kultur*, vol. 2 (Nuremburg 1917), 64.

3. A. Toynbee, *A Study of History: Abridgement of Volumes I–VI*, ed. D. C. Somervell (Oxford 1947), 39.

4. A. Willmer, *Zur Dialektik von Moderne und Postmoderne* (Frankfurt 1985).

5. A. Nandy, *The Intimate Enemy: The Loss and Recovery of Self Under Colonialism* (Delhi 1983).

6. J.-F. Lyotard, *Postmoderne für die Kinder* (Vienna 1987), 12.

7. J. Habermas, *Der philosophische Diskurs der Moderne* (Frankfurt 1985); "Die Einheit der Vernunft in der Vielheit ihrer Stimmen," *Merkur*, no. 1 (1988): 1–14.

8. J. Murphy, *Postmodern Social Analysis and Criticism* (New York 1989).

9. J. -F. Lyotard, "Can Thought Go on Without a Body?" *Discourse* 11, no. 1 ( ): 77–88. (Fall-Winter 1988-89).

10. G. Vattimo, *The End of Modernity: Nihilism and Hermeneutics of Postmodern Culture* (Baltimore 1988); F. Dallmayr, *Margins of Political Discourse* (Albany 1989).

11. Mall, "Zur interkulturellen Theorie der Vernunft, 750–74.

12. R. A. Mall and H. Hülsmann, *Die drei Geburtsorte der Philosophie: China, Indien und Europa* (Bonn 1989).

13. R. Tagore, *Boundless Sky: An Anthology*, ed. R. S. Das (Calcutta 1964), 275.

5

An Intercultural Philosophy
of Unity Without Uniformity

Preliminary Remarks

This chapter is divided into three sections. The first section lays down the fundamental principle of a regulative idea of unity as the precondition for the possibility of any intercultural understanding. Scheler has rightly remarked that our age is not just one with a particular "zeitgeist"; it is a world era (Weltalter), and the question of peace guided by unity without uniformity has become a global question for politicians and intellectuals alike. The pressing need for human solidarity today calls for a deeper, more comprehensive, and abiding foundation than the partial historical unities have ever been able to supply.

The second section deals with the application of the principle of unity in the ups and downs of human history, mostly in its abusive form of uniformity. It is not wrong to view history as a constant struggle between drive and mind, between the real and ideal factors of history. Neither of the two has ever won or lost completely, although drive has shaped human history more than mind. I also pose the historically very interesting question, "How is it that European thought tended and even, in certain quarters, tends toward expansionism, reductionism, and monocausal explanations?" In this section, I pick out, as a central theme, Hegel's metaphysics of unity, which, for all practical purposes, degenerates into uniformity.

The third section proposes an open, more comprehensive, postulative, and normative concept of hermeneutics in the center of our interculturally oriented world philosophy and hopes that such a normative philosophical hermeneutic approach might prevail in a casuistic manner. In other words, we propose a nonreductive theory of hermeneutics with its two fundamental questions: the questio facti with regard to tradition and the questio juris with regard to the regulative ideal of unity without uniformity. Our concept of hermeneutics is not only a method but goes beyond it and works out certain ways and means for the practical application of the ideal of unity. The one.Truth we are in search of has never been and will probably never be fully realized; and the truths we have realized were and are historical-philosophical expressions bound by space, time, and other traditional factors. With Jaspers, we, thus, define truth as that which unites us.

The Principle of Unity

A plurality of races, cultures, religions, and "Weltanschauungen" provides the basic data—the materials for any concrete socio-philosophical reflection. Despite factual multiplicity, different cultural patterns reveal an underlying unity among them, not so much in the sense of one absolute pattern claiming to be the paradigm for all of the others, but in the sense of being a necessary response to the physical, biological, social, and religious environment. Thus, whereas unity is a need and goes with a plurality of forms, uniformity constitutes a presumption that may, and in fact does, endanger plurality of expressions by absolutizing one particular response to the world of things and beings. There is an inherent paucity in all of our bigoted claims to be in full possession of the absolute Truth.

The philosophical reflection, which is committed less to a fundamental ontology and more to a fundamental ethics, pleads for a unity and not for a uniformity. A fundamental ethics does not try to constitute the other but starts with the conviction and commitment that our very perception of the other obliges us to live and let live. It does not entail a watering down of the concept of tolerance. Even the best type of tolerance has its limits where its own fate is at stake.

The actual historicity of human beings and their traditions is manifold, and no ideal of unity can be inductively derived from it. But the many is subordinated to the one, which does not represent any historical fact but stands for an ethical, moral, and socio-philosophical demand. This demand, again, is not the exclusiveness of any particular historicity—politically, racially, culturally, religiously, or philosophically; rather, it originates as an intuitive consciousness in the communicative situation within the manifold of different historicities. It is this consciousness of an absolute, simple historicity that, although lying beyond all particular historicities, relativizes the manifold of historicities. Of course, the experience of a multiplicity of races and cultures does not encourage us to entertain such an idea of unity. But the very being of humans consists of the fact that humans matter to one other, which leads to different forms of communication. Even the unfulfilled forms of communication, such as conflict, antipathy, and so on, point to the possibility of a unity whose absence is registered in such forms.

Although the biological-psychological constitution of human beings supports the idea of a unity, its real seat lies beyond the naturalistic observation of humans. We start with the presupposition that that which binds us is more original than that which separates us. Also, this most original bond cannot be of only biological origin. Were it so, human beings would not be able to endanger their own species. Not as a natural species are humans the seat and origin of the idea of unity, but as historical beings, who, despite the disadvantages that differences involve, learn the essential unity in the diversity of forms. The regulative idea of unity has a normative core and serves the purpose of communication.

The unity of all human beings seems to be further corroborated by the observation that similar tendencies and traits prevail in different religions and cultures. Despite great psychological and sociological differences, comparisons are possible and made; but the unity referred to here is not just an abstract universal derived from similarities between races and cultures, although their similarities are important.

An impartial study of human history shows clearly that "the good" has seldom succeeded and that "the bad" has often won the game. But, had the good been done just for the sake of success, then it should have been given up long ago. The idea of peace does not lose its right of existence simply because real human history has been far too bloody. The ideals are there to be realized, and the absence of their realization is not their failure, but ours. The so-called unity found in the modern world of science and technology is a lower type of nominalistic unity of technological formation disguising itself politically, economically, racially, culturally, and so on. It binds our heads but not our hearts. These and other similar forms of superficial unity lack the universality we philosophically and ethically postulate and try to realize in our communication with diverse cultures, religions, and so on. No single concrete unity should usurp the place of the deeper unity that lies ahead and waits for its gradual realization. For the first time in human history, we can vividly picture the connotation and denotation of one "humanity," which is not the quantitative one of a particular race, culture, or religion but the qualitative one of a regulative idea with the possibility of acting as a mediator.

The unity we mean and postulate here is an ethical proposition for realization not solely constituted by any historical fact; it stands for the ultimate goal and meaning of humanity. It is not a fact but an ideal. It represents, to use an expression of Jaspers, the will to a total, universal communication in which to differ is not to misunderstand. The very possibility of communication presupposes such an idea of unity, which allows for plurality without reduction. This methodologically postulated unity may sometimes take the form of the will to unity without the will to power, for the latter suppresses, controls, rules, and reduces. Because such a will to unity is not a fact, it must be cultivated, and every human pedagogy is committed to it. That we have never achieved such a unity in human history does not undermine its importance and status; it shows that its realization, although not impossible, is not probable.

The fundamentally ethical relevance of our concept of unity lies in its teaching us the important lesson of modesty. All individual total constructions, hypostatizing the only true message of history, have been more or less shipwrecked. We are always in search of a real philosophy of history. Any philosophical reflection on history today must bid farewell to all of the old religious-speculative, absolutistic models of understanding history, for they all (e.g., Hegel, Marx) are more or less like the Chinese well-frog, identifying the vastness of the sky with the narrow view it has of it from in the well. No one should hypostatize the one absolute historicity, and whoever claims to be in possession of it is presumptuous.

The trouble with these historico-philosophical constructions is that they treat history as a closed system with a beginning and an end. They plead either for faith or for speculation. A far truer understanding of history is our consciousness of openness. It enables us, in all openness, to wait for a future that is neither fully a chance product nor merely an aimless natural repetition. This ability to wait makes the idea of unity inevitable and bound to us. We all seem to be convinced of the idea of unity, but there is a constant tendency to commit the mistake of modeling it on a particular historical unity.

All of the different negative descriptions of what unity is can be summarized as follows: unity is neither a reality nor able to be truly pictured in any historical, philosophical, or religious vision. In contrast, it is also not just nothing; its truth exists in its character of being a symbol, a cypher whose presence we feel intensely when all of our multiple pretentious efforts to encompass the absolute historicity break down. All that remains, then, is an all-comprehensive, fundamentally ethical demand on the idea of unity as our responsibility. Its absence in reality is its guiding presence as an ideal.

The real seat of this idea of unity is our ever-present conviction that we do not accept the different forms of misunderstandings as the ultimate datum. We treat them as stepping stones to an ever-better and more comprehensive form of understanding. We feel that there really is a universal form of understandability in which we all meet. But the most crucial problem besetting our theory is this one: if the unity of one humanity is not to be found in any one particular system of belief or thought, then is it to be pursued and realized in and through the manifold of concrete historical unities, communicating with one other without any absolutistic claim? In the absence of a better answer, we must approve the second possibility. We must and should take this idea of unity as an antidote to our tendency to absolutize our own limited standpoints. To have a standpoint is what we can hardly avoid. The mistake lies in not accepting that standpoints, including our own, are standpoints. They are limited and mostly one-sided. Giving up all standpoints does not mean inventing a new standpoint of having no standpoint. An absence of standpoint represents our consciousness—an attitude that no standpoint is the standpoint.

Our concept of unity as outlined here is a concept of quality and must not be confused with any particular unity as a concept of quantity. The qualitative one is not the numerical, quantitative one. Because no quantitative expression of the qualitative unity can exhaust it, the commitment to communication is a morally binding responsibility for all of us. In real practice, it means to tolerate the historically different tradition without necessarily giving up one's own historicity. It also means that any claim to absolutism is to be suspended, for it necessarily breaks off the very possibility of the act of communication. The normative truth-claim of the concept of unity must be adhered to because the recognition of this highest value can guarantee a tolerably peaceful coexistence of different traditions, cultures, and religions. Misunderstood, unity leads to uniformity and conformity; rightly understood, unity makes room for free communication by advocating a complementary theory of truth. On this view of truth, intolerance of differences, which is the enemy of all real communication, becomes impossible. Fundamentalism as such is bad, regardless of whether it is of a religious, political, social, or even philosophical nature. The focus on qualitative unity, beyond the reach of an epistemologically oriented correspondence theory of truth, is a constant reminder of the fundamental truth that both reactionaries and revolutionaries commit the fatal mistake of secularizing this or that particular tradition. Truth in the spirit of intercultural philosophy is more committed to communication than to a metaphysical conviction or to a formal consensus. To be able to communicate, we must relinquish the idea of an exclusive possession of the Truth. The absence of consensus is not necessarily the death of communication.

A Critical Examination of Hegel's Philosophy of Unity

Even a cursory empirical survey of human history shows that cultural encounters have occurred in one of three ways:

1. The meeting of diverse cultures took the form of confrontation and ended in destruction of nearly all of the others except one. To a great extent, this scenario is the sad story history tells us about contacts between European-Christians and the inhabitants of both the American continents and between the original Persian culture and Islam.
2. They lived side by side with the lurking danger of one being destroyed at any time. In the long run, they were coerced into some kind of superficial homogeneity. The treatment of the Greek culture by the Romans and of the Greek and Roman cultures by the Christians may be cited as examples.
3. They lived together without losing their identities as was the case among Buddhism, Confucianism, and Taoism in China. The Chinese saying, "Three teachings, one family" testifies to underlying, deeper unity without uniformity. On the Indian subcontinent, cultural contacts from Aryan times until the British period took more or less such a form of coexistence. The birth of Buddha and his reformation of Hinduistic culture did not lead to a thirty-year war as was the case after Luther's reformation in Europe.

History also verifies the emergence of a new unity dominated more or less by one of the original components. The unity of European culture is a case in point. Originally, the three centers of European culture, namely Athens, Palestine, and Rome, were so opposed to one other that no optimist could think of their assimilation. The emergent unity took, of course, a long time, and the roads it traversed were stained with blood. An unbiased analysis of European culture shows clearly that differences can be and have been, to a certain extent, overcome. Western culture owes its critical, scientific spirit to Greece, its secular laws to Rome, and its religion to Palestine; but the three components of European tradition—thought, action, and faith—have rarely reached a harmonious stage. Despite this lack of harmony, Europe has always tended to mistake unity for uniformity with the added claim to a universality.

One of the reasons for this absolutistic tendency may be found in the belief of the European mind that philosophy originated in Greece alone. Traces of such conviction can be found even in the works of thinkers such as Heidegger and Gadamer as well as Hegel, a European philosopher par excellence who gave a metaphysical and absolutistic interpretation of the Christian faith.

The other reason is the conviction that Christianity is the only true religion because of its sole revelation of God through his son, Christ. This conviction led to the further conviction that the Christian religion is the point of culmination of all religions. These two beliefs, although in themselves simply the spatio-temporal and historical manifestations of philosophia or religio perennis, respectively, gathered political momentum through the development of modern sciences. The expansive tendency, lying at the back of these two beliefs, joined hands with modern technical civilization and resulted in different forms of imperialism, preaching the gospel of one philosophy and one religion.

The past fifty to sixty years have brought a real change in this one-sided outlook, making Europe one of the centers of the world. Today, we come across books on the history of philosophy that devote a few pages to non-European thought. For this change, we are thankful to the same European universalism, which, not without a touch of irony, went out to preach the gospel of the West to the East and taught the West the gospel of the East. Because the European curtain falls today and the myth of Europe being the center of the world is unmasked, we enter into an era of world history out of real sociopolitical and intercultural necessity. Our task is to learn whether this change of Western mind is just a response to a modern practical need or whether it points to a real philosophical conversion. We are afraid that the first alternative might not be far from the truth. If we define philosophy as an attempt of human thought to solve the problems with which it is confronted in its encounter with the world of things and beings, then there is no denying that philosophy originated not only in Greece but also in India and China. In 600 B.C., a genuine attempt was made to replace "myth" with "reason" in all of these three birth places of philosophy. Jaspers is one of the few far-sighted modern philosophers who seriously thought and wrote about the history of world philosophy. He introduced his revolutionary thesis of an empirically based axis of world philosophy to replace Hegel's speculative concept that identified the birth of Christ as the only axis of world philosophy.

The real spirit of a world philosophy does not take the concepts, categories, methods, and views developed by a particular philosophical tradition as the philosopher's stone. The wrong alternative—either absolutism or relativism—that philosophers put to themselves, leads them to choose one and not the other. The philosophers' inherent fear may be overcome when we realize that we do not testify to our faculty of reason by making reason itself a quality of a formal, systematic structure aimed at clarity but rather through an open-mindedness and readiness to realize the limits, weaknesses, and even presumptions of our systems.

Scheler was right when he complained that we do not have an adequate anthropology corresponding to the world era in which we live; in a similar spirit, it may be justly pointed out that we lack a hermeneutics that could do justice to the pressing need of an intercultural understanding. No philosophy can really claim to have established the absolute subject of a transethnic, universal human consciousness. An intercultural subject worthy of the name is not a subject existing side by side with empirical, historical, and temporal subjects; it is rather the name of an attitude, or a philosophical conviction, that the one Truth does not necessarily favor any one particular culture, philosophical conviction, or language.

Hegel, the great philosopher of the absolute spirit, is credited with having undertaken the great project of writing a world history of philosophy. But, at the same time, he is to be blamed for hypostatizing his philosophy of unity, which degenerates into uniformity, as the culmination of all philosophy. Hegel's metaphysics of the absolute spirit considers the whole, beyond all contradictions, as the unity that alone is real. In depicting the progress of this whole through human history, Hegel mentions three well-known phases—Oriental, Greek and Roman, and German—and asserts that the absolute spirit has come to itself in his philosophy, in Christianity, and in the Prussian state. For Hegel, German history passed through three phases after the fall of the Roman empire: the first, until Charles the Great; the second, from Charles the Great until the Reformation; and the third, from the Reformation onward. He even goes so far as to relate these three phases with the kingdom of the Father, the Son, and the Holy Ghost, respectively. Hegel, the metaphysician of dynamic unity, is overtaken by the vehemently Protestant Hegel, believing in Christianity as the only true religion and making world history a development of the nature of God. Only Christians are initiated in the providence of God as the ultimate goal of history. Hegel, to our astonishment and disappointment, even goes so far as to think of every culture as a means in the furtherance of the ultimate goal that, of course, is, for Hegel, the European-Christian culture.

Hegel's concept of unity has one merit and three defects. Its merit lies in its character of being a dynamic whole, never to be exhausted by any particular part of it. Its defects are, first, that it is far too speculative to be of any substantial use in our empirical search for an intercultural understanding; second, that it confuses metaphysics with ethics and morals, for Hegel takes the metaphysical development of the absolute spirit as ethical progress in the real history of the world; and, third, that it tends toward uniformity and conformity because it absolutizes itself. The birth of Christ is, for Hegel (as we have noted above), the axis of world history; and the Christian-oriented, Germanic-European philosophy is the only true philosophy. All other philosophies are cited as stepping stones to this one form of philosophy. Hegel's considerable ignorance of Asian philosophy and his absolutistic tendency led him to think that Asian philosophy is not even worthy of the name, although he recognizes some original philosophy in India.

Hegel's total identification of providence with the Christian version of it made him think that only Christians are in possession of the real key to world history. It is hardly necessary to comment on the dangerous character of such a philosophy in a tense climate of sociopolitical concern. Dictators are not born but made. Hegel must have been led to such theoretically dictatorial thinking because of the teaching of Christianity that the godly "reason" totally incarnated itself and appeared in person. We are tempted to think that the tendency of European-Christian thought to ontologize and hypostatize ultimate principles might have its origin herein. Only thus can we explain and understand Hegel, who speaks of circumnavigating the globe since the incarnation of the absolute Christian truth. It is Hegel's firm conviction that the world is divinely destined to be ruled by the Europeans. The countries that are not yet under their dominance are either going to be ruled soon or are not worthy of subjection. The undaunted dominance of Europe in the wake of the eighteenth century may serve as partial excuse for Hegel's incredible self-complacency. Hegel is a Christian propagandist in a philosopher's robe. Nietzsche was not far from the truth when he called Hegel a theologian in disguise.

This long allusion to Hegel's philosophy requires an excuse, which lies in my conviction that the Hegelian spirit of philosophy is still quite active in certain quarters of European philosophy, although not always explicitly. The result is that a particular philosophical, cultural, and religious tradition is given the status of a paradigm with a greater claim to truth than others. I hope to show, while elaborating on the nonreductive concept of a more comprehensive open hermeneutics, the "reductive" character of the modern hermeneutic school in Germany initiated by Wilhelm Dilthey and one-sidedly developed by Heidegger and Gadamer. Our critical examination of Hegel's philosophy of culture, religion, and history was guided by the question of whether Hegel could be of help today in our search for intercultural understanding and communication. The result is not very encouraging. The lasting merits of all other parts of Hegel's philosophy remain, of course, unaffected.

Toward a Concept of a Nonreductive, Open, and Normative Hermeneutics

The term *hermeneutics* has different connotations. Its theological origin points to its relation with sacred scriptures. The scientific interest in history in modern times led to a renewal of hermeneutics. Human history took the place of the sacred texts, and Hegel's philosophy of history allowed for only one interpretation of world history. For Dilthey, the main objective of hermeneutics was to determine the mind of the historical author. For Heidegger, and particularly for Gadamer, hermeneutics deals with the conditions and processes an interpreter uses to learn the meaning of texts and traditions.

To "understand" is not just to understand oneself and one's own tradition; it also means to understand others without transforming them in their substance. To understand others is, therefore, not to understand oneself once more. The "will to understand" and the "will to be understood" belong together and show the presence of a hermeneutic ambivalence. In understanding others, we open ourselves to them in that we start with our own self-interpretation but do not make it the only necessarily valid model. Every science of hermeneutics, which does not press the facts in a preconceived model, remains true to itself as an open process of understanding, interpretation, and application. The logic of a particular tradition does not exhaust the immense richness of the thing itself, which demands a multiplicity of philosophical traditions as responses. Hegel's mistake was that he absolutized just one particular logic of understanding history. However, an open concept of hermeneutics does not relativize the truth of one possible understanding as a sensus communis philosophicus; it simply abstains from absolutizing any particular historical form of it. Such a methodological approach is possible only under the presupposition that we, without denying our own tradition, give up the claim to absolutism, be it in the East or the West.

Viewed from its philosophical presuppositions, a "reductive theory of hermeneutics" may be characterized in the following way. First, it starts with a particular philosophy of history originating in a particular historical tradition; second, it absolutizes this one particular philosophy of history; third, it hypostatizes it either in the speculative-metaphysical spirit of Hegel or in the spirit of Heidegger's fundamental ontology; and, fourth, as a result, it raises only the problem of the questio facti and not the questio juris. The net result of such a hermeneutic model is that it deduces and reduces, for understanding is equated with self-understanding and to understand others means to understand them after transforming them into one's own categories and structures. Such a hermeneutics is one of identity, and it mainly aims at appropriating the other.

Although no philosophical theory has a universally accepted model of comparison at its disposal, the fact remains that every comparison presupposes the possible reality of a possible understanding as a common golden mean, at least as a hermeneutic demand of our philosophical responsibility. Dilthey was more farsighted than Hegel, for he tried to explain the development of other philosophical systems belonging to foreign traditions and cultures as independent expressions of a different cultural whole. The former Gadamer, in his introduction to Dilthey's book on the history of philosophy, seems to swing back to Hegel because he believes that, in Western philosophy's attempt to understand other philosophical traditions, with its sharp historical consciousness and fundamental philosophical concepts coined by the Greeks, it is left with the negative certainty to transform others in their very essence to understand them. Avowedly, such a view furthers nolens volens the cause of a reductive hermeneutics, which, because of its narrowness, either clings to the age-old sedimentations of a particular tradition or is haunted by the fear of self-alienation in its encounter and confrontation with a foreign tradition or culture. To overcome such a self-inculcated fear, it tends to transform the people, the tradition, or the culture it tries to understand, which must have been one of the main reasons for the expansive, all-appropriating tendency of the European mind in its encounter with foreign traditions. I do not minimize the importance of the powerful economic, political, ideological, and religious factors in the process of cultural confrontations; all that I want to emphasize is the poor nature of the "philosophical culture" underlying such a narrow model of a reductive hermeneutics. A philosophical culture worthy of the name believes in the efficacy of the internationality of the human mind preceding its nationality. No theory of hermeneutics can help us today if it universalizes one particular form of understanding. It is true that we cannot dismiss the necessity of starting with a particular model of understanding, but it is equally true that any ontologization of a particular model would mean the beginning of the end of all communication. In our world era, the science of hermeneutics is destined to play the most important role in intercultural, interracial, interreligious, and interpolitical understanding. An adequate logic, corresponding to our world era and following the spirit of unity without uniformity, must be one of "as well as" and not one of "either–or."

Discussed next are three approaches regarding the problem of hermeneutic understanding.

First, the phenomenological insight of Husserl, which allows "the unknown" itself to be understood in terms of some mode of the "already known," should be considered. This insight leads to the necessarily presuppositional character of all understanding, for we always approach an object with a particular anticipation of meaning. Heidegger and Gadamer were right in emphasizing the "foreproject of understanding" under the widely known title, "hermeneutic circle." A phenomenological hermeneutics no doubt starts from the fact that everyone lives in a particular, concrete "Lebenswelt," but it still points to the possibility of transcending the limits of our sedimentations. Later, Husserl was quite conscious of the fateful necessity of an intercultural understanding between the East and the West. The solely methodological Husserl must not be misunderstood as leading to the paradigmatic ontologization of a particular historical situation, which immunizes itself to the truth-claims of all other traditions. Any such absolutization changes beyond recognition the people and the traditions to be examined and understood and undertakes self-understanding while claiming to understand others. It leads again to Hegel's philosophy of unity degenerating into uniformity. Truth, in its fundamental sense, is in history, which is in the process of becoming; and no methodologically based criterion of truth should be allowed to "traditionalize" truth, thus leading to an a priori restrictive and prescriptive hermeneutics, which may be less dangerous theoretically and philosophically but can be of fatal consequences culturally and politically.

Second, we may approach the subject to be understood from an unbiased descriptive standpoint and try to work out common structures as the foundation of a theory of hermeneutic understanding, but this approach suffers from the drawback that it fails to give up the purely factual level of description. In addition, it also fails to find its way to the regulative idea of the unity of a possible understanding, which alone enables us to transcend our narrow hermeneutic models of understanding. It must also be realized that a purely descriptive hermeneutics is not always immune to the temptation of absolutizing a particular historical situation.

We plead for the third approach, a "nonreductive," open, and more comprehensive philosophical hermeneutics that considers not only the questio-facti aspect of the problem of understanding but also the questio-juris aspect of it. To understand means not only to ask how understanding really occurs but also to ask what understanding should be. If it is good that we understand what we ourselves are not and cannot be, then the ideal demand of an approximation of a possible understanding must guide every truly philosophical hermeneutics, which does not reduce because it does not absolutize. Such guidance is, however, only possible if short-sightedness, presumptive absoluteness, and conclusive understanding are avoided. Our "postulative-normative hermeneutics" rejects the very idea of absolutizing a particular objective historicity, be it concrete or speculative, in the East or the West.

Today's historical consciousness has undergone a qualitative change, and it has fully unmasked the arrogance of a philosophy of history that professed to have learned the secret of world history once and forever. There is no return to writing a history of philosophy in the spirit of Hegel because that would mean total neglect of the empirical historical evidence. Our concept of a regulative understanding consists of our insight that we are cosmic-morphological beings with the possibility of understanding one other, although, empirically speaking, we have never reached such an understanding.

To understand is not necessarily to agree. Were it so, we could have common sensations and feelings. The different cultures and forms of life are our varied reactions to the common problems we face when we come in contact with the world of things and beings. Thus, what matters is not so much our common answers but rather the common characters of our needs. Our normative postulate of the unity underlying our theory of hermeneutics serves a two-fold purpose. First, it has the advantage of explaining our more or less unending attempt at a better understanding, enabling us to use the de facto cases of misunderstanding as stepping stones toward the possible goal of real universal understanding. Second, it obliges us to take this postulate as an ethical, moral demand beyond all speculative-metaphysical or revered religious truths. Of course, the most important question regarding the limits and difficulties that the different "Weltanschauungen" face in their attempt to understand one other cannot be set aside. But, when speculation does not help, communication becomes our fate; and, because the fixation of one particular "Weltanschauung" claiming absolute truth is equivalent to an a priori determination barring the possibility of mutual understanding, we are left with the alternative of giving up the tendency of absolutizing this or that particular tradition. Thus, the question regarding the limits of our understanding turns out to be the question regarding our ability to widen our horizon of understanding. What we need today is a hermeneutic model that enables us to see that there is more in our commonly accepted but often neglected insight: human beings are human beings after all. In every concrete misunderstanding, we feel intensely the presence of something that, although in a position to make real understanding possible, somehow slips away from our grasp. Provided we do not mistake the symbolic character of our cultural patterns to be real copies of an absolute historical truth, we are led to think of the unity, yet to be realized, as underlying the concept of a universal human history. If there is a theodicee worthy of the name, then it lies in the future.

It is, no doubt, true that every understanding has a point of departure from a particular standpoint, but the insight, which is of utmost importance for our concept of hermeneutics, that all of the standpoints must be treated as standpoints is itself not to be equated with a new standpoint with concrete historical contents. To use a term from Jaspers's philosophy, it is the "encompassing" (das Umgreifende) insight, which might be motivated but is never deduced from the presence of multiple standpoints. The possible reproach that it then lacks concreteness does not hold true because the main function of such an insight, beyond all standpoints, is to enrich the different standpoints by enabling them to refrain from self-absolutization. Such an insight is not inductive, deductive, or reductive; it is rather postulative and regulative in character and owes its origin to an intuitive perception of "the other" unconstituted and unconstitutable. It is the very center of a fundamental ethics for which the presence of the other is neither a threat nor merely an oddity but a chance for practical communication. This concept of a fundamental ethics, going beyond and replacing a fundamental ontology, does not pay lip service to a superficial and modish pluralism; rather, it inculcates the philosophical conviction in us that "the other" is to be accepted and respected simply because of its being the other to me. The genuine pluralism it implies is not a syncretism but a "pluralistic unity" or a "unitary pluralism" avoiding uniformity as well as unrelatedness.

The binding truth that our nonreductive concept of hermeneutics discovers is not the historical truth of a particular philosophical convention. It is, rather, the first and the last frame of reference that really gives meaning to our various attempts at intercultural understanding. It is this truth, lying beyond all concrete history, that, as we have already mentioned, binds and does not separate us. It also frees us from our fear of historicism and relativism. It further saves us from dogmatism. That no understanding is totally presuppositionless is a commonplace of every hermeneutic science, but that no single historical situation should be absolutized still remains.

The two questions—how understanding takes place and how it should take place (the questio facti and the questio juris, respectively)—are in fact the two sides of the same hermeneutic coin. We are endlessly indebted to the normative dimension of our hermeneutics, for it is this side of it that makes us comprehend the historical limits and cultural narrowness of our traditions. This nonhistorical hermeneutic truth is historically quite potent, for it positively influences and leads our thinking in the field of intercultural understanding. We must, therefore, guard against mistaking our "ethnographic limits" to be anthropological constants. This reason must have been the main one for Hegel mistakenly seeing in his own philosophy the culmination of all philosophy whatsoever. Even the Heideggerian fundamental ontology as an analytic of being (Daseinsanalytik) succumbs to the temptation of ontologizing the being in its "hermeneutics of facticity." In our common hermeneutic undertaking, we should always aim at an approximative realization of the intended unity of a world culture, a world philosophy that is neither a bare formal logical category of unity nor a speculative metaphysical ideal only.

Our theory of hermeneutics, which bears the mark of a fundamental ethics, stands nearer to the thoughts of Vico, Schopenhauer, Collingwood, Dilthey, Misch, Scheler, Betti, and Jaspers than to those of Hegel, Heidegger, and Gadamer.

For the latter three philosophers, the relation between tradition and truth is quite ambiguous. Gadamer, following Heidegger, is, of course, right in emphasizing the importance of tradition as the precondition for the possibility of hermeneutic understanding, in so far as tradition is the historical frame in which we are all born and of which we are a part. But this must also apply to the situation in which multiple traditions and philosophical conventions penetrate and try to understand one other.

One cannot avoid the impression that, whereas Hegel absolutizes the Christian truth, Heidegger and Gadamer overrate the importance of the Greek tradition along with the sharp historicity of human consciousness. In a way, it is true that history does not belong to us, but we belong to it; then again, the question is that the history we belong to is the concrete history we are a part of. We take understanding to be an exclusive performance of history, so we must not confuse the historicity of the one absolute cosmic history we all belong to with the historicity of a particular spatio-temporally limited history. Everything forming part of this one grand cosmic life is treated with an impartiality without giving favorable treatment to any one particular species in the all-encompassing household of nature. Of course, the particular ways of different species define the special position of a species in the scheme of things. Provided we wish to avoid corseting history in a speculative metaphysical system, we must bid farewell to an absolutistic philosophy of history. We must be cognizant of the fact that there is no return to Hegel after the epoch-making, Diltheyian "critique of historical reason." No hermeneutics should be allowed to degenerate into ideology and strategy. There is an ambiguity of petitio principii if we define truth in terms of tradition, claiming thereby to clarify the relation between truth and tradition. In fact, there are two types of truth that must be kept apart: first, the truth of this or that concrete tradition; and second, the truth in this or that concrete tradition. The truth in the second sense is a framework within which all of the truths in the first sense reveal themselves. It is the open hermeneutics of one truth under different names.

Our concept of hermeneutics defines truth in terms of its approximative relationship to the one framework of truth without cutting off its relation from the truth of a particular tradition. A philosophical hermeneutics, which is true to the spirit of intercultural philosophy and is committed to it, cannot and should not avoid the question of a normative hermeneutics. To overrate the importance of human historicity leads to impatience, which, in its turn, begets short-sightedness and leads finally either to some forms of "panactivism" or "panpessimism." An empirical survey of human history does not, of course, encourage us regarding the possibility of the realization of our goal; it also does not dishearten us completely. All that it teaches us is to be humble in the face of what ultimately is beyond our control. Despite the possibility of failure, we should try to transcend the narrow conception of a philosophical objectivity based on a particular tradition.

We feel that the idea of a world culture, which seems to be in the making, may be realized only when we recognize that it is not multiplicity, but rather uniformity, that is really opposed to unity. A genuinely open understanding implies a qualitative addition to our knowledge of human nature. No violent universalization of a "crypto-anthropology" and no cultural, racial, religious, political, or philosophical provincialism can help us today. The type of anthropology we are in search of is not something ready made, just to be imitated; it is rather something to be worked out and realized with the help of a "creative hermeneutics" (Eliade) that brings about a qualitative change in our being.

6

Two Metaphors of Time-Arrow and Time-Cycle

The Thesis Defended

In this short chapter, I propose to do only one thing—to adduce a few arguments in favor of the thesis that the cyclic conception of time, rightly understood, can accommodate the linear conception of it. This chapter shows that cyclic recurrence is not just a mechanical repetition and accompanies novelty. My methodological approach is empirical, psychological, and phenomenological. There is always some sort of experience of time or consciousness of time, which underlies our various descriptions and conceptions of time. Felt time precedes any objectively measured time, which leads to the thesis that the general belief in the unreality of time is mistaken, and time is not just a mental construction but a lived experience accompanying all human and worldly processes.

It is the job of phenomenological reflection to lay bare the most foundational awareness of time, which precedes the two metaphors of arrow and cycle. The foundational character of this time awareness stands for a lived experience in the sense of an experiential subjectivity as the phenomenologically given source of evidence. The project of such an empirico-phenomenological foundation must not be confused with foundationalism through formal-logical principles. One may doubt the foundational character of formal principles and decide on a different set of principles, but the primordial, experiential evidence pointing to a deeper structure of experience is beyond doubt. Temporality, in this view, is not any physical event in the outside world but the innermost experience of a continuous flow that moves ultimately toward the last end, which is death. Although cyclic patterns repeat themselves in nature, in human history, and even in personal life, they do so in a successive manner, allowing the arrow-model its due place. The repetition involved in such a model does not mean a bare tautology, for the individuals who enjoy and suffer these repetitions are not the same. The case with groups and historical periods is similar.

An Empirico-Phenomenological Approach

An empirical and phenomenological study of time is the search for the most originary experience of succession, which must not be confused with the succession of experience, for the latter, in the sense of a phenomenologically given datum, is to be subsumed under the general heading, "experience of succession." The term *originary experience* stands for subjectively lived evidences as features of our inner consciousness. It is the most primordial character of all experiences, making an "absolute beginning," as Husserl puts it, and founding all knowledge. Husserl is very clear on this point: "No theory we can conceive can mislead us in regard to the principle of all principles: that every primordial dator intuition is a source of authority (Rechtsquelle) for knowledge, that whatever presents itself in 'intuition' in primordial form (as it were in its bodily reality), is simply to be accepted as it gives itself out to be."[1] It was the American philosopher and psychologist William James who used the term "specious present" to describe a single act of awareness that provides a unitary experience of time lasting, say, for a few seconds.[2] It has been often and rightly pointed out that it may be misleading to call this present "specious," for it is really the nonspecious time consciousness getting illegitimately mixed up with the events and processes that are experienced as the content of our time consciousness.

It seems nearly impossible to describe our time consciousness without the help of metaphors. We live, think, feel, and act in and with time consciousness. It is not, however, only the consciousness of time, or just events and processes as such, but their experienced relationship that gives rise to our time consciousness. The anthropological constant of intentionality with its emotional and expectational horizon brings in the third factor necessary for our time consciousness, for we do experience our seizing or missing opportunities in our way to fulfill our intended meanings and goals. For a being not in need of any fulfillment, time loses its meaning and also its sting. Thus, God is above time per definitionem.

Time awareness is therefore neither merely subjective, for it is something that we do not just create at our will, nor purely objective, for the intentional constitution of human nature is a necessary precondition for experiencing events and processes in terms of time. Time awareness happens to us and enables us to experience events and processes lasting longer or shorter than we wish them to. Any discussion of time must, therefore, consider that human beings are intentional and emotional creatures embedded in the cosmic household of needs and their fulfillment. This reason is also why we fear and/or desire the past, present, and future. The undeniable certainty of our death just aggravates the matter. The end, which for us is death, is of a radically different quality. Ends within the span of a life know of other beginnings, but the total end of life knows beginning.

In answering the question, "What is measured when time is measured?" we cannot name an entity divided into units unless we engage ourselves in complete abstraction and lose all contacts with life as it is lived. A lover, for example, experiences the same passage of time—for example, sixty minutes—very differently depending on whether the message of the train being one hour late while seeing off or fetching his beloved from or at the station. It is true that measured time as countable units is the same in both cases, but it is far too abstract, universal, and devoid of any meaning for human beings' lived experiences. Quantitatively measured time might claim total universality beyond cultural borders, but qualitatively felt time also possesses some sort of universality because of the anthropological constitution of human nature irrespective of other cultural differences that modify but do not override the interculturally valid anthropological overlappings. The modern anthropological insight that human beings are a bundle of wants and necessities points to a deep-rooted common structure of strategic means to satisfy these wants. The innumerable cultural devices bear, no doubt, the specific cultural marks but still the culturally invariant way to experience time in connection with the different modes of fulfillment and unfulfillment is similar beyond cultural boundaries. This fact shows the plausibility of the idea of a cross-cultural experience of time.

Time-Arrow and Time-Cycle

It is an undeniable fact of human experience that there is a repetitive pattern not only in cosmic nature but also in human history and life. The day-and-night cycle, the cycle of seasons in nature, the recurring conflicts and wars in human history, and other forms of habitual recurrence in human life are examples; but the philosophical theory of cyclic time is an inductive inference from innumerable repeated observations. Some sort of inductive generalization is also at work in the time-arrow model. The cyclic conception of time implies the idea of a beginningless and endless process. Against the cyclic conception of time, the time-arrow view pleads for the thesis of a one-way conception of time and conceives of a beginning and also of an end in and of the passage of time. If, however, we bracket the deep-rooted mythological, religious, and cultural factors, we may very well imagine the time-arrow to be beginningless and endless. In the spirit of the phenomenological method of eidetic variation we may describe the time-arrow as an endless structural repetition in the past as well as in the future. There is reasonably no sound answer to the question of why the time-arrow must have a beginning and an end.

The various alternative conceptions of time, nevertheless, make one thing clear—that time perception does vary from culture to culture with a difference is not radical but overlaps. The cyclic view of time, both at the cosmic and the human levels, has been very prevalent among the Hindus, the pre-Christian people of Central America, and the Chinese. The Western conception of time has mainly been the linear view based on the influence of Christianity. These two broad models of time, despite all of the differences, do claim to describe time, although they often, at least partly, mistake explanations and interpretations with description.

Opposing the cyclic view of time, which is less susceptible to catastrophic feelings and apocalyptic ideas, is the linear view of time, which tends either to a panactivistic or panpessimistic idea of human history. The belief in Heilsgeschichte (salvational history) is a case in point. There is a Christian belief about a divinely ordained spiritual progress in the time flow represented as the age of the Father, the Son, and the Holy Spirit. Even a fully nonreligious and secularized view of history may plead for a progressive time flow, replacing, of course, God with human agency. Thus, the climax foreseen in these progressive models of time flow may turn out to be something to be feared if we lack faith in an all-governing God or in a historical necessity. Modern man seems to be haunted by such a lack of faith. The Hindu conception of yugas and kalpas (historical and cosmic epochs) does make room for progress but lets it follow by a regress to be followed in turn by progress and so on. There is room for the image of the time-arrow within the cyclic view of time. Too much of an anthropocentric bias in our understanding of time leads to an idealistic prejudice. We deny the reality of time but it still stings.

A Critical Comparison

There is a widespread misunderstanding that the linear and cyclic views of time contradict each other because the former makes room for progress and novelty whereas the latter does not. My reflections on time try to weaken this opposition and plead for interdependence between the two views. An understanding of the cyclic view of time that is too strong and too narrow misunderstands the recurrence as identical repetition. Our understanding of the cyclic view of time emphasizes the repetition of pattern making room for novelty.

The cyclic view of time emphasizing the recurrent pattern in nature and human history points to structural recurrences that do not mean exact repetition of what has happened before. The present is not just a copy of the past and the future of the present. Life and death do repeat themselves, but those who live life and suffer death do it very differently and always individually. There is, of course, a structural pattern that is repeated as, for example, between the two world wars, when the individuals, societies, and generations experienced this general pattern with many novelties. We may think of time in terms of recurrent patterns and still experience it as full of novelties. In his book *Time's Arrow, Time's Cycle: Myth and Metaphor in the Discovery of Geological Time,* Stephen Jay Gould pleads for the thesis that the two views of time together have helped humans to understand time, history, and human destiny.[3] It is because of the cyclic view of time that we can think of lawfulness and predictability in nature, human history, and behavior. If nothing happens twice, then we are left with the dry burden of uniqueness making every communication impossible or just a matter of chance and good luck. The phenomenon of habit testifies to the fact of repetition in life.

The two views of time are found more or less in all cultures with varying degrees of dominance. When we talk of an eternal recurrence, we must not forget its mythical and religious connotation. The Hindu tradition goes to the extent of emphasizing the cycles of births and deaths, but it also suggests a way out. The religious experience of time with this sacred view is not only circular but also reversible.[4] The Indian view of time's circularity lays the main stress on the repetitive pattern of cosmic evolutions and involutions and of creation models. The empirically oriented secular view of circularity must not be confused with the religious view of it. The cosmic and historical cycles (kalpas and yugas) in Indian tradition point to a grand repetitive recurrence of changes. The various Indian philosophies (darshanas) are less interested in these cycles as such and ask instead philosophically pertinent questions, such as, "Is time subjective or objective, conceptual or real?" or "Is time just a construction or a linguistic or pragmatic convention?" There is a wide spectrum of views regarding the concept of time in Western as well as in Indian philosophical thought.

There are many perceptive minds, such as Toynbee and Tillich, who fail to distinguish between these two levels of time discussion in Indian thought and mistake these repetitive patterns as implications of fatalism, pessimism, inaction, and an impossibility of novelty.[5] These authors also misunderstand the real import of the law of karma in the cosmological and soteriological framework, for it is karma that enables us to free ourselves from these eternal circles.

The idea of karma is one of the most distinctive features of Indian philosophical and religious thinking. The theory of karma is essentially a metaphysical theory connected with rebirth and liberation. Such a theory is beyond empirical verification as well as falsification. The belief in the truth of this doctrine influences and transforms one's life. Past actions determine our present situation and, likewise, our current actions determine our future. In contrast to the deterministic theories emphasizing impersonal and collective determinants, karmic determinism is individualistic and can very well go with freedom and responsibility. The Yoga-school divides karmas into four classes: white (shukla) karmas, which excel in ethical and moral qualities and produce happiness; black (krishna) karmas, which produce pain and suffering; white-black (shukla-krishna) karmas, which give birth to both happiness and sadness; and neither white nor black (ashukla-krishna) karmas, which produce neither pleasure nor pain.[6] There are karmas that bind us and make us victims of the life-death circle, but there are also karmas that are so virtuous and flawless that they help us to get rid of this bondage. It is here that an intercultural and interreligious study of time may be of great help to clarify some of the clichés. Good karmas are those that free us from attachment and bondage, and they are meaningful not only in the religions but also in the secular context.

The idea of "eternal recurrence of the same" (ewige Wiederkehr des Gleichen) struck Nietzsche as a revelation that was not only the truest hypothesis but also a gruesome truth. The real import of Nietzsche's dictum is still a matter of debate; but Nietzsche, rather wisely, uses the term "the same" (das Gleiche) and not the term "identical" (das Identische), which does make room for novelty along with repetition. The recurrence pattern does not mean that cycles repeat themselves identically. If they do, then how can we compare them? The cycles are neither fully identical nor completely different. They have an overlapping pattern that enables us to compare them. What repeats is the generality of the recurrence pattern with the novelty of the individual cases within the same pattern. One cannot maintain that we lose all incentive to action without the prior certainty that things will radically change. The Chinese philosopher Confucius is depicted as one who used to say, "It makes no sense," although he never stopped acting.

Three Factors in Time Consciousness

There are three major factors involved in our time consciousness:

1. Without the perception of change in events and processes, we cannot have an experience of time.
2. But the continual change alone does not suffice to explain our time consciousness, although it is a necessary condition. What is needed is a primordial intuition of duration as we experience it in the living present with its retentive and protensive aspects.
3. The changes we perceive and experience are changes not only in the external world but also within ourselves. These changes are always accompanied by our desires and needs seeking fulfillment and satisfaction.

Even when we indulge in speculation and reverie, we experience that different movements get their temporal dimension from the most originary awareness, which, although itself not necessarily temporal, always becomes temporal the moment it comes into contact with the world of things and beings empirically. This foundational time consciousness is not a consciousness besides the empirical consciousness; it is only a reflective-meditative stance, an attitude that allows us to view time as linear and circular, depending on the different modes of experiencing time under different cultural and interpretative frameworks.

Time's arrow and time's cycle are two very potent metaphors for describing our views regarding time. Even when we take these two descriptions as different views of time, the question remains regarding our use of the general concept of time in both cases. In other words, some experiential time consciousness must lie at the back of these two descriptions lest they become purely formal and abstract.

Husserl receives credit for having given us a clue through his concept of the "living present" (lebendige Gegenwart), which avoids some of the drawbacks of James's specious present. Husserl's living present stands for the experience of the givenness of the flux consciousness.[7] This living present with its just past and not yet future, its retention and protension, does not necessarily subscribe to a linear view of the succession of nows although it favors it and Husserl seems to interpret the living present as a one-way view of time. But the living present, as we understand it, is as an ever-accompanying self-presence of all of our experiences during our lifetimes. The aporetic difficulties involved in the self-referencing of time are less severe when we conceive of the living present as the originary consciousness that makes the question of whether the living present itself is temporally redundant, for it is just the ever-present consciousness of the last point of reference of all of our empirical consciousness. With regard to this living present, it makes little sense to ask questions such as, "What is it that moves?" or "What is the direction it takes?" Husserl sometimes asked such questions and thought of events moving into the past, but the very use of the word *move* is metaphorical and suffers under the linguistic habit of hypostatizing events that do not change but just happen. What changes are the things; what happens are the events.[8]

An Intercultural Perspective

From an intercultural perspective, we find that both of the time models, arrow and cycle, have been prevalent in different cultures. What is undeniable is recurrence in nature as well as in human life. The cyclic view of time, because it does not mean an exact repetition, accommodates within its bounds the linear view of time. Despite the empirical evidence more in favor of the cyclic view of time than the linear view, there is a neutral sense of temporality in the Husserlian concept of the living present, which, no doubt, makes use of the above-mentioned metaphors but transcends them as well, for the temporality of the living present is experienced after bracketing physical, historical, and conceptual time. Every real experience in relation to other experiences is bound up with temporality in one endless stream of experience as a continuum of duration.[9] It is this transcendence that serves as the bedrock of our different time metaphors. Much of the puzzle that troubles philosophers in their attempt to give a neat verbal definition of time comes from the linguistic formulation of the question. Instead of asking, "What is time?" it is more fruitful to ask, "What experience is meant when we use the word *time?*"

When we ask, "What is time?" we are generally misled to expect an answer such as one answering the question, "What is a table?" But time is not something over and above the consciousness of our emotional and intentional involvement in the changing household of the cosmos as well in that of human history and life. Nothing is temporal, but feeling makes it so. I must add, lest it be mistaken, that it is not an arbitrary feeling that means that felt time is not just subjective but an anthropologically overlapping constant given to us cross-culturally. We may well fancy change without time, but we can never have time consciousness without an experience of change. Our consciousness of time's flow is, thus, our consciousness of things changing, and our division of the three dimensions of time—past, present, and future—is grounded in our anthropological-psychological activities of remembering, perceiving, and anticipating, respectively. Our experiential time's flow need not be modeled on any spatial model.[10] Our consciousness of felt time does not need any model.

Temporality and Historicity

The notion of temporality has been of utmost importance to the concept of historicity. The question, "Must a cyclic conception of time be incompatible with a concern for a philosophy of history?" may not be out of place here. There has been a general belief that philosophers not accepting the ontological reality of linear time and, tending toward a cyclic conception of it, fail to develop a deep sense for a philosophy of history. On such grounds, Indian thought was said to have failed to develop a historical sense. Jitendra Nath Mohanty is right in pointing out that it is not so much the metaphysical and religious belief in the reality or unreality of time that is responsible for the insensitivity of the Indian mind to history; it is rather a sense of the importance of history that is lacking. The reason for this lack may be the conviction of the Indian mind that ultimate values and eternal truths are not realized within history because they are transhistorical. Our interpretation of the cyclic conception of time with its broad recurrent patterns is compatible with a philosophical concern for history although it does not overrate the importance of it.[11]

The serious concern with a philosophy of history in Western thought is not really of Greek origin. Karl Löwith rightly maintains that a philosophical concern with history in Europe is of Judeo-Christian origin and culminates in modern times in the grand, speculative systems of German idealism.[12] Any deep philosophical concern for history centers around the problem of meaning and purpose in and of history. Is history a meaningful process of change? Only a positive answer to this question leads us to ask, "Is meaning inherent in history, or does it come from outside?" It is not history that just invites us to read meaning in it; it is rather our human concern that poses this question. Thus, the question of time—whether cyclic or linear—is not the whole explanation of our concern for history. The real seat of our concern for history is human nature with its drives, desires, intentions, and expectations.

History as a (meaningful) series of events and processes does not coincide with our consciousness of history because the temporality of consciousness, along with its historicity and intentionality, often experiences the unfulfillment of projected and intended meanings. What comes to an end is not so much the temporal, historical process of change but mortal, temporal, and intentional consciousness. There seems to be an essential ambiguity in the nature of the relation between consciousness and history. History is neither a totally meaningless process of change, for in that case all of our activities would be in vain, nor a fully meaningful process, for this would amount to a preordained goal—divine or human. The meaning we search in and through history can neither be a mere invention of the human mind nor something ready-made just to be noticed. It is within the historical-cultural horizon that we are led to bestow meaning to, and find it in, history.[13]

It seems to be the undeniable destiny of human consciousness not to give up its anthropologically rooted, intentional quest for meaning in life and history despite recurring negative experiences. Time's arrow and time's cycle both contain a philosophy of history, depending on the conviction of whether the ultimate value is going to be realized fully within or beyond history. An empirical survey of human history narrates a mixed story. The dream of finding heaven on earth, whether in a secular or a religious sense, may be common to both of the models with the difference that Asian thought, particularly Indian, is more skeptical about the two factors of temporality and historicity.

Concluding Remarks

Whatever theory of time we give our preference depends not only on the force of philosophical arguments but also on our philosophical and cultural dispositions and socializations. What is undeniable is the fact of our experience of repetition and recurrence, which is an essential ingredient in any conception of time. Our consciousness of temporality is not so much the consciousness of consciousness's being in time but rather the consciousness of consciousness's being itself time. All conceptions of time (mythical, cosmic, physical, historical, and so on), however remote they may appear to be, bear a relation, more or less, to this experiential temporality of human consciousness. Temporality and historicity, which are just the two sides of the coin, are experiential realities providing us with an existential framework within which all human moves occur and originate. It is this primordial framework that is the intersubjective and intercultural bedrock, with its virtual plasticity allowing for cultural differences. An intercultural perspective shows the cross-cultural overlapping in our understanding of time, giving due consideration to cultural differences that allow for the preference a particular culture possesses for the time metaphor as an arrow or as a cycle.

Notes

1. E. Husserl, *Ideas: General Introduction to Pure Phenemonology,* trans. W. R. Boyce Gobson (London 1958), 92.

2. The term *specious present,* which, according to James, was first introduced by E. R. Clay, is a fact of our immediate experience and underlines the experiential character of sensible duration. The theory of specious present has been variously interpreted, and James's version of it means that we are directly aware of both the immediate past and the immediate future. "The practically cognized present is no knife-edge, but a saddle-back, with a certain breadth of its own on which we sit perched, and from which we look in two directions into time." W. James, *Principles of Psychology,* vol. 1 (Dover 1950), 609.

3. S. J. Gould, *Time's Arrow, Time's Cycle: Myth and Metaphor in the Discovery of Geological Time* (Cambridge 1986).

4. M. Eliade, *The Sacred and the Profane: The Nature of Religion,* ed. W. R. Trask (New York 1959).

5. A. Toynbee, *A Study of History,* ed. A. Toynbee and J. Caplan (New York 1972); P. Tillich, *The Protestant Era* (Chicago 1948); J. N. Mohanty, "Time: Linear or Cyclic, and Husserl's Phenomenology of Inner Time Consciousness,"*Philosophia Naturalis* 25 (1988); A. N. Balslev, *A Study of Time in Indian Philosophy* (Wiesbaden 1983).

6. Patanjali, "The Yoga Shutras and Vyâsas' yoga-bhâsya," in *Sacred Books of the Hindus IV,* ed. R. Prasada (Allahabad 1924): chapter 4, shutras 6–8. S. N. Dasgupta, *Yoga as Philosophy and Religion* (Delhi 1987), 102–13.

7. E. Husserl, *Texte zur Phänomenologie des inneren Zeitbewußtseins (1893–1917),* ed. R. Bernet (Hamburg 1985); H. S. Prasad (ed.) *Time in Indian Philosophy* (Delhi 1992).

8. J. J. C. Smart, "The River of Time," *Mind* 58 (19): 483–94.

9. Husserl, *Ideas,* 236–37.

10. Prasad, *Time in Indian Philosophy.*

11. J. N. Mohanty, "Philosophy of History and Its Presuppositions," in *Contemporary Indian Philosophers of History,* ed. T. M. P. Mahadevan and G. E. Cairns (Calcutta 1977).

12. K. Löwith, *Meaning in History* (Chicago 1949).

13. P. Ricoeur, *History and Truth,* ed. C. A. Kelbley (Evanston 1965).

7

Metonymic Reflections on Shamkara's Concept of Brahman and Plato's Seventh Epistle

Preliminary Remarks

Both Shamkara and Plato struggle to say something positive about the ultimate one reality, but they still resist it linguisticality. Brahma-jijñâsâ, the inner-most desire to know Brahman, the nondual one, is to Shamkara and his entire philosophy the soul's desire to know the one ultimate reality, and what the hen, the agathon, is to Plato and his philosophy. Both Shamkara and Plato situate the one ultimate reality beyond language, logic, categories, and predication. Despite its nonavailability to language, the nondual one is not equated with a bare nothing. A theory of knowledge is worked out by both to pave the way for a better understanding and grasp of it. What defies language does not thereby necessarily defy its reality.

This chapter focuses on one particular but most important aspect of this reality in its relation to its availability to language and predicative judgment. Metonymy is the indubitable consciousness of the difference between the name and the named, concept and reality, which induces us to take recourse to negative expressions to describe something that claims to be positive. The metonymic figure of speech in its ultimately metaphysical import stresses the fact that the ultimate one, although in need of expression, resists the very possibility of its expressibility through language. Thus, it comes to the paradoxical situation inherent in all metaphysical teachings of this type: how to explain that which explains everything and how to say and not to say at the same time.

In the course of our metonymic reflections, we will see that the act of negation has two aspects.[1] First is the "denial" aspect, which is satisfied in rejecting any referential or experiential content; and second is the "commitment" aspect, which testifies to some noetic experience whose object is not really adequately available to language, logic, and predication. It is the second aspect of negation that is at work in the philosophy of Shamkara as well as in that of Plato. The negativity of the judgments aims at a logic of negativity without negativity. The negative descriptions of the ultimate reality are meant to draw our attention to its nonphenomenal character. It is true that Wittgenstein advises us to keep silent, but he does not corroborate the view that there is something.

Shamkara's Concept of the Nondual, the Nirguna Brahman

The nature of Brahman and its relation to the human soul is one of the central themes of Shamkara's philosophy. Upanishadic teachings like "tat twam asi"[2] (that thou art) or "aham Brahma asmi"[3] (I am Brahman) receive special treatment in Shamkara's philosophy of nonduality. The type of monism taught by Shamkara is nondualistic par excellence. On the theoretical side, it is the conception of the nirguna Brahman, of Brahman beyond the reach of any qualification as the ultimate reality.[4] His central teaching is the âtmâdvaita, which is the thesis of one, universal, eternal, nondual, and self-illuminating self. The reality of this self exists in pure consciousness without a subject (âshraya) and an object (vishaya). This consciousness alone is real. On the practical side, it is an exclusive advocacy for jñâna-mârga—that is, for metaphysical knowledge experienced as the sole means of release. Shamkara aims at an applied metaphysics.

His nondualistic philosophy, which describes the one metaphysical reality in the spirit of the upanishadic methodology of neti, neti (not this, not this), stresses repeatedly the antinihilistic character of Brahman lest his teaching be identified with the Mâdhyamika form of nihilism or negativism. Irrespective of Shamkara's rather too-negative reading of the Mâdhyamic teaching, the point to be noted in our context is that his teaching is positive regarding the nature of Brahman clothed in negative language.

The upanishadic reply to the question of what is ultimately real is not always unanimous. One of the outstanding ways to characterize Brahman was the famous neti, neti, and Shamkara took it in a strictly literal sense and arrived at his concept of nirguna Brahman.[5]

The method Shamkara uses to substantiate his thesis of the reality of the one universal, self-illuminating consciousness is the analysis of our common experience. The methodological principle he sets down is not the total rejection of reason. He allows the use of reason but only in the service of truth revealed in the scriptures and experienced by seers. Reason is important, but intuition is more important.

Shamkara's philosophy stands and falls by the acceptance or rejection of the criterion of reality that may be formulated as follows. What is real cannot be negated. What cannot be negated is consciousness because denial of consciousness presupposes the consciousness it denies. The absence of anything except consciousness is conceivable. There are different varieties of negation. Negation may be the antecedent nonexistence (prâgabhâva) before the object comes into being. It may be subsequent nonexistence (dhvamsâbhâva) after the object is destroyed. Negation may also be mutual negation of difference or absence (anyonyâbhâva), or it may be absolute nonexistence (atyântâbhâva). Because the negation of consciousness is not conceivable, none of these kinds of negations can be legitimately predicated about it. If no difference can be predicated about it and if the self-luminous, undeniable consciousness is the only reality that satisfies the criterion of being beyond negation, then things different from it are not real and cannot be real. Such a consciousness must be timeless and ubiquitous. To be known, all objects must depend on it.[6] The neutrality of consciousness is, thus, beyond the reach of judgmental predicates, such as true, false, both true and false, and neither true nor false.

The unity of consciousness, which is its nonduality par excellence, knows no parts within itself. Consciousness of blue and of red does not mean a difference in consciousness but rather one superimposed on it by a distinction between its objects, blue and red. So also is the case with the consciousness of right and wrong, truth and falsity. Shamkara claims to have established his thesis of reality as one, infinite, eternal, and self-illuminating spirit against the pluralism of Sâmkhya, Buddhists, and Nyâya-Vaisheshika. No determination of such a reality is possible, for that would amount to negation, which, as we have seen, is not possible.

To Shamkara, all knowledge commonly points to a subject as well as an object. This double implication is necessary in the emergence of knowledge. Knowledge of the round square and the son of a barren woman is really verbal. Even in the case of an illusion, there is an objective counterpart that, of course, may not be common to several persons. Anything that is a fact of experience must somehow be real. It may be rationally unintelligible and to that extent false, but for Shamkara even the false appearance is a positive entity that defies all description, for it is somewhere in between the two categories of existence and nonexistence. When he passes judgment about the falsity of the world and the empirical individual self, he really points to this third category. When we see silver instead of shell, the error is, as he maintains in his introduction to the *Vedânta-Sûtra,* a case of an illegitimate transference, or adhyâsa. But knowing that something is false is another knowledge which then allows us the discovery of the falsity of the previous knowledge. Ignorance is the cause of this adhyâsa, or superimposition.

Common knowledge is true so long as one's identity with Brahman is not realized, as dreams are until we are awake. Shamkara distinguishes between three senses of being: the merely illusory (prâtibhasika); the empirical (vyâvahârika); and the transcendental being of one, nondual, indeterminate Brahman (pârmarthika). This Brahman is designated as the svarûp-jñâna, the pure consciousness in the advaita-Vedânta of Shamkara. Recognition of this highest form of reality is what reveals that the world is not real (mithyâ) and that Brahman is the only reality. Shamkara's epistemology prepares the way to his metaphysics, which in its turn comes to an application through the constant meditation on the nonduality between Âtman and Brahman. This applied metaphysics is the religion of Shamkara with moral life as a necessary preliminary to experienced metaphysical knowledge.

The theistic conception of the Absolute is not the advaitic conception of Shamkara. For him, the theistic conception fails to solve satisfactorily the age-old problem of theodicy, of reconciling the assumed goodness of God with the undeniable presence of evil in the world.[7]

To regard the Absolute of Shamkara as the philosophic, speculative Absolute is also not very satisfactory to him. Brahman as saguna cannot be identified with the jivas or with their totality. The universe emerging from saguna Brahman is not identical with it. Thus, the phenomenon of adhyâsa prevails in the sphere of jivas, the world, and the saguna Brahman. Through mâyâ, the impersonal Brahman of Shamkara becomes a personal God.[8] But the advaitic Brahman is beyond all determinations. It is for this reason that Shamkara describes his doctrine as a-dvaita, or nondual, and not aikya, or unitary. In the name of his mâyâ-doctrine, he pleads for vivarta-vâda, which assumes the world to be a phenomenal appearance depending on Brahman as silver on the shell or the appearance of the snake on the rope. The doctrine of mâyâ fulfills the very function so urgently needed, namely that of judging the status of the world neither as really real nor fully illusory. The well-known distinction regarding the three dimensions of reality is a very ingenious way to solve or avoid this difficulty.

The most important and perplexing question for Shamkara and for us remains. What is the nature of the ultimate reality? As an infinite consciousness implied by all empirical knowledge, it is not available to empirical knowledge. When it is termed as indeterminate (nirguna), it does not amount to nothing; it only means that all that the mind can think of does not really positively belong to it. Because it can never be presented as an object of knowledge, it is beyond the reach of the familiar categories of thought. Hence, no direct, positive description is available.

The Absolute of Shamkara is not only indefinable; it is also unknowable because to be known is to be made determinate. The Absolute is also not just a speculative idea elaborated in thought and therefore only a reality in and for thought. The fact of its unknowability does not, however, exclude the possibility of its being realized in the sense of having "felt knowledge" of it.

Every negation has some positive implication, and the negative definition of Brahman does not make it a blank. The two upanishadic statements "tat twam asi" and "aham Brahma asmi" must be read, interpreted, and understood together. The first points to and testifies to the positive reality in us, whereas the second denies the possibility of any predication. The Absolute of Shamkara is, thus, something revealing itself within us. For this reason, Shamkara's teaching cannot be regarded as agnostic. It is outside of the reach of thought and reason but not outside of the world of an immediate, intuitive, inner experience. This realization of Brahman is not something to be achieved; it is the ever-present essential reality of one's own self to be realized through the destruction of the veil of ignorance. Its nature is self-illuminating (svyamprakâshatva) like the moon behind the clouds. The metaphor of light, which seems to be a topos inherent to human thought irrespective of culture, creed, and religion, is used by Shamkara (similar to Plato) to denote the real nature of the ultimate reality.[9] The type of experience that Shamkara really refers to points to a form of experience wherein to realize Brahman is by being Brahman. This higher type of experience may be rare, but it is not totally unfamiliar to us to feel one with all that exists beyond all differences.[10]

Saguna Brahman as God of religion is lower than nirguna Brahman. Through God is how Brahman really appears to an ignorant person. Our religious life is full of adhyâsas and is sustained by many dualistic concepts. Shamkara, of course, does not subscribe to the view that saguna Brahman is useless. All that he maintains is to show its inadequacy for the high goal of philosophy (âhyâmavidyâ). Apara-vidyâ, the teaching of the saguna Brahman, need not be given up; only it should be practiced with an attitude that it is not para-vidyâ, the teaching of the nirguna Brahman.

We have seen that liberation for Shamkara is not a state to be newly obtained. It is knowing and realizing by becoming what one has forever been but forgotten. The state of final release is nothing but Brahman.[11] The moral and religious discipline prescribed here to realize this goal does not so much lead us to the identity of Âtman and Brahman but does dispel the obstacles concealing the truth from us. The knowledge resulting from the removal of the obstacles must be direct and intuitive (sâtshâtkâra). It must be the name of some anubhava, intuitive, mystic experience that is the sole means of liberation. Moral perfection and religious acts may be conducive to such an experience, but they are not the sine qua non of it. Only the morally corrupt and the religiously impious will not find any taste in Brahman-jijñâsâ.

Two stages comprise the discipline to be followed. One is a preliminary qualifying us for a serious study of Advaita, and the other is the vedântic training proper that finally aims at self-realization. The first stage is the cultivation of detachment as taught in Gitâ. The latter consists of three methodical steps, shravana, manana, and nididhyâsana. The first step is the sincere study of the Upanishads with the assistance of a spiritual guru who has himself realized the truth. In addition to the fact that the ultimate Truth is to be learned from the revealed text, Shamkara also wants to emphasize the need for personal intercourse with a competent teacher, very much akin to Plato. Mere book learning does not lead us to the goal. The second step is discussing and arguing with oneself. The main aim is to remove the doubt that might linger (asambhâvanâ) regarding the truth learned to be right during the first step. At this step, reason steps in and plays its quite important role of transforming a teaching received on trust and faith into one's own true conviction. This step is also where autonomous thinking is at work. The last step is constant meditation on the identity between Âtman and Brahman. Such a practical step of meditation is needed to dispel the diverse unconscious reassertions of old habits of thought (viparita-bhâvanâ) incompatible with what has been learned as the right teaching. To know the right teaching is not necessarily to follow it. Some other mediating step must come into play to link the two. This nididhyâsana should be continued until the desired intuitive mystic experience takes place. There seems to be an element of dogmatism in Shamkara in so far as the philosophic truth is to be known through the testimony of the Upanishads, but this initial dogmatism vanishes altogether when the same truth must be verified by one's own living experience in the form of tat twam asi or aham Brahma asmi.[12]

Shamkara's is a religion without God. His Advaitavâda is a comprehensive philosophical-metaphysical system, and its center is the view of the ultimate reality as one without a second. Shamkara steers clear between the theistic absolutism of other vedântic schools and the nihilistic absolutism of the Mâdhyamikas, as he understands them.

Plato's Concept of the One and the Good (Hen and Agathon) and His Epistle VII

There is now general agreement among scholars about the authenticity and overall importance of Plato's Seventh Epistle to his entire philosophy.[13] The epistle is a letter containing Plato's political views, his connection with Athenian politics, and his relations with Dionysios I. and II. of Syracuse and Dion. It is full of political advice written in reply to an appeal for help from Dion's friends and followers. The letter must have been completed by the end of 354 B.C. or the beginning of 353 B.C.[14]

It is generally believed that those who write dialogues do not want to come forward with their ideas directly and, consequently, use various characters to say or not say what they really want to say. This belief seems accurate from Plato to Hume. The Seventh Epistle, one of Plato's longest, is written in the first person and portrays a Plato who maintains that his main teaching remains untaught and unwritten not because he did not do it but because it cannot be done. There is a short autobiographical sketch inserted by Plato at the beginning of the epistle, which shows his earnestness in matters of political principle.

The philosophical quest, according to Plato, is not meant for persons who stop short of going deep enough in search of the ultimate principle. It is a marvelous quest for a true lover of wisdom who is capable of soberly reasoning with him- or herself. "Those who are really not philosophers," Plato writes, "but have only a coating of opinions, like men whose bodies are tanned by the sun . . . , conclude that the task is too difficult for their powers; and rightly so, for they are not equipped for this pursuit."[15]

Plato knew very well the tastes of the tyrants whose heads are full of half-understood doctrines and who, nevertheless, claim to have a full understanding of the subject. It was in this fashion that Plato spoke to Dionysius. He says clearly that he did not explain everything to him, nor did he ask for it. It was also Dionysius who is said to have written a book on matters Plato and he discussed. For Plato, it is incredible that anyone could have written a book on matters that defy linguistic form. Others have written books on such matters, but Plato is sure that they do not know what they do. Plato takes this injustice done to the highest principles of philosophy as an opportunity to offer the last word on matters of ultimate philosophical principles:

> So much at least I can affirm with confidence about any who have written or proposed writing on these questions, pretending to a knowledge of the problem with which I am concerned . . . : it is impossible, in my opinion, that they have learnt anything at all about the subject. There is no way of expressing in writing about these matters, nor will there ever be one. For this knowl-

edge is not something that can be put into words like other sciences; but after long-continued intercourse between teacher and pupil, in joint pursuit of the subject, suddenly, like light flashing forth when a fire is kindled, it is born in the soul and straightway nourishes itself.[16]

This is the heart of the Seventh Epistle with regard to the teaching of the ultimate principle of philosophy, which, for Plato, remains his "unwritten doctrine."[17] Plato does not leave the matter undiscussed. He presents a theory of knowledge, and this epistemology paves the way for learning about the One beyond words. Dionysius's book on the first and highest principle of philosophy that Plato mentioned cannot, according to him, contain an exposition of his views for the simple reason that anyone who claims to know anything about these ultimate principles also knows that they cannot be expounded in writing like other knowledge. This reason must be why Plato himself refrained from writing a book about these matters. Still they can be learned through long, sincere association between teacher and pupil. Plato condemns not only Dionysius but anyone who has written or proposes to write a book on these ultimate matters. The question that forces itself on us is, "What then has Plato done in all of his *Dialogues* after all?" The Seventh Epistle is the key to understanding the entire structure of Plato's philosophy, which is therefore a prelude to say what ultimately cannot be said. The literary form of dialogue seems to be the best way to do this.

The question remains: "How do we understand Plato's own emphatic statement that he has never written anything on matters of ultimate principles?" If by the first principles we understand his theory and teaching of the ideas, then clearly it hardly makes any sense, for Plato did write about the ideas in many of his *Dialogues*. There is one train of thought that rather implicitly runs between the lines of several of the *Dialogues* as the red tape, and it is as follows: Plato feels the need for a more ultimate doctrine to support his theory of ideas. If the ideas are ultimate principles, then the ultimate principles referred to as beyond the reach of words in his Seventh Epistle are more ultimate than the ideas. The idea of the One (hen), of the Good (agathon), seems to be the ultimate source of all being, and Plato's *Socrates* does refuse to state it more fully. Plato's lectures on the Good in the Academy in the midst of his pupils are not available in black and white. In his later years, Plato seemed to traverse on the border between philosophy and poetry. In his *Dialogues*, he differentiates between philosophical wisdom and inspired guesses of poets. The earlier Plato wanted to be a philosopher minus a poet, whereas the later Plato is a poet-philosopher or a philosopher-poet.

The later Plato takes recourse in a poetic version of the One that he thinks is beyond the reach of logic, language, and even dialectics. It is therefore quite certain that Plato has noetically experienced the sudden light flashing forth like a fire in his soul, and it is this lived experience, intuition in his philosophy, that is more ultimate than anything we find in his *Dialogues* and other writings. We also know that the intimate association among the members of the Academy did deal with unwritten doctrines. They were unwritten and remained so, not because of fear of divulging a secret but because of the intrinsic difficulty of adequately putting them into writing. The way to learn it is rather analogous to upanishadic learning.

That the words, like the idea and the dialectic, so frequently in use in other *Dialogues* of Plato totally fail in this long epistle may be taken as Plato's device to show that the principles he is now trying to talk about lie far deeper than the ideas. The Seventh Epistle is less concerned with discovering the truth, a goal Plato pursued earlier, than with the teaching and the exposition of it. Thus, this letter contains a pedagogy and dialectics in the name of an epistemology. If we are to grasp the nature of any object, then there are three instruments to be employed: names, definitions, and diagrams or images. Plato does not fully deny the usefulness of these instruments; he discovers only that they are as indispensable as defective. Every teacher experiences difficulty when he or she wants to present views. The terms the teacher uses have different connotations. The metonymic chasm between the name and the named, words and things, concepts and reality, seems to be one of the main lessons of this letter and, indirectly of all of the Platonic *Dialogues.*

It is a recurring theme in Plato's various *Dialogues* that our ordinary language is incapable of adequately putting ultimate matters into words. The words and concepts we use are vested with their accidental and conventional characters. In the "Sophist," this vesting is very clearly exemplified in the verb *is,* which may stand for the relation of identity as well as for a form of predication. The philosophy of language that Plato envisages is not one that can be developed in time to meet the need of an adequate formulation; it is, rather, the inherently defective nature of language not to be able to express ultimate matters adequately.

The Seventh Epistle also makes it clear that Plato is certainly in possession of an esoteric, felt knowledge, for he mentions inadequacies and weaknesses mainly of the medium in which to impart the knowledge and not of the knowledge of the speaker as such. Of course, Plato's Seventh Epistle does not deny the possibility of real knowledge, yet he is not very optimistic about its attainability. Plato's philosophy has reserved a place for dialetic as science on the way to truth. The central teaching of the Platonic dialectic is that it is an ascent from plurality to unity, from the world of the many to that of the one. But even dialectic falls short of reaching into the heart of the ultimate principle; it rather places itself in the forefront of the area of the One and the Good. At its best, dialectic prepares our mind for illumination; it lets us be better suited for an intuitive, noetic experience of the one ultimate reality. It is less a mystic experience than an insight that goes by the name of illumination.[18] The vision of the One, the Absolute, that flashes into the mind of the seeker, cannot itself be communicated. Plato's One is more ultimate than the ideas in *The Republic.* The One as the Ultimate is beyond the being, nonbeing (epekeina te ousia). The ultimate object of the soul's quest is the One. Plato believes that the realization of this goal means an all-around contentment of the whole human—reason, imagination, and emotion. Not everybody is in a position to experience such complete satisfaction; it remains the privilege of the few. Everybody is not and cannot be a philosopher.

Reason does not become jobless in Plato's philosophy even after an assessment of his Seventh Epistle. All that happens is the indubitable insight that the One is beyond the reach of dialectic, reason, logic, and language. In *Timaeus,* Plato writes, "To discover the Maker and Father of this whole is a hard task, and when one has found him he cannot tell of him to all."[19]

Plato leaves it open to guess whether this "finding him" is just beyond language or because one finds him by being him. The latter possibility would be parallel to that of Shamkara. It amounts to a certain "Platonic irony, which recognizes the difficulty of penetrating to the real nature of justice, and the impossibility, having once penetrated there, of expounding the truth in anything but imperfect figure."[20]

If we take the main teaching of this letter to be our point of departure and try to review the entire Platonic philosophy, then we are forced to conclude that it is not the *Dialogues* that prepare the way for the noetic, esoteric, illuminatory sudden insight of light flashing into the soul, but it is just the opposite. The theology implied in the Platonic philosophy places the One, the Good, above the God of religion, although Plato rather mythologically talks of the Maker and the Father of this whole (comparable to Shamkara's Ishvara). There is no doubt that Plato's philosophy is basically rationalistic and strikingly ethical, but in the heart of its heart it is mythical and esoteric.[21]

Shamkara and Plato Compared and Contrasted

There seems to be a technique as old as human thinking itself that tries to say what cannot be said. In other words, it is negative in so far as it emphasizes the incapacities of language. Simultaneously, however, there is left a persistent and legitimate feeling of the difference between what is really said and what should have been said so that this feeling of difference is not there. The famous technique of negative theology is one of the most important ones belonging to this paradigm.

The Hen, Plato's One, plays a similar role in his philosophy as the nondual consciousness in Shamkara's works. Of course, Shamkara is linguistically more negative in his definition of the Absolute than Plato, for Shamkara terms it as nondual, a-dvaita.

Shamkara and Plato seem to deny the possibility of predication with regard to the Absolute more or less on the same ground of its being one, unique, and beyond comparison. Of course, for Plato there is his copy theory, which connects the phenomenal world of the empirical, changing things with perfect ideas, which in their turn are grounded in the One. For Shamkara, in contrast, the world of empirical things and beings shows its illusory character when it is judged from the absolute point of view. Not Plato, but Shamkara, postulates a nondual identity between the human soul and Brahman, an identity that lies hidden and only needs to be laid bare in the intuition of the ever-present identity. If Plato's One is understood as the not-many of the changeable empirical world, then, of course, it comes very near to Shamkara's nondual One. The One is equated here with not-two, not-three, and so on.

If the real teaching of the One, as the Seventh Epistle amply shows, cannot be written and communicated through discursive thought, reasoning, logic, and language, then the questions arise, "Is Plato then speaking just playfully in his differ-ent *Dialogues?*" and "Is he really not taking things solemnly and seriously?" and "If he knew about the fundamental inexpressibility of the One, why did he write and lead astray if not himself, then the readers of his writings?" Plato seems to have realized that all that is historical betrays the character of playfulness, and the One that is beyond the reach of language, time, and history defies any and every written exposition.

Shamkara, rather than Plato, presents better worked-out, methodical steps to-ward the realization of the ever-present nonduality between the human soul and Brahman. The esoteric element makes its appearance more prominently in Plato's philosophy than in Shamkara's. In the spirit of Plato's teaching, we should not be bound to the shadows of the cave but get to see the reality. But this transformation needs an illuminating revelation.

Both Shamkara and Plato subscribe to the idea of some sort of mysticism, which, of course, is not crude and allows some role for reason and discursive thinking.[22] They do not just sit and hope for the mystic experience to happen. They would have been crude mystics had they done so. Still, there seems to be a very characteristic and fundamental difference between the mysticism of Shamkara and that of Plato. The mystic experience of advaita-vedânta does not really bring about any identity; it simply lets the thick clouds of superimposition vanish. Nothing remains to be rejoined or explained, for the illusory character of everything except pure consciousness is laid bare. The Platonic mystic, in con-trast, establishes a unity forming of the whole cosmos a harmonious organic one. There is nothing in Plato that corresponds to the concept of mâyâ in Shamkara. Plato traverses a path of ascent from plurality to unity; Shamkara, from an ever-present nondual unity to a not really real plurality.

Concluding Remarks

Recently Derrida has critically picked out as a central theme the technique of neg-ative theology to say something positive by saying that nothing positive can be said about it. Both Shamkara and Plato subscribe to this paradigm. Derrida asks a very simple question, "Comment ne pas parler?" In other words, he asks how to avoid speaking. We want to put the same question in our current context and try to find out what Shamkara and Plato really want to say or aim at with their nega-tive technique.

If to speak negatively means that there is nothing to speak about, then the trou-bles these philosophers take to do so is not worth even the nihilism in which they may land: that something about which they seem to have an intuition is worth the trouble to express it negatively. It seems that both Shamkara and Plato are com-mitted to it. The negative technique is used with the intention of teaching, com-municating, conversing, and even changing human society, at least in Plato's case. It was Shamkara, not Plato, who became a sanyâsin very early in his life and led the life of a monk. Plato, in his Seventh Epistle, speaks about his ambition as a young man to enter public life and politics.

The question, "Why they do not avoid speaking by not speaking at all?" can be answered only by a commitment thesis to speak about it, a commitment they feel in themselves and that they cannot avoid fulfilling even if they desire to keep silent. There seems to be an element of inner voice that is betrayed if they really remain silent. The further questions of interest are, "Where does this commitment come from?" and "Is it something noetic, transcendental, or transcendent?" If it be something transcendent and if the acceptance of this transcendence is a sine qua non for the intuition of it, then, of course, it is not far from an ontology or a theology. The identity of Âtman and Brahman is something noetic without being arbitrarily subjective. Both Shamkara and Plato seem to subscribe to some form of mystic philosophy as a way of life (over and above philosophy as a way of thought) that steers between a purely speculative philosophy of the Absolute à la Hegel and a mystic theology that leaves room for acts of faith and prayer. The question of a religious faith and an attitude of prayer are, of course, foreign to both Shamkara and Plato. Both seem to plead for a jñâna-mârg, but with a difference. Plato and Shamkara differ to meet and meet to differ.

From what has been written above about the One of Plato and the nirguna Brahman of Shamkara, it follows that the negative description does not mean nothing, and negation is not its own telos. Because it is something that is not available to positive description and because it is also not something just to be recognized on the grounds of faith, the act of negation, of some noetically felt and intended negation to speak about the unspeakable, seems to fulfill some intention in and through this very act without thereby necessarily thinking of the ultimate reality as God, nature, and so on. The question that then arises is, "Is this Absolute then just a linguistic event?" It would go against the spirit of the philosophy of Shamkara as well as that of Plato to relegate the ultimate principle to something that takes place only in and through language. The felt-knowledge of the Absolute is something that happens. It must be an extra-linguistic event.

The pure consciousness (suddha-caitanya) of Shamkara is the underlying reality of the world, of actual as well as of possible worlds. It has nothing to do with the creation of the world. In this point, Shamkara seems to fare better, for he does not resort to any of the allegorical, mythical explanations that Plato often mentions in his works (the myth of creation in *Timaeus*). Shamkara rather takes the bull by the horns and lets everything be dependent on Brahman but not vice versa. All of the problems Plato takes the trouble to solve by bringing in the myths to play their role cease to be problems for Shamkara the moment identity with Brahman is realized. The vedântic Shamkarite mystic may intuit, experience, see, and realize the presence of Brahman along with its identity with the human soul in all beings.

Despite striking similarities and illuminating differences between the monistic concept of the One (Hen) of Plato and the nondualistic Pure Consciousness of Shamkara, they meet to differ in their concept of the mystic vision, experience. This experience teaches Plato that unity and diversity, one and all, join hands and are ultimately reconciled; it teaches Shamkara, in contrast, that there is nothing with which to be reconciled and the parasitically illusory character of all appearances is eliminated with for all time. Irrespective of the controversy of whether the world is ultimately real or illusory, the noetically mystic character of the above experience seems to be its own ground for justification, legitimacy, and truth with the additional apprehension of being in the state of perfect conciliation. Plato may join in Shamkara's conviction that the illuminatory experience of the One without a second is of self-certifying character. Both may deny the opponent the right to dispute and contest the truth of another possessing such a knowledge of Brahman and Hen, respectively, even at the risk of being branded as subjectivist.

There are two Shamkaras as there are two Platos: the exoteric and the esoteric one. The exoteric Shamkara in his hermeneutic of Indian thinking very often refers to the unquestionable authority of the Shrutis and takes them to be the ground of justification and legitimization of his views. The esoteric Shamkara, on the contrary, refers to the intuition, noetic experience (sâkshâtkâra) of the nonduality between Âtman and Brahman. The latter move is an antidote to his rather dogmatic view. The Plato of the Academy, in deep intercourse with his pupils, is the esoteric one experiencing the One (Hen) as a sudden insight of light flashing into the soul. The Plato of the *Dialogues* is the exoteric one, believing in the power of dialectics and reason to reach the truth of the One.

There seems to be inherent irony in the human quest for the Absolute. Those who have realized it cannot tell what it is really like, and those who have not cannot really know what it is like. The future of Indian as well as of European philosophy seems to lie in a balanced and critical synthesis of the roles played by authority, reason, experience, and self-knowledge.

Notes

1. I am indebted for this hint to Matilal, who differentiates these two aspects of negation in his discussion of negation and the Mâdhyamika dialectic. B. K. Matilal, *Epistemology, Logic, and Grammar in Indian Philosophical Analysis* (The Hague 1971), 162–63.

2. *Chândogya Upanishad*, VI, 13, 3.

3. *Brhadâranyaka Upanishad*, I, 4, 10.

4. The following exposition is based mainly on "The Vedânta Shutras with the Commentary by Shankarakarya," ed. George Thibaut, *Sacred Books of the East, XXXIV and XXXVIII* (Oxford 1890, 1896); *Die Sûtra's des Vedânta oder die Châriraka-Mimânsâ des Bâdarâyana nebst dem vollständigen Commentare des Chankara*, ed. Paul Deussen (Leipzig 1897).

5. S. Radhakrishnan (trans.), *The Brahma Sûtra: The Philosophy of Spiritual Life* (London 1960); K. C. Bhattacharya, *Studies in Vedântism* (Calcutta 1909).

6. *Vedânta-Sûtra by Bâdrâyana*, XXXVIII, 11, 3, 7. (Ya eva hi nirâkartâ tadeva tasya svarûpam.)

7. *Vedânta-Sûtra by Bâdrâyana*, II, 1, 34–36.

8. *Vedânta-Sûtra by Bâdrâyana*, XXXIV, XXX.

9. *Vedânta-Sûtra by Bâdrâyana*, XXXVIII, IV, 4, 3.

10. *Vedânta-Sûtra by Bâdrâyana*, XXXIV, 25, 29f.; XXXVIII, IV, 2, 14.

11. *Vedânta-Sûtra by Bâdrâyana*, XXXIV, 28; XXXVIII, III, 4, 52.

12. *Vedânta-Sûtra by Bâdrâyana*, I, 1, 2. and XXXVIII, III, 2, 24.

13. The following exposition is mainly based on G. R. Morrow (ed.), *Plato's Epistles: A Translation, with Critical Essays and Notes* (New York 1962).

14. In his Epistle VII, Plato contrasts the impact of his written work with that of the direct and esoteric contact with his pupil in the Academy and favors the latter to be the most adequate way and the real vehicle of philosophy. U. V. Wilamowitz-Moellendorf, *Platon: Sein Leben und seine Werke,* vol. II (Frankfurt 1969); J. Stenzel, *Platon der Erzieher* (Leipzig 1928); H. Richard, *Platonica* (London 1911); F. Egermann, *Die Platonischen Briefe VII und VIII* (Berlin 1928); L. A. Post, *Thirteen Epistles of Plato* (Oxford 1925); G. Hell, *Untersuchungen und Beobachtungen zu den Platonischen Briefen* (Berlin 1933).

15. Morrow, *Plato's Epistles,* 340.

16. Morrow, *Plato's Epistles,* 341.

17. K. Gaiser, *Platons ungeschriebene Lehre* (Stuttgart 1968).

18. J. Stenzel, "Der Begriff der Erleuchtung bei Platon," in *Kleine Schriften zur griechischen Philosophie* (Darmstadt 1956).

19. Plato, *Timaeus,* 28.

20. Morrow, *Plato's Epistles,* 80.

21. H. J. Krämer: "Das Problem des esoterischen Platons," in *Arete bei Platon und Aristoteles* (Heidelberg 1959).

22. R. Otto, *Mysticism East and West* (New York 1932); K. Albert, *Über Platons Begriff der Philosophie* (St. Augustine 1989).

8

The God of Phenomenology in Comparative Contrast to Those of Philosophy and Theology

Husserl's Religious Leanings

Auch Gott ist für mich, was er ist, aus meiner eigenen Bewußtseinsleis-
tung.

—Husserl

Husserl, who was born in a liberal Jewish family, was baptized and became a protestant Christian in 1886. He seems to have remained a believing Christian of the "Free Christians" sort throughout his life.[1]

Husserl later in his life used the metaphor of "religious conversion" to describe faithfully and analogically the impact and importance of transcendental reduction (cf. *Hua* VI 140).[2] In a letter written on 21 February 1926, Husserl refers to a phenomenological process of creation in human cast when he writes that "a systematic phenomenology of world constitution shows from below, how God, in eternal creation, creates the world."[3] The question about what type of theodicy Husserl's phenomenology of religion really entails receives a Hegelian answer when we think of Husserl's firm conviction that it is the essence of reason to march one-sidedly in the necessary process of realizing its infinite task.[4]

Although in Husserl's published work he is less explicit about the problems of religion, God, faith, and mysticism, he nevertheless discusses these and other related problems in his unpublished manuscripts. Four of his published works contain a great deal of material concerning religious themes.[5] The relevant unpublished manuscripts thematize less the problem of the fruitfulness of the phenomenological method concerning religious matters and focus more on how they can be shown to be valid beliefs.[6] Like Hume, Husserl seems to have struggled with the problem of God. Despite this similarity in philosophical orientation,

Husserl is more positive about God than Hume was. Their temperamental differences might have been one of the reasons for this variation. Husserl was fully aware of the futility of the so-called "proofs" for the existence of God, and he never explicitly poses the question, "Does God exist?" Nevertheless, he tries to incorporate God into his teleology of reason.[7]

Husserl's Concept of Teleology

Man cannot be the original source of a universal teleology, and Husserl brings into his phenomenology the concept of God's transcendence as a means to make room for a nonanthropocentric foundation of teleology. While referring to God's transcendence, Husserl speaks of a "wonderful teleology" that focusses on the particular nature of God's transcendence and His absoluteness in opposition to the transcendence of the world and the absoluteness of consciousness.[8] A systematic study of all teleologies points to theology. Husserl writes,

> We pass by all that might lead to the same principle from the side of the religious consciousness, even though its argument rests on rationally grounded motives. What concerns us here, after merely touching on the different groupings of such rational grounds for the existence of a "divine" Being beyond the world, is that this existence should not only transcend the world, but obviously also the "absolute" Consciousness. It would thus be an "Absolute" in totally different sense from the Absolute of Consciousness, as on the other hand it would be a transcendent in a totally different sense from the transcendent in the sense of the world.[9]

Husserl's concept of God is neither anthropocentric nor pantheistic. The transcendence and absoluteness attributed to God seem to bear no analogy to human categories, which may be the reason we have recourse only with negative descriptions. Different philosophical and religious traditions in the East and the West testify to this fact.

Husserl firmly believes in the teleological structure of the world and life in it. He writes, "Menschsein (ist) ein Teleologischsein" (to be human is to be teleologic), and this teleology is at work in "allem und jedem ichlichen Tun und Vorhaben."[10] What the concept of intentionality is to his phenomenological analysis, teleology is to his phenomenology of religion and God. Husserl, who was quite critical of Hegel, seems to subscribe to the idea that there is a historical intentionality that realizes itself in the course of human history. Husserl speaks of a teleological beginning, which he anchors in the thinking of the Greeks, and sees it renewed in modern philosophical humanity, which is the legitimate heir to the grand Greek tradition. Husserl is convinced of a teleological process in human history. He often uses the word the Greek word *Urstiftung*, meaning the first and foremost beginning of the European spirit.[11]

Whether teleology is grounded in God is a question Husserl neither explicitly affirms nor fully denies. In the spirit of Hegel, he seems to think of an Absolute that is absolutely necessary. For Husserl, the Aristotelian philosophy is fully autonomous and represents an eternal task; and an autonomous philosophy, according to Husserl, culminates in a teleology and philosophical theology. Husserl regards this philosophy as a way to God, who is not necessarily bound to a particular denomination.[12] This view might be interpreted as a nontheological (i.e., the philosophical-metaphysical) way to God. We will see that the attempt to assert the absolute necessity of an extremely sensible instance as needed by the contingency and irrationality of the world is a metaphysical and religious move and is not in the spirit of phenomenology as is radical and open philosophizing. The real spirit of phenomenology is opposed to any privileged treatment of a particular point of view.

Two Paths to God: The Historical and the Philosophical

There are two ways to God, according to Husserl: the historical—that is, the way of historical revelation—and the nonhistorical—that is, the way of philosophy to God.[13] Husserl often equates universal religion with universal ethics, which remain abstract and represent pure forms. The philosophical way to God is via universal ethics, which is not necessarily dependent on any revelation through historical persons. Husserl regards the way to God through autonomous philosophical knowledge as valid even for atheists. Such ascience leading to God is the essence of general humanity as the substratum for a supranational, suprahistorical, and supra-empirical novum.[14]

According to Husserl, the Aristotelian philosophy represents an autonomous philosophy par excellence. As an endless task, it necessarily comes to a teleology and even to a philosophical theology. This way to God is not bound to any religious denomination. Husserl feels that the type of religion he is in search of cannot be inferred from the Aristotelian metaphysics as it stands. He does expect an autonomous philosophy to account for the essential necessity of the world, and human beings therein, in a historical religion. The autonomous in this sense is a tool in the hands of theology. Husserl is sometimes pained to find philosophical arguments in favor of the absolute truth of a historical religion, such as Christianity.[15] Husserl aims at a theology of the true religion.

The Program of Phenomenology in Relation to Teleology and Theology

The original phenomenological program aims at the ideal of being presuppositionless. The two trends of Husserl's phenomenology—the essentialist and the descriptive—accompany it from the beginning and point to a persisting tension.[16] To favor an essentialist move, which Husserl, of course, never fully relinquishes, is to side with a particular metaphysical thinking. Phenomenology as an essentialist approach to philosophical problems, including religious ones, participates in the grand tradition inherited from the Greeks.

Phenomenology's most original and unprejudiced proposal is its unending search for the most originary given because the only foundation beyond all doubt is to be found in lived experiences. The method helping us to discover this dimension is epoche, or reduction. Phenomenology, thus, is an attempt to regress as far as possible and discover the domain of consciousness that alone makes us and others understand what it means to speak understandably of anything, even of God, religion, and faith. Transcendental subjectivity possesses the status of an ultimate principle in the sense of being the most fundamental ground for all constituted meanings. This subjectivity can make room only for an immanent God as the constituted one. Transcendental phenomenology, true to its spirit, cannot give privileged treatment to any particular sense of God or to any particular religion.

The methodological proposal of description does not speculate, postulate, or hypothesize. The constitutive analysis describes all objects as noemata of experienced acts. This analysis makes phenomenology essentially a descriptive philosophy committed first and foremost to the clarification of meaning. A true phenomenologist qua phenomenologist must be radical in his or her search, for sedimented interpretations and personal beliefs may sometimes pretend to be self-evident truths. The eidetic correlation between noetic acts and noematic achievements is one of the far-reaching insights of Husserlian phenomenology. The given qua given is the object of phenomenological description. To understand the phenomenon of God means to ask the question, "How does an intenional act refer to the intended object, namely God?" We cannot start with God and then try to fit it within the noetic-noematic correlationship.

Husserl's faith in God is, of course, faith in a God who is there before all constitutions. The "Cartesian way" tries to show the transcendence of God in that it accepts its anouncement in human consciousness but resists the idea of pure immanentism. That Husserl does not remain fully faithful to his phenomenological program becomes obvious from his tendency to posit transcendence in human consciousness before it really announces itself. The peculiar mode of this givenness in consciousness can at most testify to the view of God being a noema, an intended object but not an existence, for that would mean a fulfilled intention.

In the case of intersubjective connections, Husserl's transcendental philosophy of subjectivity rightly stresses the point of empathy among human beings. Empathic understanding with others is neither an inductive nor a deductive step; it is also not just an analogical argument. It is really an immediate, intuitive, lived experience of a fundamental resemblance between me and you and you and me. But, when we talk of God, it is not really the same empathy that is at work between human consciousness and God, the absolute consciousness. If Husserl maintains that God as monas summa is still given to and in human consciousness, then he may undoubtedly describe his lived experience, provided he further concedes that the grace of God and faith are at work here. It is this second move that is not really phenomenological. God being one without a second cannot be justly modeled after the intermonadic relationship.

The search for the originary, the desire to trace things back to their most originary sources of meaning, is central to the method of phenomenology. Through this method is how Husserl discovers the life-world as the matrix of all further constitutions, whereby the life-world itself is constituted. Human nature is destined to constitute even as a biological organism with needs, instincts, and wants.

In our attempt to work out a phenomenology of God, we must look for the appropriate intuitive evidence, for the noetical lived experience constituting the meaning of God, religion, and faith. The phenomenological reflection as the method of understanding and clarifying meaning is less concerned with the problem of the truth of God and religion. That point is one whose decision lies outside of this method. It is naive to think that there may be an ontology or metaphysics of God without there being at the same time constituted unities of meaning.

Husserl very rightly emphasizes the need to constantly rediscover the genesis of meaning in originary experience, and he asks us to start fresh and remain faithful to the spirit of a new beginning. To think, as Husserl often does, that teleology must lead to theology[17] is to side with one metaphysical tradition, for there are cases (e.g., Sâmkhya-philosophy[18]) where it need not be. It is also possible to think of an unconscious teleology without any intelligent principle guiding the whole process of means and ends. The eternal cycle of being, with its recurrent phases of coming to be and going out of existence, may be an evolutionary and involutionary model. To think of a purpose beyond this one may be overrating the importance of human wants and desires. The Confucian Weltanschauung believes in the possibility of a teleology without any theology. To the question, "Why does the good often remain unrewarded and the bad unpunished in this world?" a Confucian philosopher would reply that this is how things are, and we human beings often fail to be just and good.

Stephan Strasser is strongly of the opinion that Husserl believes in the concept of a transcendent God.[19] Strasser does not, however, clearly show that Husserl, the untiring phenomenologist, and Husserl, the believing Christian, are like the two souls in one's breast.

Phenomenology of Religion

Irrespective of the outcome of an application of the phenomenological method to sublime religious themes, the methodological analysis concerned with lived experience must remain unbiased and thematize our affective, religious, and mystic areas. If we begin our study of religious phenomena like God, faith, and so on by affirming their ontological truth, nature, and stature, then we do nothing but put the cart before the horse. The more proper way (and also the way more in tune with the phenomenological philosophy) is to start with the transcendentally purified life of consciousness with its richness of noetic-noematic correlations that finally allows us to understand and clarify the meaning of religious concepts as intended noemata. The life of consciousness is the life of its own intentionality. There are different modi of the lived experience of this consciousness. The two most important among them are the mode of fulfillment and the mode of non-fulfillment—that is, of disappointment. What remains unfulfilled in the second mode is not that the intended, noematic object "God" becomes unintelligible; all that happens is that the "real" content of faith in its existence does not form a constitutive part of the noetic-noematic structure. Were it otherwise, there would be no atheism worthy of the name.

It follows that the phenomenological philosophy of religion as worked out by Gerardus van der Leeuw[20] better confirms the real spirit of Husserlian phenomenology than the one propounded by H. Duméry.[21] In opposition to Duméry, who pleads for the real possibility of a phenomenological explanation of religion at an ontological level, van der Leeuw holds that all religious phenomena must be discussed, understood, and explained from within the phenomenological perspective. Whoever thematizes and absolutizes only one religious faith is phenomenologically guilty of biased treatment. What is un- or suprahistorical and atemporal in the phenomenological analysis is the universal correlativity between noesis and noema and not the concrete religious phenomena and their constitution through different types of sedimentation. Angela Ales Bello seems to fear that a merely descriptive attitude with the phenomenologist as a "disinterested" spectator may lead to exclusively "formal" results and, consequently, she thinks that van der Leeuw's approach "remains insufficient."[22] Granted, there is the lurking risk of a phenomenology of religion being exclusively formal and contentless, but it nevertheless remains to be asserted that the fear and the risk are themselves the result of thinking that considers God and religion as singular. Because no philosophy and no phenomenology, at least, can start with a monistic preference of one particular world view, religious matters may very well be dealt with as historical phenomena. The concept of one God and one religion can, at the most, claim the status of a regulative concept leading to better communication and understanding among diverse standpoints that overlap beyond the fictions of total commensurability and incommensurability.

The problem of a monistic interpretation of world and religious matters gained importance as Husserl realized the diversity in the history of humankind and its cultural formations. His manuscript A VIII 5 testifies to this realization and thematizes topics such as "living in the world, open world, open mankind, in global historicity, in the unity of global historical tradition, relativity of the surrounding world, correlation of humanity," and other related matters.

In the spirit of Confucius but, of course, with a different intent, Husserl starts with his own experience, experience in the family, the neighborhood, the city, the nation, and the world, and speaks of an openness to the surrounding world. The idea of unity, which should lie at the root of all cultural and religious formations, along with the inherent tendency of this idea to incarnate itself historically in one philosophy (here phenomenology) and religion (here Christianity) is something that Husserl does not take to be itself historically sedimented and constituted in the concrete life of a certain cultural, philosophical, and religious tradition. This view might have been the blind spot in Husserl's otherwise very clear and sincere phenomenological optics.

In the spirit of Buddhism and Taoism, Husserl connects the idea of religion with that of universal ethical behavior. Husserl, who often read Neumann's translation of the original Buddhist literature and made ample notes in his private copies, is full of praise for the Buddhist way of liberation, which is the result of a radically new way of intuitive seeing. It is our destiny, Husserl thinks, to come to terms with this new Indian religiosity. Husserl seems to be fascinated by Buddhism.[23] But he does not traverse this path very long and leaves it in favor of a theory of a universal religion that incarnates itself in one people preaching one God of revelation beyond the reach of ethnic groups with polytheistic religions.

Hume, Husserl, and Hegel

In opposition to Hume, who favors polytheism and, despite existing tensions between theism and polytheism, praises its ability and tolerance, Husserl tends to side with monotheism with its claim to be a religion of universal interest. Plurality of gods and different mythical powers are objects belonging to the same category as the plurality of animals and human beings. For Husserl, the idea of God knows no plurality.[24] It is Christianity that deserves this status. If God's grace and faith in Him fail, no philosophy, not even phenomenology, can bridge the gap between theism and atheism. Hume was right in pointing out the vain character of the controversy between the two. He wrote, "The theist allows, that the original intelligence is very different from human reason: The atheist allows, that the orignial principle of order bears some remote analogy to it. Will you quarrel, Gentlemen, about the degrees, and enter into a controversy, which admits not of any precise meaning, nor consequently of any determination."[25]

In the spirit of Hegel, Husserl speaks of a "substantial" point of view that surpasses the narrow, cultural, and religious dimensions of different individuals and groups and places itself over them with the further claim that it is inclusive of all of them. Husserl is convinced that the European philosopher is in a position to lay bare the style not only of his own world but also of the foreign world. In a rather prejudiced hermeneutic view of eighteenth- and nineteenth-century Europe, Husserl poses many rhetorical questions, such as "Who scrutinizes the world scientifically?" and "Who interprets and explains the structure of one's own homeworld and that of the other?" The answer is *Europe*. Husserl flatly denies such an ability to other cultures, to the nonhellenized Romans and the Chinese. Husserl reminds one of Hegel, with his claim that the European understanding of the non-Europeans is the only true and real understanding.[26] It is this inclusivism of Husserl's philosophy of religion that gets little or no phenomenologically methodical support.

Because "the primitives," according to Husserl, remain prescientific, there is little theoretical possibility of coming to mutual understanding in religious matters.[27] Contacts and cooperation are possible from just the practical point of view. Unknowingly, perhaps, Husserl theoretically justifies the practice of certain missionaries in non-European countries, who also undertook much trouble to learn foreign languages, customs, habits, and manner just to convince them of one universal faith. For these missionaries, it was more important to be understood by others than to understand them. For Husserl, Europe is obligated to export philosophy, culture, and religion to non-Europeans. One wonders about Husserl's self-complacency when he was otherwise a sincere phenomenologist and philosopher ever ready to start anew.

There is a strange line of argument in the manuscript, A VII 9. Husserl maintains that the very fact that the Europeans pose such questions about the difference between the logic of the primitives and that of the Europeans or the question concerning the universality of religion, culture, and philosophy is a sure indication of the superiority of the Europeans over the "primitives." Husserl expects the charge of Eurocentrism and dismisses it. He rhetorically poses the following question: "Does it make any sense if we accept objections like this is your European way of thinking?" Husserl dismisses such a question as meaningless and is convinced that the only real understanding of the universe of the other is one's own understanding of it. Even if we accept the genuine truth in Husserl's remark, we still wonder why it cannot be also the other way round. The best way is, of course, mutual critical understanding among cultures.[28] If philosophical rationality culminates in Husserl's phenomenology, then religious universality comes to its self-realization in Christianity. The crux of this way of arguing in favor of only one religion lies in the inability to see that the phenomenon of the need for universality, be it in philosophy or religion, is itself a noematic object that gets its meaning in the lived noetic experience. To think that this felt need is also fulfilled borders on self-fulfilling prophecy. Sympathetically and truly, Bello comments on this problematic aspect of Husserl's thinking: "Husserl was profoundly interested in the confrontation of cultures and the interpretation of the salient stages in the development of Western civilization: its fundamental characteristic appeared to him to be the aspiration to universality."[29]

Husserl and Scheler

It may be appropriate to point to a very illuminating difference between Husserl and Scheler on the problem of God. Scheler, who, no doubt, confines the reduction to the eidetic, delineates the affective and religious spheres of the lived experiences not in the sense of a concept of God who is fully transcendent and existent before and from the beginning of the world. He develops the idea of a God-in-becoming, a God who is thought to possess a comradeship in cosmic solidarity with humans. Humans, according to Scheler, play a very important role in the self-realization of God.[30] In his manuscript B II 2, Husserl approaches Scheler and seems to side with pantheism. God is defined here as the will of the good. As ultimate reality, it comes to its full realization when the good is the fulfilled will of God—in other words, the fulfilled realization of God. This is the ideal of the fulfilled realization of the good and of God in relation to whom every action is good as an approximation toward this goal. The one all-encompassing God can be thought of only as an infinite life, an infinite love, and an endless will. It is the only activity that entails infinite fulfillment and infinite happiness. God, for Husserl, is the will to do good. Humans are God in proportion to the realization of this good in themselves, in their lives, and in the world.[31] Husserl speaks of the ideal of the ethics of universal love, and humans realize God in everything noble and good they do. Humans and nature become God by realizing the will of the good by the fulfilled will of God. Not very consistently, God is entelechy, or energy, for Husserl.

Husserl's Phenomenology and the Problem of God's Transcendence and Immanence

In my attempt to draw a systematic picture of Husserl's religious thought, I have consulted his published and unpublished literature. Husserl never claimed to have already worked out a unified theory about God. This fact is also testified to by what Husserl says about God in different places, such as the phrase, "fulfilled realization of God." All that phenomenology can say is that it is an unfulfilled noetical act as lived experience. Husserl's phenomenology of religion offers him the ideal of an immanent God, but he wants to press out of his phenomenology, although he has little success, however, a transcendent, loving God.[32]

The science of phenomenology as the most radical method of philosophizing about any subject of human interest is not directly interested in reintroducing the old philosophical and theological arguments for the existence of God—that is, those that are ontological, cosmological, moral, and so on. All that this science really strives to achieve is to come to some originary experience in which God is not only constituted but, over and above, makes his existence felt in it. This is what, as we have seen, phenomenology cannot afford to do.

Husserl's phenomenology of religion and his concept of God seem to have imbibed much of what characterizes the God of philosophy and metaphysics. The Aristotelian element of teleology and entelechy leading to an argument for the existence of God is no less present in Husserl's concept of God than the idea of the prime mover. For Husserl, the facticity of transcendental subjectivity as the flowing present and as the reservoir of all meaning-giving acts is, no doubt, absolute and most originary. It knows no beginning and no end. The ever-flowing, transcendental life as the bedrock of all that happens in time cannot come from nothing and cannot vanish into nothing. It must be, Husserl says, immortal because dying makes no sense for such a life. After reading such passages in Husserl's unpublished manuscripts, one has the impression that he tends toward some type of pantheism but stops short because he is also a believing Christian.[33]

There seems to be another facticity of a still higher order and potency that functions as sufficient reason for the facticity of transcendental human subjectivity. It is this "other" absolute that seems to take the place of God. Husserl is not very clear regarding how this absolute makes its passage into human consciousness. There is one quite ambiguous hint in his manuscript B I 14, where Husserl speaks of a mystical, nonintentional feeling in our consciousness. This feeling, instead of founding God as its correlate, is itself the affection generated by God. This

God, this something that is not dependent on us, is beyond the reach of human language. In this area, Husserl seems to side with the negative theologians of all religions.[34]

The best way to reconcile these two conflicting motives in Husserl's person and philosophy is "to render to Caesar the things that are Caesar's, and to God the things that are God's." In other words, the concept of a noematic God as found in the noetic-noematic structure is credited to the phenomenologist Husserl; the concept of God as a transcendent existence knocking at the door of human consciousness is what is contributed by the believing and even mystical Christian Husserl. Both may live side by side, if not simultaneously, which is quite difficult to achieve, and then alternately. The personal religiosity of Husserl, although not a philosophically relevant argument, sheds some light on the problem at hand.[35] Hume seems to be right when he thinks that it is not only in poetry and music, but also in philosophy, that taste matters.

Husserl even tends to a moral argument in favor of the belief in the existence of God, for he often points to the presence of moral life in humans. He joins hands here with Thomas Aquinas. Thus, Husserl also subscribes to God as an idea, but he is less emphatic concerning the problem of demonstrating the existence of God and is rather satisfied with felt needs and indications. It is the precategorical attitude with its characteristics of fulfillment, evidence, and intuition that fit with religious attitude. The categorical attitude remains at the discursive level in search of proof and demonstration. Despite the fact that God, for Husserl, is constituted in human consciousness, he is far from inventing Him, for He is the highest transcendence. Husserl's constitutive phenomenology deals with the performances of human consciousness, and these performances are essential for our understanding of the world of things and beings. Husserl is very clear on the point that the transcendent God is not an invention of human consciousness.[36]

God in the theological perspective is, of course, an object of faith. Although Husserl does subscribe to such a faith and seems to be a theist in its religious connotations, he still feels the need to pre-prepare the human mind in search of faith. For the believer Husserl, faith no doubt sprang from tradition and claims absolute validity independent of experience, intuition, and understanding. Husserl classifies all religions in two categories: the revelatory and the nonrevelatory. Faith is an act of freedom, and Christian science is there not to produce faith but to mediate between natural theology and revelation and to justify the latter before the eyes of reason.[37] Here, Husserl fails to realize that the absolute validity he thinks of in relation to Christianity may be equally claimed by believers of different denominations.

Husserl, the Phenomenologist, and Husserl, the Believer

The most crucial question that any post-Husserlian phenomenology of religion must answer today is how to avoid exclusiveness or inclusiveness of a faith. The idea of pluralism of religion is now no more an idea, and it really never has been.

Today, it has become a desideratum of the so-called modern-postmodern period. Humanity does not need only one religion, if it needs any. The crucial question regarding the problem of communication among this plurality of religions can be solved neither by accepting the fiction of one religion for all of us nor by denying any possibility of communication among them but by looking for the more or less overlapping structures among them. Jaspers is right in essentially connecting the idea of truth with the possibility of communication. The will to communicate has primacy over truth, which means that any absolutistic claim to truth must be given up to make room for communication. It is here that Jaspers was very critical of Christianity and expected—in fact, demanded—from the latter to dispose of the devil of absoluteness.[38]

The God of phenomenology, in contrast to that of philosophy and theology, must be a noematic correlate of a noetically lived experience. To this extent, every phenomenologist believes in the meaningful idea of God. The noetic acts may contain all of the various qualities (e.g., infinity, unity, simplicity, incorporeality, inmutability, eternity, goodness, omniscience, omnipotence) commonly attributed to God by traditional metaphysics and theology. Still, the chasm between the God of phenomenology and that of theology will remain unbridged until it is bridged by either fulfillment of the intended meaning of the concept of God or the reality of God making its entrance into human consciousness via the routes of mystic experience, revelation, faith, or grace. The path phenomenology legitimately has to traverse is only the former and not the latter. Husserl might have reconciled the two in his own person, but that is a different story. There is some evidence that Husserl lived through the tension between being a radical phenomenologist and being a believing Christian.[39]

It is against the spirit of phenomenology to give special treatment and privileged position to a particular philosophical, cultural, or religious tradition. A phenomenologist qua phenomenologist does not belong to a particular culture because of his or her neutral descriptive attitude and commitment to the originary and evidential sources of meaning. Husserl often oscillates here when he treats European philosophy as the only philosophy, European culture as the only true universal culture, and Christianity as the highest religion. In contrast, Husserl is not a believer of the naive sort, and he is, at times, far too inquisitive. Husserl does pose questions, in a rather indecisive, pathetic, and tragic mood: "Are there really not many revelatory religions?" "Are they equal in status?" and "Is not, in a way, even religious life autonomous?"

Notes

1. Cf. Karl Schuhmann, "Malvine Husserls Skizze eines Lebensbildes von E. Husserl," *Husserl Studies*, no. 5 (1988): 106–25.
2. *Hua* VI, 140.
3. Karl Schuhmann, *Husserl-Chronik* (The Hague 1977), 295.
4. *Hua* VI, 338–39.
5. *Hua* VI, VII, XIII, and XIV.

6. A V 19; A V 21; A V 22; A VII 9; BI; E III 1; E III 4; E III 7; E III 10.

7. Like Hume, Husserl was very interested in theology, as testified to in a letter Husserl wrote to Gustav Albrecht on 2 August 1917: "Das Leben ist überhaupt hart und ich sehne mich sehr nach der Ruhe, die den natürlichen Abschluß dieses irdischen Seins bilden muß. Ich fühle mich freilich noch nicht genug religiös vorbereitet und das Ende meines philosophischen Lebens sehnt sich nach dem letzten religions-philosophischen Abschluß. Leider fordert die Pflicht, meine langjährigen Arbeiten zu Vollendung und Druck zu bringen, zumal sie durchaus für eine Versöhnung zwischen der naturalistischen Weltanschauung, die die abgelaufene Epoché beherrschte, und teleologischer Weltanschauung die wissenschaftlichen Fundamente bieten. Die teleologische aber ist die endgültig wahre. Ich kämpfe ständig mit der Ungunst der Umstände, zum Teil solchen, die in mir selbst, in meinen schwachen Kräften liegen." Schuhmann, *Husserl-Chronik*, 212–13.

8. Edmund Husserl, *Ideas: General Introduction to Pure Phenomenology*, trans. W. R. Boyce Gobson (London 1958), 174.

9. Husserl, *Ideas*, 174.

10. K III 6, 253.

11. "Uns gilt es, die Teleologie in dem geschichtlichen Werden der Philosophie, insonderheit der neuzeitlichen, verständlich zu machen, und in eins damit, uns über uns selbst Klarheit zu verschaffen, als ihre Träger, in unserer persönlichen Willentlichkeit ihre Mitvollzieher . . . . Wir sind eben, was wir sind, als Funktionäre der neuzeitlichen philosophischen Menschheit, als Erben und Mitträger der durch sie hindurchgehenden Willensrichtung, und sind das aus einer Urstiftung, die aber zugleich Nachstiftung und Abwandlung der griechischen Urstiftung ist. In dieser liegt der teleologische Anfang, die wahre Geburt des europäischen Geistes überhaupt." *Hua* VI, 71–71.

12. E III 10, 18: "Eine autonome Philosophie, wie es die aristotelische war und wie sie eine ewige Forderung bleibt, kommt notwendig zu einer Teleologie und philosophischen Theologie—als inkonfessioneller Weg zu Gott."

13. A VII 9, 20: "Universale Ethik und Religion ist offenbar nur reine Form, in ihrer universalen Allgemeinheit abstrakt, offen unbestimmt lassend die Konkretionen von Mensch und Umwelt."

14. A VII 9, 20–21: "Der Weg über die Philosophie, der unhistorische Weg, der durch den Durchbruch der autonomen Erkenntnis und einer durch diese motivierten neuartigen universalen Normierung der Praxis. Der auf dem einen Wege entsprungene Gott aller Menschen und aller Welt ist, nachdem historische Offenbarung überliefert ist, für alle in dieser Tradition stehenden Menschen ohne weiteres als offenbarter mitverstanden—auch für den 'Atheisten.' Demnach ist die nachträglich erwachsende Wissenschaft, sofern sie mit ihm rechnet, . . . eo ipso theologisch. Eine Wissenschaft aber, die nicht Offenbarung voraussetzt, eine Weise der universalen Wissenschaft, die keine Offenbarung kennt oder als vorgegebene Tatsache (obschon nachher erkenntnismäßig zu behandelnde) anerkennt, atheistisch. Demnach wenn eine solche Wissenschaft doch zu Gott führt, wäre ihr Gottesweg ein atheistischer Weg zu Gott, wie ein atheistischer Weg zum echten unbedingt allgemeinen Menschentum, und dieses verstanden als Substrat für eine übernationale, überhistorische Normierung dessen, was echtes Menschentum überhaupt, überzeitlich, überempirisch ausmacht."

15. E III 10, 18: "Philosophische Theologie als Kulmination der Philosophie, konfessionelle Theologie die Philosophie als Werkzeug nutzend . . . Eine autonome Philosophie, wie es die aristotelische war und wie sie eine ewige Forderung bleibt, kommt notwendig zu einer Teleologie und philosophischen Theologie—als inkonfessioneller Weg zu Gott—aber eine solche Philosophie, indem sie Rechenschaft gäbe von der Wesensnotwendigkeit der

Welt als Welt mit und für Menschen und damit des menschlichen Daseins in einer historisch sich gestaltenden Religion, muß auch Rechenschaft dafür abgeben, wie historisch konkrete Religion die Zielgestalt der Religion sub specie aeterni ist und in ihr ewige Notwendigkeit in sich trägt; es bedarf daher einer / philosophischer Theologie eines zweiten Sinnes, einer auf dem Boden der Konfession stehenden. Hier ist autonome Philosophie das Werkzeug, um verständlich und einsichtig zu machen, warum der zeitlich gewordene, mit Vorstellungen der historischen Situation in der Sprache einer Zeit sich mitteilende Glaube sich rechtmäßig als absolute Wahrheit ausgeben könne, und das auch totz des Wandels der religiösen Formen, von Interpretationen, auch von philosophischen Interpretationen."

16. R. A. Mall, "Phenomenology—Essentialistic or Descriptive?" *Husserl Studies,* no. 10 (1993): 13–30.

17. *Zur Phänomenolgie der Intersubjektivität,* III (The Hague: 1973), 378–86.

18. The original Sâmkhya pleads for a teleological evolution that is atheistic. The original matter (prakrti) evolves into things and beings of phenomenological nature. This theory is based on a particular theory of causality advocated by Sâmkhya. According to this theory of causality (satkâryavâda), an effect is implicitly present in the cause. The original matter is the very matrix of all differentiations. The prakrti evolves for the sake of the experience (bhoga) of the selves. S. C. Banerjee (trans.), *The Sânkhya Philosophy: Sânkhyakârikâ with Gaudapada's Scolia and Narayana's Gloss* (Calcutta 1909); S. Radhakrishnan and C. A. Moore (eds.), *A Source Book in Indian Philosophy* (Princeton 1957).

19. S. Strasser, "Das Gottesproblem in der Spätphilosophie E. Husserls," *Philos. Jahrbuch der Görres-Gesellschaft* 67 (1959): 130–32.

20. G. van der Leeuw, *Phänomenologie der Religion* (Tübingen 1956). Much light has been thrown on the problems of religion, God, and mysticism from a phenomenological perspective by K. Stagenhagen, *Absolute Stellungnahme: Eine ontologische Untersuchung über das Wesen der Religion* (Erlangen 1925).

21. Henry Duméry, *Phénoménologie et Religion* (Paris 1962).

22. A. A. Bello, "Archeology of Religious Knowledge," in *Phenomenology and the Numinous* (Pittsburgh 1988), 11.

23. "Für uns, für alle, die in dieser Zeit des Zusammenbruchs unserer durch Veräußerlichung entarteten Kultur sehnsuchtsvoll Umschau halten, wo noch seelische Reinheit und Echtheit, wo friedvolle Weltüberwindung sich bekunden, bedeutet dieses Sehendwerden für die indische Art der Weltüberwindung ein großes Erlebnis. Denn daß es sich im Buddhismus—so wie er aus seinen reinen Urquellen zu uns spricht—um eine religiös-ethische Methodik seelischer Reinigung und Befriedigung von einer höchsten Dignität handelt, durchdacht und betätigt in einer inneren Konsequenz, einer Energie und einer edlen Gesinnung fast ohnegleichen, das muß jedem sich hingebenden Leser bald klar werden. Nur mit den höchsten Gestaltungen des philosophischen und religiösen Geistes unserer europäischen Kultur kann der Buddhismus parallelisiert werden. Es ist nunmehr unser Schicksal, die für uns völlig neue indische Geistesart mit der für uns alten und sich in diesem Kontrast selbst wieder verlebendigenden und kräftigenden verarbeiten zu müssen." *Hua* XXVII, 125–26.

24. "Götter im Plural, mythische Mächte jeder Art, sind umweltliche Objekte von derselben Wirklichkeit wie Tier oder Mensch. Im Begriffe Gott ist der Singular wesentlich." *Hua* VI, 335.

25. D. Hume, *Dialogues Concerning Natural Religion,* Part XII, ed. N. K. Smith (London 1947), 218.

26. A VII 9, 23–24, *Hua* XXVII, 73–74: "Und schließlich: Wer stellt alle diese Betrachtungen an? Wer legt analytisch den Stil der eigenen Heimwelt, der Fremden aus . . . und gibt

davon eine "wissenschaftliche" Auskunft, eine "Theorie"? Sage ich: ich der Europäer, ich in der Geschichtlichkeit der griechischen Wissenschaft und im Besitz ihrer methodischen Habitualitäten, und sage ich: der Primitive, der im Mythischen lebende Römer, der nicht helenisiert war und dgl., könnte das nicht, und der Chinese heute kann es auch nicht, wenn er nicht europäisiert worden ist—so setze ich eigentlich wieder voraus, daß ich Europäer Wissen von Primitiven etc. habe, die "nüchterne" objektive Wissenschaftlichkeit und im besonderen Wissenschaftlichkeit der Historie?"

27. A VII 9, 27.

28. A VII 9, 25–26: "Hat es einen Sinn, den Einwand gelten zu lassen: das ist Deine europäische (und schließlich Deine persönliche) Denkungsart, sie ergibt europäische Wahrheit, europäische Logik, europäische Weltanschauung . . . ? Wer sagt das? Zu mir, als Einwand? Doch der Mensch, der für mich in meiner Welt ist, und als solcher, für den ich dann in seiner Umwelt bin, was ich aber selbst in meinem Bewußtseinsleben erkenne, als Bestand in meiner Welt habe! . . . Ist es da nicht ein Unsinn, daß das Universum meiner Wahrheit und meines Seins mit dem Universum des Erkennbaren irgenwelcher Anderen, etwa Primitiver, in unlöslichem Widerstreit stehen könnte, wenn doch diese Primitiven und ihr Universum (nach allem, was ich darüber in Wahrheit sagen kann) in meinem Universum enthalten sind?"

29. Bello, "Archeology of Religious Knowledge," 15.

30. Scheler's concept of God-in-becoming is mainly ethical. Scheler writes, "Wir lehnen dieses 'Jenseits'und 'Diesseits,' diese zwei Substanzen, ferner die Lehre von dem absolut allmächtigen guten und weisen Gott als Grund der Welt ab. Der Grund der Dinge ist Werdesein und mit der Welt als Geschichte gegenseitig *solidarisch.* Es kann also auch in Gott nicht 'vollkommener Friede' sein, sofern er nicht in der Welt ist. Auch in Gott besteht die Urspannung von Geist und Drang. Wir sind weder 'Knechte,' 'Diener' noch 'Kinder Gottes,' sondern Freunde und Mitkämpfer um den solidarischen Frieden in Gott und Welt. Die Selbstrealisierung Gottes vollzieht sich nicht ohne die Weltgeschichte, die Geschichte des Menschen. . . . Den gleichzeitigen 'Gottesfrieden'und Weltfrieden zu realisieren gehört uns also zu den identisch gemeinten Zielen des theogenetischen Prozesses und des Weltprozesses. Was wir hier scharf ablehnen, ist die Geste aller derer, die mit dem Finger zum Himmel deuten, wenn das Wort Friede fällt—und damit den Menschen trösten oder entschädigen wollen für den mangelnden Weltfrieden. Es ist nach unserer festen metaphysischen Überzeugung nicht ein bißchen mehr Friede in Gott als in der Welt." M. Scheler, *Die Idee des Friedens und der Pazifismus,* ed. M. S. Frings (Munich 1974), 21–22; M. S. Frings, "Gott und das Nichts," *Phänomenologische Forschungen,* no. 6/7 (1978): 118–40; E. Avé-Lallemant, "Religion und Metaphysik im Weltalter des Ausgleichs," *Uit Tijdschrift voor Filosofie* 42, no. 2 (1980): 266–93.

31. B II 2, 53-54; R. Sokolowski, *Moral Action: A Phenomenological Study* (Bloomington 1985): "Natürlich kann das Allich, das alle Ichs in sich und alle Wirklichkeit in sich und nichts außer sich hat, nicht wie ein empirisches Ich gedacht werden, es ist unendliches Leben, unendliche Liebe, unendlicher Wille, sein unendliches Leben ist eine einzige Tätigkeit, und da es unendliche Erfüllung ist, unendliches Glück. Alles Leid, alles Unglück, allen Irrtum lebt Gott in sich nach, und nur dadurch, daß er es im strengsten mitlebt, mitfühlt, kann er seine Endlichkeit, sein Nichteinsollen überwinden in der unendlichen Harmonie, zu der es da ist. Gott ist überall, Gottes Leben lebt in allem Leben. . . . Gott als Wille zum Guten ist letzte Wirklichkeit, erhält letzte Realisation, wenn eben das Gute ist, und so ist das realisierte Gute der erfüllte Gotteswille, die erfüllte Gottesrealisation. Alles andere ist gut als Handlung zu diesem Ziel hin. In allem Edlen und Guten das ich in mir realisiere, bin ich also realisierter Gott, erfüllter Gotteswille, bloße Natur, die zu Gott geworden ist, zum erfüllten Gott."

32. H. Hohl, *Lebenswelt und Geschichte: Grundzüge der Spätphilosophie E. Husserls* (Munich 1962), 83–88.

33. K III 6, 394 and 399: "Urtümliches Leben kann nicht anfangen und aufhören. Aber wie steht es mit dem strömenden urtümlichen Leben, in dem die Zeitigung und Weltigung statthat? Als phänomenologisierend Erkennender erkenne ich diese Zeitigung, diese Selbstobjektivation, in allen Strukturen. . . . Aber das Transzendentale urtümliche Leben, das letztlich weltschaffende Leben und dessen letztes Ich kann nicht aus dem Nichts werden und ins Nichts übergehen, es ist "unsterblich", weil das Sterben dafür keinen Sinn hat etc."

34. B I 14, XIII 16: "Mindest denkbar, mindest möglich ist, als ein Seinsbereich, der uns unzugänglich bleibt, oder als ein 'Nichts,' das nicht gebunden ist an unsere Seinsbewährungen und Seinsausweisungen, das irgend im Gefühl oder wie immer mystisch in unserer Bewßtseinsphäre anklopft, auf das nur die Sprache unseres Bewußtseins nicht paßt."

35. It is interesting to note here that Lévinas also pleads for a philosophical theology with a transcendent God and opposes the phenomenological thesis of immanence. He introduces the concept of track or footprint left behind by a transcendence that eludes our understanding and is beyond our control. The absent presence of the transcendent God are the footprints left behind in our consciousness and in the world. E. Lévinas, *Die Spur des Anderen* (Munich 1987); E. Lévinas, *Wenn Gott ins Denken einfällt* (Munich 1985).

36. "Auch Gott ist für mich, was er ist, aus meiner eigenen Bewußtseinsleistung, auch hier darf ich aus Angst vor einer vermeneintlichen Blasphemie nicht wegsehen, sondern muß das Problem sehen. Auch hier wird wohl, wie hinsichtlich des Alterego Bewßtseinsleistung nicht besagen, daß ich diese höchste Transzendenz erfinde und mache," *Hua* XVII, 222.

37. "Also Glaube als echte Bekehrung oder echte ursprüngliche Nachfolge ist freie Tat. Und Erneuerung dieser Freiheit in der echten Bekennerschaft ist das Thema ursprünglicher christlicher Predigt. Dasselbe gehört zu jeder ursprünglich gestifteten Religion gegenüber dem gewachsenen und nicht gestifteten Mythus der mythischen Religion. Eigentliche Religion ist also ein Durchbruch der Freiheit. . . . Die christliche Wissenschaft hat nicht die Funktion, den Glauben zu erwirken, sondern ist zunächst Mittel der Apologetik und soll dazu dienen, den in Einwendungen geltend gemachten Widerstreit zwischen "natürlicher Vernunft" und Offenbarung (offenbartem Gehalt) aufzulösen und diesen vor der "Vernunft" zu rechtfertigen," *Hua* XXVII, 103.

38. K. Jaspers, *Der philosophische Glaube* (Munich 1981).

39. E III 10, 21 and 23: "In allen Mächten, in allen Geistern herrscht ein Gott, ein einziger über alle, in allem, alles zum universal Guten bestimmend, für uns Menschen. Aber wir sterben, die Nationen sterben, alles ist vergänglich—Unsterblichkeit . . .—gibt es nicht wirklich viele Offenbarungsreligionen? Stehen sie einander gleich? . . . Ist nicht in gewisser Weise auch religiöses Leben autonom?"

9

The Concept of the Absolute—
An Intercultural Perspective

Preliminary Remarks

In search of the one Absolute, several kinds of anchorage have been discovered, constructed, and invented—for example, metaphysical, ontological, speculative, ideological, theological, and humanistic. The term *absolute* as used by philosophers represents the independent reality regarded as one, perfect, and complete as well as the very source of plurality. Such a philosophy of the absolute betrays its theological kinship and still fails to overcome the tension between the absolute of the philosophers and the God of the theologians. This approach locates the absolute outside of the only world in which human beings live, act, and die—which leads to the legitimate suspicion that the absolute is just a projection of the finite.

In this chapter, I am not going to pick out any one of these theories as my central theme. Instead, I work out a theory of an overlapping value structure following the spirit of interculturality and interreligiosity and leading to a binding absolute that is the exclusive possession of no one alone.

Peter Frederick Strawson has distinguished between two kinds of metaphysics—descriptive and revisionary.[1] One might maintain that the same applies to the concept of the absolute. Our intercultural perspective favors the descriptive rather than the revisionary kind of absolute and tries to develop a concept of the absolute that allows for communication among different cultural perspectives without ignoring their differences.

There seems to be an inherent irony in our search for the absolute. Those who claim to have found and realized it cannot describe it exactly, and those who have not cannot conceive of what it is like. There has always been a tension between absolutism and relativism with a rather comic effect that the very presence of more than one absolute leads automatically to relativism, be it in philosophy or religion.

In the current world context of global formation, the battle between absolutists and relativists has become even more dominant. One of the main reasons for this battle seems to lie in our unfulfilled longing for a fixed, all-pervasive, universal Archimedian point. Richard Bernstein uses the expression "Cartesian anxiety" for the conviction of a universal foundation.[2]

The either–or situation of a deadly and exclusively two-valued logic denies the pluralistic approach of various roads leading to one absolute goal. The one absolute, in whatever field, is always in need of understanding, interpretation, and expression. There is no absolute text, for the one absolute has no one mother tongue, be it Arabic, Chinese, Greek, German, or Sanskrit. As there is no absolute text, so also there is no absolute interpretation. Interpretations have their own history.

That there is no absolute value in this sense does not mean the acceptance of an absolute relativism (subjectivism, individualism) leading to total incommensurability. All that it means is that the moment the telos of one absolute is linguistically, culturally, philosophically, and religiously interpreted, understood, and realized, it becomes a relative absolute, which means that the binding universality of the absolute expresses itself in various ways. Thus, the absolute is what is applicable to various value systems in that it shows its presence in them and also transcends them. It is not the absolute value that thereby becomes relative; only the different value systems are relative to it. The absolute is the overlapping structure that rejects the fictions of total identity as well as of total difference among cultures, philosophies, and religions enabling us to understand and communicate.

The various religious and philosophical traditions testify to this fact: the Indian rigvedic dictum of one Truth under different names; the Christian dictum of Nicholas of Cusa, "una religio in rituum varietate"; the Chinese saying, "three teachings, one family"; and one of the Hadiths of Islam, "the ways of God are like unto the breathings of all created beings." The cry for absolute values combined with the claim of universal acceptance is theoretically unsound, practically dangerous, and religiously blasphemous.

Toward the Concept of an Overlapping Absolute

The true spirit of interculturality and interreligiosity proclaims as its motto that the desire to understand and the desire to be understood go hand in hand and are the two sides of the same interculturally oriented, hermeneutic coin. The mere desire to understand may turn out to be empty, and the total desire only to be understood may become blind. In the long period of colonization—whether in culture, religion, or politics—the desire to be understood was most powerful on the part of the colonizers. Furthermore, it is not always wrong to maintain that orientalists and ethnologists played a conspiratorial role for a long time.

The intercultural study of cultures and religions shows fundamental similarities and illuminating differences. This complex pattern of similarities and dissimilarities forms an important basis for intercultural dialogue. *Interreligiosity* is the name of an ethos connecting all religions as their overlapping center. In the absence of such an ethos, all interreligious dialogues are samples of no real value. Methodologically and from the point of view of conviction, it belongs to the essence of such an interreligious ethos that there are various ways to the same religious truth. The claim to absolute truth is not necessarily bad if it is just for the person or the group; but, the moment it demands universal following, it becomes absolutistic in the fundamentalist sense.[3]

An interreligious hermeneutics based on such an ethos rejects not only the fiction of total religious commensurability but also that of complete incommensurability among religions. The ethos of interreligiosity testifies to the fact of religious overlapping, which is the sine qua non of any sincere religious dialogue. The interreligious hermeneutics we plead for starts from the concept of overlapping as its methodological postulate and tries to realize it as its supreme goal. For example, whereas Hindus and Buddhists appeal to the religious hypothesis of the karma doctrine and rebirth in their search for heavenly justice, Christians and Muslims do the same by taking recourse in the will of God. The hermeneutics at work here may be termed *analogous hermeneutics,* which allows for polymorphic theological anchorage, opposing the hermeneutics of identity, which is far too exclusive in nature. Interreligiosity does not stand for any particular religion; it is rather an overarching religious framework preceding the theory and practice of any particular religion and also accompanying them.[4]

If the hermeneutic dilemma exists in the seemingly paradoxical situation that we cannot understand without having certain prejudices and that we fail to understand if we have only prejudices, then the task of finding a way out is incumbent on us. To say that we are caught in this hermeneutic circle does not help much. The way out seems to lie in the interreligious conviction of one Truth under different names. Such an attitude enables us to respect the plurality of religions. It also frees us from the worry we might have about the truth of our religion in the face of other religions. From the premise, "My religion is true" does not follow the falsity of another's religion unless I define the truth of my religion as essentially constituted by the falsity of the other's religion. Interreligiosity, as understood it here, approves of experiential pluralism, which differentiates but does not discriminate.[5]

An Interreligious Hermeneutics

The intercultural and interreligious hermeneutics we plead for stands not only for a way of thought but also for a way of life. It is wrong to think that such a polytheological anchorage betrays the idea of religious earnestness. Sometimes Buddhism and Hinduism are accused of such an attitude, but those who make this argument fail to realize that they confuse earnestness with fighting spirit. Human history supplies enough examples for the thesis that polytheism is as a rule more tolerant than monotheism. The prefix *mono* has always been impatient and tends toward a deadly logic of either–or, leaving no room for compromise, cooperation, and dialogue. That is why there lurks a danger in overrating the importance of consensualism. Reciprocal understanding needs acquiescence not because of consensus but because of disensus. The Indian poet-philosopher Rabindra Nath Tagore puts it very pointedly and rightly: "If humanity ever happens to be overwhelmed with the universal flood of a bigoted exclusiveness, then God will have to make provision for another Noah's Ark to save his creatures from the catastrophe of spiritual desolation."[6] The intercultural and interreligious dialogues might save us from such an end.

Fundamentalistic thinking is by nature nihilistic. If it is too radical, then it leads to total individualism without having any overlapping moral values as objects of shared experiences. It is interesting to note that fanatics legitimatize their practice by pointing out its correspondence to the theory in which they believe. That is why there is a point to saying that fanatics are too sincere, but this sincerity is so exclusive that it may represent some type of mental derangement badly in need of therapy. It is theoretical fanaticism that must be erradicated first because practical fanaticism originates from the theoretical one. There is, thus, a limit to the practice of tolerance, and the dictum does make some sense: tolerate the tolerant! It is a shabby and feeble argument by the intolerant to demand tolerance from the tolerant because of the latter's being tolerant.

The absolute from an intercultural perspective is, thus, polyphonic and polymorphic, and its richness unfolds in and through polylogues. The "bigoted exclusivism" of the one Absolute loses its sting, and we learn to write more than one absolute allowing none of them to usurp the one Absolute. That plurality is God's will and is testified to by verse 14 of sure 49 of the Koran, where God is said to have created various races and tribes to live in love, peace, and harmony.

An intercultural and interreligious perspective allows for an absolute that favors unity but not uniformity; that is fundamental but not fundamentalistic; and that does not unnecessarily give privileged treatment to any one particular religion, culture, or philosophy. Such an interculturally oriented absolute stands in a metonymic relation to the different philosophical and religious traditions. It, of course, needs them but does not become exhausted by any of them. Such an absolute maintains close contact with experience and does not confuse one's subjectively lived experience of the absolute with the absoluteness of one's experience. One and the same moon may shine in different waters; the same holds true for the concept of the absolute, which binds and does not separate us.

Philosophy of Values and the Absolute in Indian Thought

Despite India's rich and varied tradition, Indian thought is unanimous in advocating for an integral theory of personality. Nearly all Indian thinkers accept two functions of knowledge—one that is theoretical and reveals the existence and the nature of the object (arthaparicchitti) and the other that is practical and helps in the attainment of some purpose in life (phala-prâpti). These two functions of knowledge are closely connected, which leads to the conception of philosophy both as a way of thought and a way of life.

The Sanskrit word for *value* is *ista,* which means "that which is desired." Disvalue is that which is shunned (dvista). Because Indian philosophy takes a pragmatic view of knowledge, it has always allotted a central place to value in the integral scheme of life. We cannot consider here the general question of whether we desire things because they are of value or they are of value because we desire them.

The four well-known values in Indian thought (catur- varga) are dharma (ethical and moral value), artha (wealth and possession), kâma (pleasure), and moksa (self-realization). Values may, of course, be either instrumental or intrinsic. When we are thirsty, water is of instrumental value, and the quenching of thirst by means of water possesses an intrinsic value. In addition to these four values, earlier Indian philosophical and religious literature refers only to the first three (tri-varga). Artha (wealth) stands for economic and kâma for psychological values. Artha is an instrumental value, for it is helpful in satisfying the various needs of life. In all religions, there is an imperative to help the needy. Islam asks us to lend money without asking for interest. The satisfaction that results is kâma and is an intrinsic value. These two values are sought not only by human beings but by all creatures. The main difference is that, whereas other creatures seek it instinctively, human beings do it knowingly.

The value that stands higher in the hierarchy of values is dharma—moral value—and is to be found only in the sphere of human beings. Dharma in atheistic systems, such as Buddhism, stands mainly for moral value, but its connotation becomes wider when we come to orthodox Hindu-systems, where it also includes religious values. Yâjnavalkya, the noted upanishadic philosopher, speaks of nine moral values: noninjury, sincerity, honesty, cleanliness, sense-control, charity, self-restraint, love, and forbearance.

If dharma is of higher standing, then the question arises regarding its relation to artha and kâma. Kâma, or pleasure, is welcome to all of us. All that we value is undoubtedly desirable, but not all that we desire is valuable. A sick person may desire a particular kind of food that the doctor has forbidden. Thus, we must distinguish between the two types of kâma. Dharma provides the criterion. The pleasure that serves the purpose of dharma is the real value to be desired. Dharma, thus, functions as a regulative principle. Those who act in the spirit of dharma will be rewarded at some time. This line of thinking seems to have a very deep intercultural anchorage. Kant's postulate that the good will be rewarded belongs to this type of moral thinking. Indian theories of rebirth and Kant's postulate of the immortality of the soul are further cases in point.

There is, of course, another conception of dharma that makes it an intrinsic value. This conception comes very near to Kant's theory of the categorical imperative, for it, too, demands total respect for the moral principle beyond our likes and dislikes. The Indian view tends, as a whole, to make dharma a value that is a prerequisite for the attainment of the highest value, which is self-realization. This value is the absolute end for which all other values are instrumental. The term *value,* in the absolute sense, should be predicated only by this ultimate goal.

The search for the truth aims at removing ignorance (avidhyâ) about the ultimate reality, which is the objective of all philosophy. Thus, both the good and the true are ladders leading to moksa. Mere intellectual conviction is not enough, however. What is needed is direct experience of the absolute truth. To know what is good is one thing, but to do what is good requires something more, a change of character in the person concerned. "Hence all the Indian schools prescribe a proper course of practical discipline to bring about this consummation, viz transforming a mere intellectual conviction into direct experience."[7] The age-old yoga discipline in Indian thought brings about this transformation.

The ideal of self-realization is the Absolute worthy of the name and stands for the absence of ignorance—that is, for the knowledge of truth and for the state of absolute bliss, which is the absence of all pain and suffering. Thus, the integral theory of values in Indian thought does not give absolute status to any of the three values but only to what they lead us to, namely to the absolute ideal of self-realization. This absolute value of self-realization is characterized by freedom from all egoistic bindings, which means conviction in the cosmic unity of things and beings resulting in love for others. Of course, the ideal of self-realization may be and really is a progressive process of attainment with the firm conviction that it will be achieved one day as a culminating stage.

From an intercultural perspective, the concept of the Absolute is to be discussed at two levels. At the first, mostly culturally bound, first-order level, the search for the Absolute is normally characterized by conflicts among points of view, religions, ideologies, moral systems, and even theories. These conflicts produce tensions and strong likes and dislikes among different circles. At the second, higher-order level of interculturality, the search for the Absolute leaves a battlefield dominated by warring points of view and takes an impartial attitude to discover the truth of the Absolute, which is everywhere and is also nowhere in toto. This absence of all points of view is a higher-level experience of the shared Absolute enabling us to think, feel, and will in a reciprocal, communicative, and tolerant spirit. Justice is, thus, done to all points of view when no one single point of view is *the* point of view.

An Intercultural Concept of Tolerance

The age of modernity, which began with the European spirit of setting up a universal pattern for the whole of humanity in the name of expansionism, colonialism, imperialism, and missionarism, has also led to the phenomena of interculturality and interreligiosity. It is rather ironic that this spirit ended nolens volens with the recognition of plurality in religion, culture, philosophy, and so on.

Today's cultural and religious dialogues bear the stamp of interculturality over and above their intracultural character. The problem of tolerance is also a hermeneutic problem, and no religion can claim to speak in the name of God alone and exclusively. It is we human beings who make this claim. The more absolute this claim, the more difficult the interreligious dialogue. To be too monistic in one's Weltanschauung is to be too discriminatory. Polytheism, rightly understood, is by nature more tolerant. It does not, of course, satisfy the greed for monism, which is God.

There is a hermeneutics of one Truth under different names. This hermeneutics leads to a liberal, democratic attitude even in the field of religion, which is good. There is tension associated with our commitment to tolerance. Our confession to truth and tolerance is a reciprocal relation; and truth without confession to tolerance becomes blind, whereas tolerance without truth is empty. The age-old parable of the lame and the blind is of much heuristic and pedagogical value.

There is an overlapping core of commonness among different cultures, philosophies, and religions, which is amply testified to by the wise sayings and proverbs to be found in all cultures and religions. A few examples are "Ekam sad, viprâ bahudhâ vadanti" (Rigveda); "una religio in rituum varietate" (Nicholas of Cusa); and "san jiao, yi jia" (a Chinese proverb).

Intercultural and interreligious discourses following the spirit of an overlapping, analogous hermeneutics help us avoid the evils of both indifferentism and syncretism. The modern–postmodern debate revolves around the overly enthusiastic statement of similarity and dissimilarity, respectively. An intercultural and interreligious enlightenment helps us to search, find, and foster overlapping centers among cultures and religions, enabling us to overcome the fictions of total identity and complete difference.

The interreligious understanding advocated here agrees to the regulative idea of an overlapping unity; but it refuses the disruptive idea of uniformity. We must avoid the temptation of confusing the truth in one's own religion with the religion of truth in an absolute sense. Whoever absolutizes one's own religion lacks the inner, spiritual character of interreligiosity and fails to overcome provincialism. An overlapping, binding plurality is a value and not an irritation.

Our religious pluralism is a desideratum that we all must accept without becoming unfaithful to our own culture and religion. It is not perspectivism, which is wrong, but our greed to put our own perspective in an exclusive, absolute position. Absolutistic claims and tolerance have always been like fire and water. The idea of tolerance and intolerance with regard to content is found in nearly all cultures and religions to some degree. Most striking is that European liberalism and tolerance went hand in hand with imperialism, colonialism, and intolerance.

Tolerance, rightly and positively understood, is a diffident attitude in theory and practice allowing the spirit of truth to blow in more than one place. Any real turning away from fundamentalism in its various facets may occur either through a theoretical, reflexive insight resulting from a methodological, epistemological, moral, metaphysical, political, and religious diffidence or through an act of will and determination practically to give up all claims to absolutism and fundamentalism in the face of the de facto presence of pluralism in all walks of life. To be tolerant out of strategic reason or because of cowardice and weakness is not real tolerance. Tolerance worthy of the name is the ability to understand, accept, and respect the other without necessarily agreeing with it.

The famous German comparative religionist Gustav Mensching differentiates between two types of tolerance: formal tolerance and tolerance with regard to content. A formally tolerant religion allows other religions to exist but may still believe itself to be the only true religion. Chistianity under the influence of enlightenment and other social and political changes accepts the idea of secularism without necessarily giving up the conviction of being the only true religion (revelatio specialis).

The religious scene on the Indian subcontinent from time immemorial seems to have witnessed a very lively pluralistic religious stage. This reason might apply to a different reading of the concept of secularism in Indian context. Whereas the concept of secularism in Western context is partly an anti-religious move and stands for the absence of religion in worldly affairs, the Indian context allows for secularism in the sense of plurality of religions combined with equal respect for all religions. Gandhi tended to some such type of secularism. No religion has the right to be given a privileged position by the state. Indian nationalism, patriotism, and secularism, thus, go hand in hand and reject the idea of any particularizing fundamentalism and fanaticism, regardless of denomination in religion, race, or language.

Tolerance regarding content is real tolerance worthy of the name, for it recognizes and respects other religions. Contrapuntal to these two forms of tolerance are two forms of intolerance: formal and regarding content. The worst form of intolerance is intolerance for content, for it fights other religions and is destructive, aggressive, and violent. The militancy of such an intolerance ends in and with the destruction of other cultures, religions, and ideologies. Such militancy is not just a sign of religious fundamentalism. History tells us that the French revolution in its early reaction against the church was more persecuting and less tolerant. The "Kulturkampf" in Germany in the 1870s is another case in point. The communist revolution of 1917 in Russia practiced militant intolerance against Christianity.

Persons, groups, and communities led by such an intolerance may even go so far as to claim to act in accordance with God's will. A God in whose name intolerance is allowed does not really deserve this name just per definition. A fundamentalist is one who says that anyone who does not think the way he or she does makes a mistake, which is a fatal mistake in the eyes of a fundamentalist.

The following sensitive and fragile questions are often posed: "Is tolerance limitless, or is there some limit to tolerance?" "Does it make sense to talk of an unconditioned tolerance?" "What would happen to our commitment to the idea of tolerance regarding content if we practiced tolerance unconditionally?" "Where is the limit when one is committed to stop being tolerant in the name of, and for the sake of, tolerance?" and "Is there any neutrality in the face of exclusivism, fundamentalism, and absolutism?" The philosopher Jaspers says no. All of these and other related questions are far too complex and defy quick and ready-made solutions.

The other side of the dictum, tolerate the tolerant, is as follows: an intolerant position does not deserve my tolerance, not because I do not like the person who holds this position and perhaps also not because he is intolerant but mainly because his position forces me to be untrue to my commitment to tolerance. There are grades of tolerance and intolerance in thought, speech, and action. To a certain degree, tolerance may, therefore, tolerate intolerance; but it depends on the degree and intensity of the intolerance, lest the possibly bearable conflict produced by intolerance degenerate into warfare. The limit is at this point.

For this reason, we can normally get on with formal intolerance, but formal intolerance may lead to theoretical fanaticism that is more ridiculous than harmful. Practical fanaticism (fundamentalism) born out of the theoretical one and in alliance with social, political, and other worldly powers is very dangerous, indeed. Fundamentalistic thinking is bad, but fundamentalistic thinking in possession of power is worse.

Is fundamentalism a disease, a mental derangement? How does one face the argument of a fundamentalist who really and sincerely declares that he does what he believes? It is not so much his action, but rather his conviction, that is primarily in need of therapy. Schools, colleges and universities, seminars, congresses, and other forms of meetings are committed to fighting this theoretical fundamentalism in the spirit of interculturally and interreligiously enlightened secularism. It may be too late if theoretical fanaticism becomes practical.

Tolerance as understood here is a positive attitude and not a state of indifference compatible with any content whatsoever. Such a concept of tolerance committed to, as well as born out of, the values of interculturality and interreligiosity proclaims as its motto: tolerate the tolerant and think, feel, and act in the spirit of the wisdom in live and let live, read and let read, believe and let believe.

Those who accuse this theory and practice of tolerance of being intolerant confuse a formal, empty, and irresponsible tolerance with a positive and responsible one. It is the latter—namely, a responsible tolerance—that we so badly need today. Thus, the dictum is as follows: there is a limit to tolerance points to a theory and practice of tolerance in the name and for the sake of tolerance.

Of course, there are innumerable ways to protest intolerance. It may range from Buddha, Jesus, and Gandhi to Buber, Jaspers, and other forms of active and passive defense of the ideal of tolerance.

Notes

1. P. F. Strawson, *Individuals: An Essay in Descriptive Metaphysics* (London 1959).

2. R. J. Bernstein, *Beyond Objectivism and Relativism* (Oxford 1989), 16.

3. R. A. Mall, "Der Absolutheitsanspruch: Eine religionsphilosophische Meditation," *Loccumer Protokolle*, no. 7 (1991): 39–53.

4. W. Duprès, "Implicit Religion and the Meaning of Interreligious Dialogue," *Studies in Interreligious Dialogue*, no. 1 (1991): 129–45.

5. P. S. Knitter, *No Other Name? A Critical Survey of Christian Attitude Toward World Religion* (New York 1986).

6. R. Tagore, *Boundless Sky: An Anthology*, ed. R. S. Das. (Calcutta 1964), 275.

7. M. Hiriyanna, "Philosophy of Values," in *The Cultural Heritage of India*, vol. 3 (Calcutta 1975), 652.

10

Europe in the Mirror of World Cultures—On the Myth of the Europeanization of Humanity: A Non-European Discovery of Europe

Historical Remarks

In Raimon Panikkar's work relevant to history and in writing about the long relation between the orient and occident, he describes knowledgeably, critically, and in a balanced way the history of European advances into Asia; European domination in India, China, and Japan; and, finally, the retreat of whites from the greater Asian region.

Europe knew about India long before Alexander the Great went to India, because by 480 B.C. Indian soldiers fought on Greek soil under a Persian banner. In addition to political and economic reasons, European expansion always had as its aim the spread of Christianity. "The crusader spirit," as Panikkar wrote, "was substituted by a conversion zeal."[1]

Even if it is true that "the Christian offensive" against Asian religions failed and that, for the Europeans, Asia remained a religious, cultural, and philosophical challenge, and indeed a disappointment, it cannot be denied that the Asian adoption of modern European ideas (for example, democracy in the widest sense, natural sciences, historical research, the idea of nationalism, and so on) influenced Asia, although, of course, without breaking off its Asian traditions. European efforts for unity stood and still stand in contrast to Asian diversity.

In the newspaper *Die Zeit* dated 11 July 1997, Eckhard Nordhofen asks, "What makes Europe Europe? Seen from the viewpoint of other cultures . . . the antitheses of nationalities and mentalities of different confessions shrink down to the diffuse term 'western.'"[2] Although Nordhofen emphasizes Europe's diversity and tolerance, he overlooks, nonetheless, that despite its diversity, humanism, and liberalism at home, Europe in the mirror of other cultures has appeared universalistic, imperialistic, and missionary.

This chapter's title, "Europe in the Mirror of World Cultures," represents a non-European, extra-European discovery of Europe. It is certainly correct that Europe has been the continent with the greatest urge for discovery and was hardly, if ever, an object of discovery itself. In contrast to the adventurous, geographical, and hegemonic European discovery of non-European continents, the non-European discovery of Europe is concerned with the critical consideration of a situation that has arisen in the wake of a European modernity. There is a fateful dialectic between the discoverer and the discovered. Wilhelm Halbfass is, therefore, correct in saying that the Europeans have become used to "seeing themselves as the discoverers par excellence. . . . In the name of their philosophy and science, and also in the name of the Christian religion, the Europeans presented themselves as the bearers and harbingers of a true, trans-cultural universality. In discovering and understanding the other, in by what Husserl and Heidegger called the 'Europeanisation' of the earth and humanity, there lacked ever so often the willingness for self-questioning and self-discovery."[3]

Georg Lichtenberg wrote the following words two hundred years ago in a sad and historically pregnant tone: "The American who first discovered Columbus made a bad discovery"[4]; this tone can apply in milder form to the discovery of Europe by the non-Europeans. Since Alexander the Great and until the end of colonialism and of imperialism in this century, the dialogue among cultures was, in fact, more or less a European monologue. Despite various kinds of dependency, the dialogue among cultures is today no longer a one-way street, which is good.

Today, the reception among the cultures, philosophies, religions, and other forms of world view is of a completely different quality from what it has been. This renewed reception of Asia, Africa, and Latin America by Europe, and vice versa, is characterized by a situation in which the non-European cultures, each with its own voice, participate in the discussion. New in this reception is that the de facto hermeneutic situation entails two additional dimensions apart from the two hermeneutic dimensions of the self-understanding and foreign-understanding of Europe—namely, the self-understanding and the foreign-understanding of non-European cultures. Thus, we have a four-dimensional hermeneutic, dialectical situation.

The institutionalized disciplines of oriental studies and ethnology, for example, are an indication that Europe almost always presented itself as the subject and was supported in it by extra-philosophical factors. Because reciprocal understanding today no longer is, nor can remain, a one-way street, the question is, "Who understands better or best whom, when, how, and why?" This is true both interculturally as well as intraculturally. Self-understanding is indeed at work with every understanding (this is the hermeneutic circle), but is not the only criterion. If this were not the case, then every understanding of the foreign would be a double self-understanding. It might surprise Europe even more that today it has become interpretable, even on behalf of non-Europeans.

Mircea Eliade speaks of a second "unsuccessful Renaissance" and means the promising discovery in the eighteenth and nineteenth centuries of the Asian spirit, the Sanskrit language, the Upanishads, and Buddhism in contrast to the successful first Renaissance in which the discovery of the Greek spirit was taken seriously not only by philologists but also by trained philosophers, theologians, historians, and literati. Eliade rightly sees the reason for the failure of the second Renaissance in that it was taken seriously only by the indologists and not by trained philosophers, theologians, and historians. If today we are on the threshold of a third Renaissance, or if we are already in it, then all of us are called on and committed to take it seriously and help it succeed.

Derrida describes the self-admiration of Europe quite appropriately: "Europe cultivates its own identity in the figure of the Cape, in the being-for-itself of its own difference as a difference with itself. . . . From Hegel to Valéry, from Husserl to Heidegger, this traditional discourse—despite the differences—is a modern discourse."

The question of identity leads to several problems. The idea sounds promising, but the identity sought does not disappear completely in what is found. That is why the idea of a complete purity of identity is a myth, a fiction. Everything human seems to be subject to its becoming and its perishing. The problem of identity is both intracultural and intercultural.

On the Myth "Europe"

Even if we cannot succeed in giving a completely clear explanation of the name "Europe" or in confining this name purely geographically to Central Greece, the myth of the "abduction of Europe" is indeed very clear in its language about "from where" and the implicit "to where."

The beautiful daughter of Phoenician King Agenor is said to be observed by Zeus while she was bathing. He fell in love with her, transformed himself into a bull, abducted her, and carried her away on his back from Asia to a country that did not yet have a name but was then named Europe.

This naming is very dazzling, but behind the myth's mask, much is hidden that later becomes true. If Europe is the result of a robbery, then from Alexander the Great until today, Europe undertook the features of robbery. Furthermore, Europe preached universalism to the world and even practiced it. Europe, who was herself robbed, is now the robber. What an irony! The European emerges out of the conquest. In his Nobel Prize acceptance speech in 1986, Wole Soyinka gave a talk with the highly suggestive title, "This Past Has to Confront Its Present" (Zurich 1988). What the non-European world is today, it owes Europe, without wanting to. The Eurocentric circle is in fact the hermeneutic circle.

As for the question determining the position of philosophy, the ancient Greeks themselves had contrary views. One argued about the origin of philosophy—India or Greece. Whereas Lukian von Samosata saw the goddess of philosophy first descend on the Indians and then the Greeks, Diogenes Laertius spread the view that philosophy is an invention of the Greeks and not of barbarians.[5] In the long history of the encounter between the occident and the orient, several reasons contributed to the fact that the view of Diogenes Laertius developed into a philosophical dogma. The political constellation was largely responsible. Heidegger says very clearly, "The statement: philosophy is in its nature Greek, says nothing else but that: the occident and Europe, and only they, are originally philosophical in the course of their intrinsic history."[6]

"European" as an Adjective to the Name Philosophy

By definition, adjectives serve the function that whatever they modify should not be given absolute status. Accordingly, *European philosophy* means philosophy from Europe. When one turns the pages of books on the history of philosophy, excluding a few published recently, one realizes that they exclusively and, as a matter of course, thematize the history only of the philosophy of Europe. Therefore, the expression *European philosophy* is a tautology because—according to a deeply rooted view, although one based on ignorance, false information, dilettantism, prejudice, and arrogance—philosophy could only be European. In fact, Heidegger says, "The often heard expression 'Western-European philosophy' is in truth a tautology."[7] One is tempted to ask whether this expression is simply an analytical tautology, such as, "Bachelors are unmarried," or whether it is concerned with philosophy itself. Certainly, Heidegger does not simply mean the analytical tautology. Contrary to Heidegger, Jaspers lets the spirit of philosophy also float in China and India and thereby frees it from the narrowness of a single tradition. The well-known thesis of the axial period is proof.

On European Reason

Paul had already taught the Greeks and said that what they respect and worship as the unknown was now named for the first and last times. He referred to the Christian God, the Father, revealed by Christ, His son.

The Greek idea of reason claims for itself, beyond its local, sedimented form, a universality that it alone can identify. The Latin American philosopher Leopoldo Zea rejects this "magistral" claim on the logos by reinstating the original meaning of *logos* as reason and language. The ability to convey what is comprehended with the help of language is an anthropological constant and not a characteristic only of the Greek and European spirit.[8]

I have often asked myself how it is that Christian Europe—apart from a few states with the so-called only true political world views until the recent past—pleads for a republican, pluralistic form of democracy in its own history of thought but rejects a pluralistic theology in religion. The present intercultural and interreligious scene makes it clear that it is false and dangerous to make the one philosophia perennis or the one religio perennis the possession of a particular culture, philosophy, or religion.

Indeed, this danger is relevant when designating anything. If we simply do not wish to suspend the metonymic difference (between a name and the named) by a definitional, nominal trick, then we have to think not only of Lao Tzu and the Rigveda but also of Cusanus and Goethe. As Lao Tzu says, "The name that can be named is not the eternal name." The Rigveda speaks of a truth that the wise ones name differently. In a conversation between Faust and Gretchen in Martha's garden, Goethe describes metonymy in its perfected form.[9] The one with the many names is not absorbed by any of the names, a metonymy that applies to reason as well. Indeed, it is always in need of a language, a name, yet it is not absorbed by it. Reason needs language, but reason still is not at language's complete disposal. European reason is of a certain and special form. No one can call the one reason exclusively his or her own. Even talk of one reason is problematic and can at best be understood as a "regulative idea." This fact is true both intraculturally and interculturally.

European Culture

If European culture is what European philosophy, European reason, and European occidental Christianity have produced, then the following question arises: "From where does the universalistic claim of this culture come?" With Hegel, we found an urge for a secret identity between being and ought, which occurred at the philosophical as well as the political and religious levels. Therefore, Hegel's philosophy can also be read as a legitimation of Europe's universalistic claim. It may appear to a critical thinker that with this claim the European identity would be cryptic, but today's globalization appears to transform this cryptic identity into a concrete reality. Hegel certainly speaks as a European, but the subject, the "we," he speaks of is universal. Today, it must be grasped in all clarity that no subject can, may, or should make its own notion of self-realization the only goal for the whole of humanity.

Whoever regards Europeanization without universalization as impossible seems to behold the proper telos of humanity, in the European spirit, becoming universal. One can, nonetheless, ask the justified question, "Is European universality not indeed a Eurocentric claim?" In contrast, it has to be noticed that this so-called European universality is relativized in the followers themselves. One cannot resist the impression that the European spirit confuses "westernization" and globalization of European technological formation with the "Europeanization" of the European spiritual and religious categories as such.

In his lecture, "Die Krisis des europäischen Menschentums und die Philosophie" ("Philosophy and the Crisis of European Humanity"), given to the Wiener Kulturbund May 7 and 10, 1935, in Vienna, the phenomenologist Husserl speaks of the real form of Europe as spiritual, and not geographical, technological, nor civilizational. Husserl thinks he can discover in Europe something unique, beyond the scheme of strangeness and familiarity that applies everywhere:

> We experience this precisely in our Europe. There is something unique in it which, even for other groups of humanity, is experienced in us, as something which, apart from all considerations of use, is a motive for them indeed always to Europeanise themselves in an unbroken will to spiritual self-preser-

vation, whereas we, if we understand ourselves properly, would never, for example, Indianise ourselves. I mean we feel (and in all unclarity this feeling indeed has its right) that in our European humanity an entelechy is inborn.[10]

Is this a new edition of the theory of inborn ideas in the field of cultural philosophy? Husserl sees philosophers as functionaries of a single, true humanity. Paul Feyerabend accuses Husserl of astounding ignorance because, "What does Husserl know about the true being of the culture of the Nuer?" In fact, Feyerabend speaks of Husserl's phenomenal conceit and considerable contempt for those who think differently. In Feyerabend's words, "I think it shows an astounding ignorance (what does Husserl know about the 'true being' of the Nuer?), a phenomenal conceit (is there a single individual who has sufficient knowledge of all races, cultures, civilisations to be able to speak of 'the true being of humanity'?) and, of course, a sizeable contempt for anybody who lives and thinks along different lines."[11]

The prejudices of diverse provenances that are at the base of such a reading of European and non-European cultures are, in fact, too public to require a learned, academic refutation. But, because they still operate in many philosophical heads, they must be addressed critically.

In contrast to those who regard the universality of the technological formation as evidence for Husserl's thesis, Husserl himself was far removed from confusing this hardware—the external, global universality and uniformity of European science and technology—with the software—the inner, spiritual cultural form. Husserl was concerned with the spiritual universality of European culture, the assumption of which was not an external but an internal matter.

In another connection helpful in our context, Franz Martin Wimmer has shown in his book *Interkulturelle Philosophie* (*Intercultural Philosophy*) that external taking over does not eo ipso signify one's own inner change. Since sixth-century Japan was under the influence of Chinese technology, organization, and even science, "A Sinologised island country has not in the meantime emerged out of it."[12]

Husserl may have flirted with the idea of a universalized Christianity, but empirically it has not occurred. In the term *God,* the singular is particularly essential, according to Husserl. Does not his concept of "culture" also claim a similar singularity? It is Europe's old claim not only to be able to understand itself but also to understand others better than they can themselves. Precisely in this sense, Husserl thinks he helps the others toward better self-understanding and brings them closer to their own self-preservation. It need not be emphasized here that the European categories of thinking and understanding universalize themselves as a matter of course, as if they were naturally beyond all cultural sedimentation. For a long time, Europe raised its particularity to universality, promoted chiefly by extraphilosophical factors and political hegemony.

What Husserl strove for in his phenomenology Hegel had already maintained (in the sense of his scheme of theoretical stages) through his presentation of the history of philosophy—namely, with the Asians belonging to the age of infancy and the Christian-Germanic Europeans belonging to the mature (spiritual) old age. Since the mid-eighteenth century, in fact, the sun of European colonialism, imperialism, and its missionarism has not set, a fact that may have encouraged not only Hegel to see confirmation of the idea of "Europe" in it. Hegel's cultural philosophy is characterized by its exclusion of other cultures. He ascribes to the Africans a wildness and unruliness that make it impossible for the Europeans to understand these people: "If we want to understand them, then we would have to abandon all European notions. . . . That is precisely why we cannot really understand their nature, as little as that of a dog."[13]

Jaspers is one of the few modern philosophers who, through his thesis of the axial period—that is, the simultaneous philosophical, cultural movement in China, India, and Greece—ascribes a befitting meaning to the adjective *European*. Unfortunately, this thesis was not taken seriously in all of its consequences.[14]

Later, Scheler at least pleads for equalization of Asia and Europe under a complete change of the Eurocentric notion. Scheler was often accused (unjustly) of wanting to make the occident the orient and to convert the Christian to Buddhism. The relativization of the European spirit in Scheler's philosophy of equalization, however, is not an end in itself but serves the aim of equalization. According to him, the aim is determined by the view "that the national spirits of people are called upon in all purely cultural matters to complement one another . . . in fact complement one another incovertibly."[15]

The universality that is projected in the adjective *European* expresses itself in a way that the philosophical truth is defined by the European tradition and the latter by the former. A petitio principii is entailed and thus obstructs intercultural communication and understanding. Heidegger consequently sees a tautology in the expression "western-European philosophy."[16]

In reading Samuel P. Huntington's work *The Clash of Civilisation* closely, one notices that Huntington deeply regrets the loss of European universalism.[17] However, as a realpolitik-thinker, he knows that Europe can no longer reestablish its old universality, which is why he suggests stronger unity among all Europeans against the dangers threatening Europe.

The one Truth, if such a thing exists, is not the privilege of a particular adjective, be it European, Indian, Chinese, or anything else. Karl Löwith rightly thinks that thoughts in connection with history show no preference for the occident.[18] An adjective coincident with universalism admires only itself.

It was Hegel who assumed that the real key to the truth was given to Christian-Germanic Europe, and he made Asia the beginning and Europe the end of history. To think that this statement is indeed merely idealistically metaphysical is inadequate.[19]

The consciousness-history of the adjective *European* owes for its universal claim a power structure that, with the discovery of the non-European area, opened up a one-sided discourse. This discourse, introduced by Europe, made the universalism of the European a constitutive element of the discourse, as if the problem of universalism were merely a matter of definition. Edward Said pointed this out convincingly in his book *Orientalism*. The theory of deconstructivism can help us infer the right of other adjectives. Similar events may be understood as being fortunate or unfortunate, depending on the standpoint. The discovery of both of the Americas is both fortunate and unfortunate—fortunate for the Europeans and unfortunate for the original inhabitants. Discovery and covering go together here.

Taking for granted the universal claim in the adjective *European* has a long history. Already the Greeks laid the foundation for it through their distinction between the Greeks and the barbarians. Alexander's marches of conquest played their part in it as well. In his article "Kritik der Globalphilosophie" ("Critique of Global Philosophy"), Rafael Angel Herra speaks of an "Aristotelian syndrome."[20] The intercultural viewpoint is not an extension and expansion of a particular culturally based point of view; this would be a new version of the old practice with the aim, once again, to monopolize the discussion.

Christianity set out to teach the heathens and to show them the only right way to God. This missionarism proceeded with great success, which also consolidated the universal claim of the adjective *European*. In the eighteenth and nineteenth centuries, Europe was blessed with a triumphant march, which must have moved Hegel to make the remark, "The world is circumnavigated and for the Europeans it is round. What they do not yet control is either not worth the effort or is determined still to be controlled."[21] Does Hegel here bring in "the spirit of the times to the term?" Today, one can hardly understand the tremendous euphoria and arrogance in Hegel's statement.

Europe's heritage still continues in this view and, in fact, sees in the technological formation of the world today a confirmation of the unified European idea.[22] Manfred Henningsen writes in his article "Vom Anspruch und Elend des europäishen Universalismus" ("On the Claim and Misery of European Universalism"):

> The Euro-centric emphases which in Kant, Hegel, Marx and Engels consciously-unconsciously reflect a predominance of Europe can further still be noticed in German and other European universities in the organisation of the study of history [and even in the disciplines of theology and philosophy, to name just two more]. . . . The history that is taught as the ancient, medieval and modern, is European. . . . Historians live and think for the occident.[23]

On the Idea of European Unity

Since its beginnings, European culture had the fortune (or misfortune) to assert itself. It, therefore, rarely developed a mature humility in its association with foreign cultures. The multiplicity of cultures is an anthropological fact and presents an intercultural desideratum. Europe's educated people are accustomed to seeing Europe as a unity created out of the idea. This fact may have been true here and there, wherever and whenever they identified themselves as Europeans in non-European countries. They practiced a difference that they had set. Today, there are some voices in Europe who think that European unity is running the risk of losing itself through the presence of non-European cultures and religions in the heart of Europe. The Europeans themselves did not pose this question when they made the non-European countries multicultural and multireligious by their own presence.

We know that Europe has three birth places: Athens, Rome, and Jerusalem. The idea of "Europe," thus, has three fathers and/or mothers. From early Roman-Christian times, through the Middle Ages, until now, these three centers implicitly or explicitly have been in a relation of tension. They were all differently inclined. Athens did not have a religion of revelation but possessed science. With Jerusalem, it was exactly the opposite. Rome was rather practically, pragmatically inclined, thinking more highly of institutions and legal codes than religion and science. The so-called occidental unity conceals the essential differences among these three streams. Something similar occurred with the doctrine of the trinity: the Aryans saw a plurality of gods in it but were banned in the council of Nicaea in 325 B.C. Of course, there was no philosophical council that philosophically dogmatized the unity of the Europeans. The fact remains, however, that the Europeans appeared, at least outwardly, with noteworthy unanimity.

Europe has many fathers and the adjective *European*, therefore, cannot be so unified, despite the religious, historical, and philosophical ideologies of unity. The history of Europe bears traces of violence. The French historian Jean-Baptiste Duroselle describes it aptly: "If someone tells me that Europe is a land of justice, then I think of arbitrariness; if a land of human dignity, then I think of racism; if a land of reason, then I think of romantic fancy."[24]

Helping to Give the Adjective Its Right

It is time for Europe to know and recognize its genesis and to free itself from the prejudice for which it itself is largely responsible—namely, that it is the only true paradigm of philosophy, culture, religion, and so on. It is hardly helpful to set differences arbitrarily and then to emphasize, teach, and practice them. In this sense, India for the indologists is largely an invention and orientalism, a western projection of study and research in the academic institutions of Europe.[25] Identity and difference, however, should be seen as equally original and equally important, as with speaking and silence. Whoever sees in silence merely an incapability to speak and thinks that one will be able to speak eventually makes the logos carry a heavy burden that it may not bear.

It is not a good empirical or moral practice among philosophers to want only to subdue the thorny relation to the world with differences, multiplicities, and other oppositions by letting them disappear in consciousness, thinking, theory, and reflection. Going beyond the fictions of total commensurability and incommensurability, a many-voicedness of philosophy, reason, culture, and religion should be assumed as something desired by nature or by God, to bear it and perhaps also to endure it. In this sense, the development of an authentic philosophical culture is more important than philosophy itself because the latter depends on the first.

A layperson has no problem in ascribing the adjectives *European, Indian, Chinese, Japanese, African,* or *Latin American* to the names *dance, music, cooking,* and so on. Why can the philosopher not learn from the unprejudiced practice of laypersons? Is the situation really something different? A metonymy obtains in the expression *dance* or *music* as much has it does in the expressions *philosophy, logos, tao, brahman, jen, dharma,* and so on.

The example of the frog in the well given by Chuang Tzu can help us to overcome not the limitedness of an adjective—that is, of our standpoint—but only its absolutization, its singularization. What Christina Boidi says about the task of Latin American philosophy is valid as a partial duty of all non-European philosophies:

> The so-called objectivity also has its starting point also in the subject who postulates it. It is not a matter of forgetting the good old Hegel, or to cross out Plato from our books; it is a matter of understanding universal philosophy, or let's say: European philosophy, as it is, namely, as the philosophy of a culture that presents itself as the only universal, all-encompassing one. And for this reason Latin American philosophy also has a negative task, in that it rejects the concealing categories of European philosophy, in the name of which a domination (of other cultures) was pursued.[26]

The adjective *European* originally had a political connotation, then a civil one, leading to cultural, philosophical, and religious ones, because, since Homer's time until our century, Europe was the dominating moment in the dialogue: occident and orient.[27]

To say that Europe is the continuation of Asia toward the West may have had a partial justification at some time. Today, however, it is rather inadequate and inapplicable. The opposites, Asia and Europe, have often been emphasized, and one has talked about a danger for what is European on the part of what is Asian. Such almost conspiratory theoretical efforts could lead to a self-fulfilling prophecy. Not only the old historians and thinkers of Europe, but even the great German philosopher Heidegger wrote in a lecture held in Rome in 1936 that today it is a matter "of the rescue of Europe, or its destruction." This rescue, Heidegger further says, exists in "the test of the European peoples against the Asian." What must be overcome, according to Heidegger, is "the eradication and splitting up" of Europe.[28] One is reminded here of several passages in Huntington's writings on the fight of cultures.[29] Europe's fear of losing its identity seems to be irradicable. Even Emperor Wilhelm II drew a picture of the archangel Michael who calls on Europe to be watchful of Asian danger. Karl Jaspers, Heidegger's former friend and later rival, warns against such exaggerations and rejects any metaphysical hypostatization of the Europe–Asia dichotomy. One talks oneself into believing that Europe could possibly lose itself in Asia.[30] Today, in the context of world peace, a different thinking is called for, namely a thinking that the original ground, or what bears and endures everything, is neither only Asian nor only European, but an eternal reservoir that offers innumerable models of interpretation. Indeed, there is neither an absolute text nor an absolute interpretation.

On the Place of Eurocentric Difference

From Hegel to Heidegger, one strove over and over again to store away European identity and universality in the mere idea "Europe," beyond the geographical and relative culture. Husserl speaks of a spiritual geography of the Europe idea. This identity ascribed by itself and in itself maintained for a long time, indeed for too long, has been facilitated by political power relations.

One did not consider encountering the other as being anything difficult, as it has been shown to be the case today, because the other cannot be handled by definition. Whenever Europe suspected the loss of its so-called spiritual, cultural identity, universality, and singularity, it spoke of a crisis of Europe, as if the loss of its invented universality were identical with the loss of European identity. Derrida says quite clearly, "Everyone says the crisis of Europe is the crisis of spirit at the moment when the boundaries, the outlines, the eidos, the aims and the ends and the endlessness of Europe display themselves, this means, when the reserves of the idiom, of the capital on endlessness and universality are in danger."[31]

Husserl also speaks of a crisis of European humanity, and Heidegger regrets the deprivation of the spirit, which is equal to the dethronement of the West. All of these anxieties rotate around the loss of home-made claims. There are different views of the Europeanization of the world. First is the idea of a uniform picture of the world emerging from the uniform pattern of a certain culture. Expressions like *world-Christianity, world-Islam, world-Buddhism,* and *world-communism* aim at it. The utopian trait in this view cannot be overlooked. Second is the idea of a universalization as a consequence of modernity and in the name of natural science and technological formation. Heidegger seems rather to indicate this external Europeanization with his expression "Europeanization of the earth." Third is the Husserlian "Europeanization of humanity," which universalizes European reason, European culture, and in fact even Christianity. The fact is that each idea of unity is always valid in the face of diversity and the alternative means neither unity and diversity, neither unity nor diversity, nor unity nor diversity, nor both unity and diversity. Furthermore, modernization, for example of Islam, is not equal to the Islamization of modernity because modernity wears different faces.

The true place for the universal "European," for Hegel, is "the coming-to-itself of the spirit in absolute knowledge"; for Husserl, it is the transcendental community of a "we subjectivity"; and for Heidegger, the uncovering of being. If there is such a thing as a "destiny of being," then all of these philosophers claim it, as if being has nothing to do with what is not European!

It is an error to think that these three Europeans limit European universality to technological globality; it is a claim on the transcendental idea, on the absolute spirit, and on the uncovering of being that exists not only in the idea. The transcendental idea of Europe is simultaneously voluntaristic and does not allow the other to be different because being different is either merely a step on the way to the absolute or something relative. This spiritual Europe is not against communication but it would like to see the philosophical, cultural, and religious discourse (under the mask of transparency) guaranteed by an absolutization of its own hermeneutic model. The genesis of Europe is a history of continuous absence of the other because its own projection does not let the otherness of the other come within view.

A large number of the European learned dislike defining truth in the plural because, so they think and fear, the fate of the one European truth is then at stake.[32]

Europe is not the world, not even spiritually. It is not only a matter of recognizing this but also of drawing its consequences because only then can one overcome the almost a priori universalism and let Europe be European in view of what is not Europe, nor was, nor indeed can ever be. I am inclined, in the spirit of Hülsmann's thesis of an "anthropocentric difference,"[33] to speak here of a "Eurocentric difference," namely a difference from which the adjective *European* first receives its meaning and from which the claim can be derived that it indeed believes itself to have.

Europe and the Term *History*

The exaggerated emphasis on the categories "temporality" and "historicity" is one of the special features of Christian-European identity. Whether it concerns the philosophia perennis or the religio perennis, this thinking is inclined toward possessing exclusively the one Absolute and putting it into one particular concrete system, politics, person, or religion. This thinking may be traced back partly to the secret of the Christian trinity. The hermeneutic of the revelatio specialis is proof.

If a culture emphasizes the factors of time and history, then it overexerts itself, leaving little space for what transcends time and history, which ultimately leads to suffering what is beyond history as the victor, as fate. Beyond the question of the truth of time and history one can rightly notice that Asian and Indian thought on temporality and historicity in their relation to being do not assign an ontological meaning as European thought does. In Indian thought, incidents have a greater priority than time itself, and the values, the realization of which signify freedom, liberation, nirvana, and so on, are beyond time and history. For this reason, history and temporality are ascribed lesser significance.

The present political situation demonstrates that there is, and was, also a history beyond Europe. Even the European area histories—note the plural—are narrated, even though one speaks of world history and universal history religio-philosophically and even ideologically, when actually one means European history. The concept of European history as world history represents a claim. In it, people are spoken of who are not only without history but devoid of any historicity. This concept is a European standard and not a universal one. To want to measure the world of history only by European standards is evidence of one-sidedness and arrogance. Even European history has been jointly constituted of Egyptian, Persian, Arabic, and Turkish influences, to name a few. Today, we know that not only the ancient Greeks but also the Indians in their early history had public gatherings and other democratic institutions. Christian Meier thinks rightly that he must give the Europeans the following advice: "One would possibly do well not to speak of 'world history' and 'universal history', because both these terms are quite burdened by their past, thought too much from the point of view of Europe, as if Europe were the aim of world history."[34] With his three-fold thesis of the axial period, Jaspers pluralizes the singularity of the Greek-European axis but unfortunately remains bound to the European prejudice that true history can only be a written tradition. In almost a Hegelian manner, he makes the African people a people without history and thinks that one cannot conduct proper discussion with them. Jaspers seems here to cling to logocentricism. The myth–logos dichotomy is not sequential, but concurrent, because even in cultures dominated by myths there have been proverbs that bear evidence of the presence of the logos beside its myth.

The term *world history* should be understood in the sense of a horizon, rather than being the quintessence of history. Today, we cannot carry on as if the ancient classical-occidental model of history were still valid. It must be stated that Greek historical thought is closer to the Asian than the Christian-European. The hermeneutic situation demands from all of us the desire to want to know the other and the desire to be understood by others as two sides of the same hermeneutic coin.

Until only the recent past, Europe has experienced how the non-Europeans see Europe. This change of perspective helps both sides, provided everyone removes his or her blinkers. This horizon of an intercontinental change of perspective helps us to see through the standardizing tendency of the one history and to see world history as the world of histories. Every comparison has to start methodically from such an insight. "We could become provincial," the historian Meier says, "if we are not careful. Or have we been that already for a long time, if we then spiritually—according to Toynbee—still stand at the stage of Vasco da Gama's circumnavigation of the Cape of Good Hope, when the putative 'world historical' horizon encompassed only Europe and a few neighbours."[35] Not only the actual history of Europe and the one that has become effective worldwide but also the idea of history itself is to be seen as one among several equal ideas of history.

Our meditation on the adjective *European* has ultimately become a meditation on every kind of adjective, with the result that it is the adjective that qualifies the noun and not the opposite, irrespective of the fact that the adjective is *Chinese, Indian, European, Arabic, African, Red Indian, American,* or *Latin American.* The Europeanization of humanity is itself a myth, because a good philosophy, culture, and religion are not the exclusive possessions of a single tradition. It goes beyond the orient–occident dichotomy. Furthermore, it must be seen that the phenomenon of Europeanization of the world also transforms Europe.

If it is true that achievements such as philosophy, culture, and religion are not exclusively European feats, then the often-used thesis of a "Europeanization" of the world is empty. If, however, Europeanization means that the non-European countries should take over Western science and technology, and as a consequence of this adoption change themselves, then this as a trend of the times is undoubtedly true. But it has to placed in a world-encompassing framework, reminding us of Egyptian, Indian, Chinese, and Arabic influences on the Greek-European tradition. Indeed, not without justification, one can pose the almost provocative question, "How European are the European philosophy, culture, and religion?"

From what has been said, one should not automatically conclude that the claim to universality is foreign to non-European cultures. We know today that such a claim is also part of the Chinese and Indian cultures, however with the difference that in practice these cultures have hardly waged a destructive cultural war. A closer analysis of different cultural encounters in the history of humanity bears this evidence.

The conclusion is that if philosophy, culture, and religion are universal (which they, in fact, are), then they cannot possess an exclusive relativity to a particular philosophy, culture, and religion, be it Greek, Chinese, Indian, African, or Latin American.

The intercultural reflection on "Europe in the mirror of world cultures" and on the adjective *European* presented here should not conceal the fact that apart from the Europe that arrives from its triumph and either incorporates or neglects the other as something different, there is also the other Europe, the Europe of liberalism, of tolerance, of humanism, of enlightenment, and of human rights. Indeed, the non-European countries have barely or hardly known this Europe. Nonetheless, it is a historical fact that many fighters for liberation, primarily Gandhi and Nehru, among others, knew this Europe and have learned, expected, and demanded from it to be European itself in this sense. Enno Rudolph refers to such a Europe and its identity.[36]

The Indian poet-philosopher Rabindra Nath Tagore writes the following: "If humanity ever happens to be overwhelmed with the universal flood of a bigoted exclusiveness, then God will have to make provision for another Noah's Ark to save his creatures from the catastrophe of spiritual desolation."[37] As an addition and confirmation of this prediction, an important voice from Latin America may be quoted here. The Mexican writer Carlos Fuentes recalls in his article written as a letter titled "Das andere Gesicht Europas" ("The Other Face of Europe") on "Eurocentric self-complacency": "A continent [Latin America] tells Europe: 'I am your other face, a face which reflects neither the metaphysical entirety nor the enlightened modernity which you yourself have ceased to believe in, but the manifoldness, the active difference, the dialogue in which you have to participate.'"[38]

Europe searched for and found non-Europe. This finding has led to non-Europeans discovering Europe, albeit a discovery that relativizes the centuries-old self-understanding of Europe and compels Europe more and more to look at itself in the mirror of world cultures.

Notes

1. K. M. Panikkar, *Asien und die Herrschaft des Westens* (Zürich 1955), 430.

2. "Die Farbe Bunt," *Die Zeit*, no. 29 (11 July 1997): 40.

3. W. Halbfass, "Die indische Entdeckung Europas und die Europäisierung der Erde," in *Philosophische Grundlagen der Interkulturalität*, ed. R. A. Mall and D. Lohmar (Amsterdam 1993), 210–11.

4. *FAZ* 13, no. 2 (1992).

5. R. A. Mall and H. Hülsmann, *Die drei Geburtsorte der Philosophie: China, Indien, Europa* (Bonn 1989), 23.

6. M. Heidegger, *Was ist das—die Philosophie?* (Pfullingen 1963), 3.

7. Heidegger, *Was ist das—die Philosophie?* 13.

8. L. Zea, *Signale aus dem Abseits—Eine lateinamerikanische Geschichte der Philosophie* (Munich 1989), 23.

9. J. W. Goethe, "West-östlicher Diwan," in *Goethes Werke*, vol. 2, ed. G. von Stenzel (Salzburg 1951), 731.

10. E. Husserl, *Die Krisis der europäischen Wissenschaften und die transzendentale Phänomenologie*, vol. 6 (The Hague 1962), 320.

11. P. F. Feyerabend, *Farewell to Reason* (New York 1987), 274.

12. F. M. Wimmer, *Interkulturelle Philosophie: Geschichte und Theorie*, vol. 2 (Vienna 1990), 155.

13. G. W. F. Hegel, *Vorlesungen über die Philosophie der Weltgeschichte*, vol. 171 (Hamburg 1955), 218.

14. K. Jaspers, *Vom Ursprung und Ziel der Geschichte* (Munich 1983), 76; Mall and Hülsmann, *Die drei Geburtsorte der Philosophie*.

15. M. Scheler, *Gesammelte Werke*, vol. 5 (Bern 1976), 386.

16. Heidegger, *Was ist das—die Philosophie?* 13.

17. S. P. Huntington, *The Clash of Civilizations*, vol. 12 (New York 1996).

18. K. Löwith, *Geschichtliche Abhandlungen: Zur Kritik der geschichtlichen Existenz* (Stuttgart 1960), 175.

19. H. Hülsmann, *Nietzsche und Odysseus: Eurozentrismus und Anthropozentrische Differenz* (Munich 1990), 106.

20. Herra, R. A. "Kritik der Globalphilosophie," in *Vier Fragen zur Philosophie in Afrika, Asien und Lateinamerika* ed. F. von Wimmer (Vienna 1988), 14.

21. Hegel, *Vorlesungen über die Philosophie der Weltgeschichte*, 763.

22. H.-G. Gadamer, *Das Erbe Europas* (Frankfurt 1989); K. Held, "Husserl's These von der Europäisierung der Menschheit," in *Phänomenologie im Widerstreit*, ed. C. von Jamme and O. Pöggeler (Frankfurt 1989), 13–39.

23. M. Henningsen, *Merkur*, vol. 8 (1983).

24. H. Schulze, "The Return of Europe," *FAZ* 17 (28 April 1990).

25. E. W. Said, *Orientalism* (London 1978), 92; A. A. Malek, "Orientalism in Crisis," *Diogenes*, no. 44 (1963): 107.

26. C. Boidi, "Ist ein freies, unabhängiges, eigenständiges Denken in Lateinamerika möglich?" *Conceptus* 22, no. 56 (1988): 116.

27. Said, *Orientalism*, 5.

28. M. Heidegger, "Europa und die Deutsche Philosophie," in *Europa und die Philosophie*, ed. H.-H. Gander (Frankfurt 1993), 31.

29. Huntington, *The Clash of Civilizations*, vol. 3, 6–7.

30. Jaspers, *Vom Ursprung und Ziel der Geschichte* 96.

31. J. Derrida, "Kurs auf das andere Kap—Europas Identität," *Liber*, no. 3 (1990): 11.

32. Derrida, "Kurs auf das andere Kap—Europas Identität," 13.

33. Hülsmann, *Nietzsche und Odysseus*.

34. C. Meier, "Jenseits von Europa," *Die Zeit*, no. 13 (1989): 54.

35. Meier, "Jenseits von Europa," 54.

36. E. Rudolph, "Mit Blick auf Europa selbst," *Dialektik*, no. 2 (1997): 11–31.

37. R. Tagore, *Boundless Sky: An Anthology*, ed. R. S. Das (Calcutta 1964), 275.

38. C. Fuentes, "Das andere Gesicht Europas," *Liber*, no. 2 (1989): 20.

Bibliography

Abraham, W. E. *The Mind of Africa.* Chicago 1970.

Acharya, R. S. (ed.). *108 Upanisaden (Sanskrit und Hindi).* Bareli 1974.

Adorno, T. W. *Negative Dialektik.* Frankfurt 1973.

Albert, K. *Über Platons Begriff der Philosophie.* St. Augustine 1989.

Amery, J. "Hegel—Befreier oder Oppressor?" in *Der integrale Humanismus.* Stuttgart 1985.

Apel, K.-O. *Diskurs und Verantwortung: Das Problem des Übergangs zur postkonventionellen Moral.* Frankfurt 1988.

Aster, E. v. *Geschichte der Philosophie.* Stuttgart 1980.

Atreya, B. L. *The Elements of Indian Logic.* Benares 1934.

Aurobindo, Sri. *The Life Divine.* Calcutta 1947.

Avé-Lallemant, E. "Religion und Metaphysik im Weltalter des Ausgleichs." *Uit Tijdschrift voor Filosofie* 42, no. 2 (1980): 266–93.

Bahm, A. J. *Comparative Philosophy: Western, Indian and Chinese Philosophies Compared.* Albuquerque 1977.

Baiculescu, M. "Freiheit mit Reiseleiter." *Der Falter,* no. 8 (1985): 13.

Balslev, A. N. *A Study of Time in Indian Philosophy.* Wiesbaden 1983.

Banerjee, N. V. *The Spirit of Indian Philosophy.* New Delhi 1974.

Banerjee, S. C. (trans.). *The Sânkhya Philosophy: Sânkhyakârikâ with Gaudapada's Scolia and Narayana's Gloss.* Calcutta 1909.

Barua, B. *Prolegomena to a History of Buddhist Philosophy.* Calcutta 1918.

Beky, G. *Die Welt des Tao.* Munich 1972.

Bello, A. A. "*Archeology of Religious Knowledge.*" In *Phenomenology and the Numinous.* Pittsburgh 1988.

Berlin, I. *The Crooked Timber of Humanity.* London 1990.

Bernstein, R. J. *Beyond Objectivism and Relativism.* Oxford 1989.

Bhattacharya, H. (ed.). *The Cultural Heritage of India,* vols. 1–4. Calcutta 1975.

Bhattacharya, K. *Alternative Standpoints in Philosophy.* Calcutta 1953.

———. *Philosophy, Logic and Language.* Bombay 1965.

Bhattacharya, K. C. *Studies in Vedântism.* Calcutta 1903.

———. *Studies in Philosophy,* 2 vols. Calcutta 1955–1957.

Bhattacharya, S. "Philosophy as Self-Realisation." In *Indian Philosophy Today,* edited by N. K. Devaraja. New Delhi 1975.

Biderman, S., and B.-A. Scharfstein. (eds.). *Rationality in Question: On Eastern and Western Views of Rationality.* Leiden 1989.

Bishop, D. H. (ed.). *Indian Thought: An Introduction.* New Delhi 1975.

Bochénski, J. M. *Formale Logik.* Munich 1970.

Bodde, D. "On Translating Chinese Philosophical Terms." *Far Eastern Quarterly* 14 (1955): 235–37.

Boidi, C. "Ist ein freies, unabhängiges, eigenständiges Denken in Lateinamerika möglich?" *Conceptus* 22, no. 56 (1988).

Bühler, G. (trans.). *The Law of Manu with Extracts from Seven Commentaries.* Oxford 1886.

Burckhardt, J. *Weltgeschichtliche Betrachtungen.* Stuttgart 1978.

Burkert, W. "Platon oder Pythagoras? Zum Ursprung des Wortes Philosophie." *Hermes* 88 (1960): 59–177.

Burr, J. R. *Handbook of World Philosophy.* London 1981.

Burt, E. A. *In Search of Philosophic Understanding.* New York 1965.

Chan, W. T. *The Way of Lao Tzu: A Translation and a Study of the Tao-te Ching.* New York 1963.

———. *A Source Book in Chinese Philosophy.* Princeton 1973.

———. "Chinese Philosophy." In *The New Encyclopaedia Britanica,* vol. 4. London 1978.

Chatterjee, S. C. *The Nyaya Theory of Knowledge.* Calcutta 1950.

Chatterjee, S. C., and D. M. Datta. *An Introduction to Indian Philosophy.* Calcutta 1968.

Chattopaddhyaya, D. *Lokayata: A Study in Ancient Indian Materialism.* New Delhi 1959.

Chaudhuri, A. K. R. *The Doctine of Maya.* Calcutta 1950.

Cho, K.-K. *Bewußtsein und Natursein: Phänomenologischer West-Ost-Diwan.* Munich 1987.

———. "Restauration of Universism: Toward an Ethics of Accord Beyond Human Society." In *The World Community in Post-Industrial Society,* no. 5 (Seoul 1988): 2–19.

Chraust, A.-H. "Philosophy: Its Essence and Meaning in the Ancient World." *Philosophical Review,* no. 27 (1947).

Conze, E. *Buddhism: Its Essence and Development.* London 1951.

Copleston, F. C. *A History of Philosophy,* 8 vols. Oxford 1946–1966.

———. *Philosophies and Cultures.* Oxford 1980.

Creel, H. G. *Thought: From Confuzius to Mao Tse-tung.* Chicago 1953.

Dallmayr, F. *Margins of Political Discourse.* Albany 1998.

Dascal, M. (ed.). *Cultural Relativism and Philosophy.* Leiden 1991.

Dasgupta, S. N. *A History of Indian Philosophy*, 5 vols. Cambridge 1922/Delhi 1975.

———. *Indian Idealism*. Cambridge 1962.

———. *Philosophical Essays*. Delhi 1982 (1941).

———. *Yoga as Philosophy and Religion*. Delhi 1987.

David, T. K. "Philosophy in Contemporary China." *Far Eastern Economic Review*, no. 23 (1957).

Davidson, D. "On the Very Idea of Conceptual Scheme." *Proceedings of the American Philosophical Association*, no. 17 (1973–74).

———. *Inquiries in Truth and Interpretations*. Oxford 1984.

Dawson, R. *Confucius*. Oxford 1981.

Daya Krishna. *Indian Philosophy: A Counter Perspective*. Delhi 1991.

de Bary, W. T. (ed.). *Sources of Chinese Tradition*. New York 1960.

de Bary, W. T., and A. T. Embree. *A Guide to Oriental Classics*. New York 1975.

Derrida, J. "Mythologie blanche." *Poetique*, no. 5 (1971): 1–52.

———. *Randgänge der Philosophie*. Frankfurt 1976.

———. *Vom Geist: Heidegger und die Frage*. Frankfurt 1988.

———. "Kurs auf das andere Kap—Europas Identität." *Liber*, no. 3 (1990).

Desai, M. D. (trans.). *The Naya-Karnika*. Arrha 1915.

Deussen, P. *Allgemeine Geschichte der Philosophie*, 7 vols. Leipzig 1894–1917.

———. *Sechzig Upanishads des Veda*. Leipzig 1899.

——— (trans.). Die Sûtra's des Vedânta oder die Shârîrakamîmânsâ des Bâdarâyana nebst d. vollständigen Comm. des Shankara, Leipzig 1887.

Deutsch, E. (ed.). *Culture and Modernity: East–West Philosophical Perspectives*. Honolulu 1991.

Dhar, S. *Canakya and the Arthasastra*. Bangalore 1957.

Dilthey, W. *Der Aufbau der geschichtlichen Welt in den Geisteswissenschaften*, edited by M. von Riedel. Frankfurt 1981.

Duala-M'bedy, M. *Xenologie: Die Wissenschaft vom Fremden und die Verdrängung der Humanität in der Anthropologie*, Freiburg i. Br. 1977.

Dubs, H. H. "Comparison of Chinese and Greek Philosophy." *Chinese Social and Political Science Review*, no. 17 (1933): 307–27.

Duméry, H. *Phénoménologie et Religion*. Paris 1962.

Duprès, W. "Implicit Religion and the Meaning of Interreligions Dialogue." *Studies in Interreligious Dialogue*, no. 1 (1991).

Durant, W. A. *Kulturgeschichte der Menschheit*, vols. 3 and 4. Frankfurt 1981.

Dussel, E. *Philosophie der Befreiung*. Hamburg 1989.

Dutt, M. N. (trans.). *The Dharma Sutras*. Calcutta 1908.

Edgerton, F. *The Beginnings of Indian Philosophy: Selections Rig Veda, Atharva Veda, Upanishads and Mahabharata*. Cambridge 1965.

Edwards, P. (ed.). *The Encyclopedia of Philosophy*, vols. 3 and 4. London 1972.

Egermann, F. *Die Platonischen Briefe VII und VIII*. Berlin 1928.

Eliade, M. *Le Yoga, immortalite et liberte,* Paris 1954.

————. *Yoga, Immortality and Freedom.* New York 1958

————. *The Sacred and the Profane: The Nature of Religion,* edited by W. R. Trask. New York 1959.

————. *The Quest.* Chicago 1969.

————. *Die Sehnsucht nach dem Ursprung.* Vienna 1973.

————. *Kosmos und Geschichte: Der Mythos der ewigen Wiederkehr.* Frankfurt 1984.

Erdmann, J. E. *Grundriß der Geschichte der Philosophie.* Berlin 1930.

Eucken, R. *Geschichte der philosophischen Terminologie im Umriß.* Hildesheim 1964.

Fanon, F. *Die Verdammten dieser Erde.* Hamburg 1969.

————. *Schwarze Haut, weiße Maske.* Frankfurt 1980.

Fatone, V. *El Budismo Nihilista.* Buenos Aires 1962.

————. *The Philosophy of Nagarjuna.* translated by K. D. Prithipaul. Delhi 1981.

Feyerabend, P. F. *Farewell to Reason.* New York 1987.

Finkielkraut, A. *Die Niederlage des Denkens.* Hamburg 1989.

Fischer, K. *Geschichte der neueren Philosophie,* 9 vols. Heidelberg 1897–1907.

Flint, R. *History of the Philosophy of History.* London 1893.

Flintoff, E. "Pyrrho and India." *Phronesis* 25, no. 1 (1980): 88–108.

Forke, A. *Geschichte der neueren chinesischen Philosophie.* Hamburg 1938.

Fornet-Betancourt, R. *Kommentierte Bibliographie zur Philosophie in Lateinamerika.* Frankfurt 1984.

————. *Filosofia intercultural.* Mexico 1994.

———— (ed.). *Diskursethik oder Befreiungsethik.* Aachen 1992.

Frank, M. *Die Grenzen der Verständigung,* Frankfurt 1988.

Franke, W. *China und das Abendland.* Göttingen 1962.

Frauwallner, E. *Geschichte der indischen Philosophie,* 2 vols. Salzburg 1953–1956.

Frings, M. S. "Gott und das Nichts." *Phänomenologische Forschungen,* no. 6/7 (1978): 118–40.

Fuentes, C. "Das andere Gesicht Europas." *Liber,* no. 2 (1989).

Gadamer, H.-G. (ed.). *Grundriß der allgemeinen Geschichte der Philosophie von W. Dilthey.* Frankfurt 1949.

————. "Begriffsgeschichte als Philosophie." *Archiv für Begriffsgeschichte,* no. 14 (1970).

————. "Hermeneutik." *Historisches Wörterbuch der Philosophie,* vol. 3. Darmstadt 1974.

————. *Truth and Method.* New York 1975.

————. *Wahrheit und Methode.* Tübingen 1975.

————. *Das Erbe Europas,* Frankfurt 1989.

Gaiser, K. *Platons ungeschriebene Lehre.* Stuttgart 1968.

Gander, H.-H. (ed.). *Europa und die Philosophie.* Frankfurt 1993.

Gandhi, M. K. *The Story of My Experiment with Truth.* Washington 1960.

Geertz, C. *The Interpretation of Culture.* New York 1973.

Geldner, K. F. (ed.). *Der Rig Veda* (Kommentiert). Wiesbaden 1951.

Geldsetzer, L. *Was heißt Philosophiegeschichte?* Düsseldorf 1968.

Gestering, J. J. *German Pessimism and Indian Philosophy: A Hermeneutic Reading.* New Delhi 1986.

Giles, A. (trans.). *Chuang Tzu, Mystic, Moralist, and Social Reformer.* London 1961.

Gilson, E. *Der Geist der mittelalterlichen Philosophie.* Vienna 1950.

———. *Unity of Philosophical Experience.* London 1955.

Glasenapp, H. v. *Das Indienbild deutscher Denker.* Stuttgart 1960.

———. *Die Philosophie der Inder.* Stuttgart 1974.

Glockner, H. *Die europäische Philosophie von den Anfängen biszur Gegenwart.* Stuttgart 1958.

———. *Beiträge zum Verständnis und zur Kritik Hegels sowie zur Umgestaltung seiner Geisteswelt.* Bonn 1965.

Goethe, J. W. "West-östlicher Diwan." In *Goethes Werke,* vol. 2, edited by G. von Stenzel. Salzburg 1951.

———. *Zahme Xenien,* vol. 1. Munich 1981.

Goodwin, W. F. "Ethics and Values in Indian Philosophy." *Philosophy: East and West* 4 (1955).

Gopalan, S. *Hindu Social Philosophy.* New Delhi 1979.

Goshal, U. N. *A History of Hindu Political Theories.* London 1927.

Gould, S. J. "Human Equality Is a Contingent Fact of History." In *The Flamingo's Smile.* New York 1985.

———. *Time's Arrow, Time's Cycle: Myth and Metaphor in the Discovery of Geological Time.* Cambridge 1986.

Granet, M. *Das chinesische Denken.* Frankfurt 1985.

Guthrie, W. K. C. *A History of Greek Philosophy.* Cambridge 1962.

Habermas, J. *Der philosophische Diskurs der Moderne.* Frankfurt 1985.

———. *Die neue Unübersichtlichkeit.* Frankfurt 1985.

———. "Die Einheit der Vernunft in der Vielheit ihrer Stimmen." *Merkur,* no. 1 1988.

———. *Die Moderne—Ein unvollendetes Projekt.* Frankfurt (1988).

——— (ed.). *Hermeneutik und Ideologiekritik.* Frankfurt 1971.

Hackmann, H. *Chinesische Philosophie.* Munich 1927.

Hadot, P. *Philosophie als Lebensform: Geistige Übungen in der Antike.* Berlin 1991.

Halbfass, W. "Hegel on the Philosophy of the Hindus." In *German Scholars on India.* New Delhi 1973.

———. "Indien und die Geschichtsschreibung der Philosophie." *Philosophische Rundschau,* no. 23 (1976): 104–31.

————. *Indien und Europa*. Stuttgart 1981

————. *India and Europe*. New York 1990.

————. "Die indische Entdeckung Europas und die Europäisierung der Erde." In *Philosophische Grundlagen der Interkulturalität*, edited by R. A. Mall and D. Lohmar. Amsterdam 1993.

Hamburger, M. "Aristotle and Confucius: A Study in Comparative Philosophy." *Philosophie* 31 (1956).

Harding u. Reinwald (ed.). *Afrika—Mutter und Modell der europäischen Zivilisation*. Berlin 1990.

Harlez, C. (ed.). *Textes Taoistes*. Paris 1891.

Harré, R., and M. Krausz. *Varieties of Relativism*. Oxford 1996.

Hatori, M. *Dignâga on Perception*. Cambridge 1968.

Heer, F. *Europäische Geistesgeschichte*. Stuttgart 1953.

Heftrich, E. *Hegel und Jacob Burckhardt: Zur Krisis des geschichtlichen Bewußtseins*. Frankfurt 1967.

Hegel, G. W. F. *Vorlesungen über die Philosophie der Weltgeschichte*, vol. 171. Hamburg 1955.

————. *Werke in 20 Bänden*. Frankfurt 1971.

Heidegger, M. *Unterwegs zur Sprache*. Pfüllingen 1960.

————. *Was ist das—die Philosophie?* Pfullingen 1963.

Heimann, B. *Studien zur Eigenart des indischen Denkens*. Tübingen 1930.

————. "Europa und die Deutsche Philosophie." In *Europa und Philosophie*, edited by H.-H. Gander, Frankfurt 1993.

————. *Indian and Western Philosophy: A Study in Contrasts*. London 1937.

Heimsoeth. H. *Die sechs großen Themen der abendländischen Metaphysik*. Stuttgart 1965.

Heinemann, F. (ed.). *Die Philosophie im XX. Jahrhundert*. Stuttgart 1963.

Held, K. "Husserls These von der Europäisierung der Menschheit." In *Phänomenologie im Widerstreit*, edited by C. von Janne and O. Pöggeler. Frankfurt 1989.

Hell, G. *Untersuchungen und Beobachtungen zu den Platonischen Briefen*. Berlin 1933.

Henningsen, M. *Merkur*, vol. 8. Munich 1983.

————. "Vom Anspruch und Elend des europäischen Universalismus." *Merkur* 8, no. 37 (1983): 894–902.

Henrich, D. (ed.). *All-Einheit*. Stuttgart 1985.

Herder, J. G. *Ideen zur Philosophie der Geschichte der Menschheit*, edited by B. von Suphan. Berlin 1877–1913.

————. *Auch eine Philosophie der Geschichte zur Bildung der Menschheit*. Frankfurt 1967.

————. *Briefe zur Beförderung der Humanität*. Vol. 1. Berlin 1971.

Herra, R. A. "Kritik der Globalphilosophie." *Vier Fragen zur Philosophie in Afrika, Asien und Lateinamerika*, edited by F. von Wimmer. Vienna 1988.

Hinman, L. M. "Quid Facti or Quid Juris? The Fundamental Ambiguity of Gadamer's Understanding of Hermeneutics." *Philosophy and Phenomenological Research* 40, no. 4 (1980): 512–35.

Hiriyanna, M. *The Essentials of Indian Philosophy*. London 1948.

————. *Outlines of Indian Philosophy*. London 1958.

————. "Philosophy of Values." In *The Cultural Heritage of India*, vol. 3. Calcutta 1975.

Hocking, W. E. "Value of Comparative Study of Philosophy." In *Philosophy: East and West*. New Jersey 1946.

Hoffmann, G.-R. (ed.). *Wie und Warum entstand Philosophie in verschiedenen Regionen der Erde?* Berlin 1988.

Hohl, H. *Lebenswelt und Geschichte: Grundzüge der Spätphilosophie E. Husserls*. Munich 1962.

Holenstein, E. *Menschliches Selbstverständnis*. Frankfurt 1985.

Hollis, M., and S. Lukes. (eds.). *Rationality and Relativism*. Oxford 1982.

Hopkins, E. W. *The Great Epic of India*. New Haven 1928.

Hörisch, J. *Die Wut des Verstehens: Zur Kritik der Hermeneutik*. Frankfurt 1988.

Horkheimer, M. *Gesellschaft im Übergang*. Frankfurt 1981.

Horkheimer, M., and Adorno, T. W. *Dialektik der Aufklärung*. Frankfurt 1983.

Horner, I. B. (trans.). *The Book of Discipline (Mahavagga): Sacred Book of the Buddhists*, vol. 4. Oxford 1951.

Hountondji, P. J. *African Philosophy: Myth and Reality*. London 1983.

————. "Reason and Tradition." *Philosophy and Culture*, edited by H. Odera-Oruka and D. A. Masolo. Nairobi 1983.

————. "Aspects and Problems of Philosophy in Africa." *Teaching and Research in Philosophy: Africa*, edited by UNESCO. Paris 1984.

Hsiao, K. C. *A History of Chinese Political Thought*, vol. 1. Princeton 1979.

Hu, S. "Ch'an (Zen) Buddhism in China: Its History and Method." *Philosophy East and West*, no. 3 (1953): 3–24.

Hufnagel, E. *Einführung in die Hermeneutik*. Stuttgart 1976.

Hughe, E. R. *Chinese Philosophy in Classical Times*. London 1942.

Hülsmann, H. *Die technologische Formation*. Berlin 1985.

————. *Nietzsche und Odysseus: Eurozentrismus und Anthropozentrische Differenz*. Munich 1990.

Hume, D. *Dialogues Concerning Natural Religion*, Part XII, edited by N. K. Smith. London 1947.

Hume, R. E. *The Thirteen Principal Unpanishads*. Oxford 1931.

Huntington, S. P. *The Clash of Civilizations*. New York 1996.

Husserl, E. "Über die Reden Gotamo Buddhos." *Zeitschrift für Kunst und Literatur* 2, no. 1. Munich 1923.

————. *Ideas: General Introduction to Pure Phenomonology*, translated by W. R. Boyce Gobson. London 1958.

————. *Die Krisis der europäischen Wissenschaften und die transzendentale Phänomenologie*, vol. 4. The Hague 1962.

————. *Cartesianische Meditationen und Pariser Vorträge*, vol. 1. The Hague 1963.

————. *Zur Phänomenologie der Intersubjektivität III: 1929–1935*, vol. 15. The Hague 1973.

————. *Texte zur Phänomenologie des inneren Zeitbewußtseins (1893–1917)*, edited by R. Bernet. Hamburg 1985.

Huxley, A. *The Perennial Philosophy*. London 1990.

Ingalls, D. H. H. *Materials for the Study of Navya-Nyaya Logic.* Cambridge 1951.

Izutzu, T. *Philosophie des Zenbuddhismus.* Hamburg 1983.

Jaeger, W. *Paideia.* Berlin 1933.

——. *Aristoteles.* Zürich 1967.

James, W. *Principles of Psychology,* vol. 1. Dover 1950.

——. *The Will to Believe.* New York 1956.

Jaspers, K. *Die großen Philosophen,* vol. 1. Munich 1957.

——. *Einführung in die Philosophie.* Munich 1972.

——. *Lao-tze, Nagarjuna: Zwei asiatische Metaphysiker.* Munich 1978.

——. *Die maßgebenden Menschen: Sokrates, Buddha, Konfuzius, Jesus.* Munich 1980.

——. *Der philosophische Glaube.* Munich 1981.

——. *Weltgeschichte der Philosophie.* Munich 1982.

——. *Vom Ursprung und Ziel der Geschichte.* Munich 1983.

Jayaswal, K. P. *Hindu Polity,* 2 vols. Bangalore 1955.

Jha, G. (trans.) *Manu smrti: The Laws of Manu with the Bhasya of Medhatithi,* 5 vols. Calcutta 1920–1926.

——. *Purva Mimamsa in its Sources.* Benares 1942.

—— (trans.). *The Yoga-darsana, The Sutras Patanjali with Bhasya of Vyas.* Bombay 1907.

Joad, C. E. M. *Counter Attack from the East: The Philosophy of Radhakrishnan.* London 1933.

Johnston, C. (trans.). *The Yoga Sutras of Patanjali.* New York 1912.

Jolly, J., and R. Schmidt (trans.). *Naradiya Dharmasastra, or the Institutes of Narada.* London 1876.

Kaltenbrunner, G.-K. *Hegel und die Folgen.* Freiburg 1970.

Kane, P. V. *History of Dharmasastra (Ancient and Medieval Religions and Civil Law in India),* 4 vols. Bombay 1930–1953.

Kapp, E. *Der Ursprung der Logik bei den Griechen.* Göttingen 1965.

Kekes, J. *The Morality of Pluralism.* Princeton 1993.

Kiesewetter, H. *Von Hegel zu Hitler.* Hamburg 1974.

Kimmerle, H. *Philosophie in Afrika: Annäherungen an einen interkulturellen Philosophiebegriff.* Frankfurt 1991.

——. *Die Dimension des Interkulturellen.* Amsterdam 1994.

Klaus, G., and M. Buhr *Philosophisches Wörterbuch.* Leipzig 1969.

Kluckhohn, C. *Common Humanity and Diverse Cultures: The Human Meaning of the Social Sciences,* edited by D. Lerner. New York 1959.

Knitter, P. S. *No Other Name? A Critical Survey of Christian Attitude Toward World Religion.* New York 1986.

Koslowski, P. *Die postmoderne Kultur.* Munich 1987.

Kramer, F. *Verkehrte Welten—Zur imaginären Ethnologie des 19. Jahrhunderts.* Frankfurt 1977.

Krämer, H. J. "Das Problem des esoterischen Platons." In *Arete bei Platon und Aristoteles.* Heidelberg 1959.

Kranz, W. *Die griechische Philosophie.* Basel 1980.

Kroeber, A. *The Nature of Culture.* Chicago 1960.

Kroeber, A., and C. Kluckhohn. *Culture: A Critical Review of Concepts and Definitions.* New York 1952.

Kropp, G. *Von Lao-Tse zu Sartre, Ein Gang durch die Geschichte der Philosphie.* Berlin 1952.

Krumpel, H. *Philosophie in Lateinamerika: Grundzüge ihrer Entwicklung.* Berlin 1992.

Laertius, D. *Leben und Meinungen berühmter Philosophen,* edited by O. von Apelt. Hamburg 1921.

Lahiri, K. *Comparative Studies in Philosophy.* Calcutta 1963.

Larson, G. J., and E. Deutsch (eds.) "Interpreting Across Boundaries: New Essays in Comparative Philosophy." *Philosophy East and West* 39 (1989).

Legge, J. *The Sacred Books of the East,* vol. 39, The Texts of Taoism, Oxford 1891.

———— (trans.). *The Chinese Classics.* Hong Kong 1961.

Lévinas, E. *Totality and Infinity.* The Hague 1969.

————. *Wenn Gott ins Denken einfällt.* Munich 1985.

————. *Die Spur des Anderen.* Munich 1987.

Lichtenberg, G. *FAZ* 13, no. 2 (1992).

Liu, W. *A Short History of Confucian Philosophy.* Baltimore 1955.

Long, A. A. *Hellenistic Philosophie.* London 1974.

Löwith, K. *Meaning in History.* Chicago 1949.

————. *Weltgeschichte und Heilsgeschehen.* Berlin 1953.

————. *Von Hegel zu Nietzsche.* Stuttgart 1958.

————. *Geschichtliche Abhandlungen: Zur Kritik der geschichtlichen Existenz.* Stuttgart 1960.

————. "Geschichte und historisches Bewußtsein." In *Vorträge und Abhandlungen, Zur Kritik der christlichen Überlieferung,* edited by K. Löwith. Stuttgart 1966.

Lyotard, J.-F. *Postmoderne für die Kinder.* Vienna 1987.

————. *Das postmoderne Wissen: Ein Bericht.* Bremen 1982.

————. "Can Thought Go on Without a Body?" *Discourse* 11, no. 1 (19??): 77–88.

Madhavacarya. *Sarva-Darsana Samgraha,* translated by U. S. Sharma. Varanasi 1964.

Mahadevan, T. M. P. *Gaudapada: A Study in Early Vedanta.* Madras 1952.

Maitra, S. K. *An Introduction to the Philosophy of Sri Aurobindo.* Benares 1945.

Malek, A. A. "Orientalism in Crisis." *Diogenes,* no. 44 (1963).

Malkani, G. R. *Vedantic Epistmeology.* Amalner 1951.

Mall, R. A. *Studie zur indischen Philosophie und Soziologie: Zur vergleichenden Philosophi und Soziologie.* Meisenheim am Glan 1974.

————. "Marxism and Gandhism." *Die Dritte Welt* 4, no. 2 (1975).

————. "Schelers Konzept der kosmopolitischen Philosophie, Grenzen der Vergleichbarkeit verschiedener Weltanschauungen." *Trierer Beiträge: Aus Forschung und Lehre* 11 (1982).

————. "Hermeneutik." *Tradition und Innovation*, 13. Bonn 1984.

————. "Unity Without Uniformity, Prolegomena to Any Theory of Hermeneutics." In *Focus on Quality, Selected Proceedings of a Conference on Qualitative Research Methodology in the Social Sciences*, edited by R. Singh and W. M. Venk, no. 21. Durban 1985.

————. "Die orthafte Ortlosigkeit der Hermeneutik: Zur Kritik der reduktiven Hermeneutik." *Widerspruch* 8, no. 15 (1988).

————. *Die Herausforderung: Essays zu Mahatma Gandhi*. Hildesheim 1989.

————. *Buddhismus—Religion der Postmoderne?* Hildesheim 1990.

————. "Der Absolutheitsanspruch: Eine Religionsphilosophische Meditation." *Loccumer Protokolle*, no. 7 (1991): 39–53.

————. "The God of Phenomenology in Comparative Contrast to Theology and Philosophy." *Husserl Studies* 8 (1991).

————. "Philosophie als Denk- und Lebensweg." In *Probleme philosophischer Mystik*, edited by E. von Jain and R. Margreiter. St. Augustine 1991.

————. "Die orthaft ortlose philosophia perennis und die interkulturelle Philosophie." *Das Begehren des Fremden*, edited by L. J. von Bonny Duala-M'bedy. Essen 1992.

————. "Meditationen zum Adjektiv 'europäisch' aus interkultureller Sicht." In *Der technologische Imperativ: Heinz Hülsmann zum 75 Geburtstag*, edited by W. von Blumberger Munich/Vienna 1992.

————. "Metonymic Reflections on Shamkara's Concept of Brahman and Plato's Seventh Epistle," *Journal of Indian Council of Philosophical Research* 9, no. 2 (1992): 89–102.

————. "Phenomenology—Essentialistic or Descriptive?" *Husserl Studies*, no. 10 (1993): 13–30.

————. "Interkulturalität und Interreligiosität." In *Verantwortlich leben in der Weltgemeinschaft: Zur Auseinandersetzung um das "Projekt Weltethos,"* edited by J. von Rehm. Gütersloh 1994.

————. "Schelers Idee einer werdenden Athropologie und Geschichtsteleologie." In *Phänomenologische Forschungen*, edited by E. W. von Orth and G. Pfafferott. Munich 1994.

————. "Überlegungen zu einer interkulturellen Vernunft." In *Sein—Erkennen—Handeln, Festschrift für Heinrich Beck zum 65. Geburtstag*, edited by E. von Schadel and U. Voigt, Frankfurt 1994.

————. "Zur interkulturellen Theorie der Vernunft: Ein Paradigmenwechsel." In *Vernunftbegriffe in der Moderne*, edited by H. F. von Fulda and R.-P. Horstmann. Stuttgart 1994.

————. *Philosophie im Vergleich der Kulturen: Interkulturelle Philosophie—eine neue Orientierung* (Darmstadt 1995), 41–42.

————. "Interkulturelle Philosophie und die Historiographie." In *Ethnozentrismus*, edited by M. Brocker and H. Nau. Darmstadt 1997.

————. "Orthafte Ortlosigkeit der Menschenrechte—Eine interkulturelle Perspektive unter besonderer Berücksichtigung indischer Traditionen." In *Voigt Die Menschenrechte im intterkulturellen Dialog.* Frankfurt 1998.

————. "Philosophy and Philosophies—Cross-Culturally Considered." *Topoi,* no. 17 (1998): 15–27.

Mall, R. A., and H. Hülsmann. *Die drei Geburtsorte der Philosophie: China, Indien, Europa.* (Bonn 1989).

————. *Philosophie im Vergleich der Kulturen: Interkulturelle Philosophie—eine neue Orientierung* (Darmstadt 1995).

Mandelbaum, M. " A Critique of Philosophies of History." *Journal of Philosophy* (1948).

Mann, G., and Neuß. A. *Weltgeschichte,* vol. 1. Berlin 1961.

Marquard, O. *Abschied vom Prinzipiellen.* Stuttgart 1981.

————. *Schwierigkeiten mit der Geschichtsphilosophie.* Frankfurt 1982.

Martin, G. (ed.). *Sokrates in Selbstzeugnissen und Bilddokumenten.* Hamburg 1967.

Masson-Oursel, Paul. *La Philosophie comparée.* Paris 1923.

Matilal, B. K. *Epistemology, Logic and Grammar in Indian Philosophical Analysis.* The Hague 1971.

————. "Indian Philosophy: Is There a Problem Today?" In *Indian Philosophy—Past and Future,* edited by S. S. Ram Pappu and R. Puligandla. Delhi 1982.

————. *Logic, Language, and Reality.* Delhi 1990.

Mckeon, R. "Philosophy as an Agent of Civilization." *Philosophy and Phenomenological Research* 41, no. 4 (1981): 419–36.

Mehlig, J. (ed.). *Weisheit des alten Indiens,* 2 vols. Leipzig 1987.

Mehta, J. L. *Martin Heidegger: The Way and the Vision.* Honolulu 1976.

————. *Philosophy and Religion: Essays in Interpretation.* New Delhi 1990.

Meier, C. "Jenseits von Europa." *Die Zeit,* no. 13 (24 March 1989): 54.

Mensching, G. *Toleranz und Wahrheit in der Religion.* Munich 1955.

Métraux, A., and B. Waldenfels. (eds.). *Leibhaftige Vernunft.* Munich 1986.

Michel, W. *Das Fremde und das Eigene,* edited by A. von Wierlacher. Munich 1985.

Mill, J. S. *Utilitarianism.* London 1993.

Misch, G. *Der Weg in die Philosophie.* Munich 1950.

Mohanty, J. N. "Philosophy as Reflection on Experience." *Indian Philosophy Today,* edited by N. K. Devaraja. Delhi 1975.

————. "Philosophy of History and Its Presupposition." In *Contemporary Indian Philosophers of History,* edited by T. M. P. Mahadevan and G. E. Cairns. Calcutta 1977.

————. "Indian Philosophy." In *The New Encyclopaedia Britanica,* vol. 9. London 1978.

————. *The Possibility of Transcendental Philosophy.* Dordrecht 1985.

————. "Time: Linear or Cyclic, and Husserl's Phenomenology of Inner Time Consciousness" *Philosophia Naturalis,* vol. 25 (1988).

————. *Reason and Tradition in Indian Thought: An Essay on the Nature of Indian Philosophical Thinking.* Oxford 1992.

Mookerjee, S. *The Buddhist Philosophy of Universal Flux.* Calcutta 1935.

————. *The Jain-Philosophy of Non-Absolutism: A Critical Study of Anekantavada*. Calcutta 1944.

Moore, C. A. *Philosophy East and West*. Princeton 1944.

————. *Philosophy and Culture—East and West*. Honolulu 1962.

————. *Indian Mind*. Honolulu 1967.

————. (ed.). *Essays in East-West Philosophy: An Attempt at World Philosophical Synthesis*. Honolulu 1967.

Morrow, G. R. (ed.). *Plato's Epistles: A Translation, with Critical Essays and Notes*. New York 1962.

Müller, F. Max. *The Six Systems of Indian Philosophy*. London 1928.

———— (ed.). *Sacred Books of the East*, 51 vols. Oxford 1875.

Munro, D. *The Concept of Man in Early China*. Stanford 1969.

Murphy, J. *Postmodern Social Analysis and Criticism*. New York 1989.

Murti, K. S., and K. R. Rao. *Current Trends in Indian Philosophy*. Waltair 1972.

Murti, T. R. V. *The Central Philosophy of Buddhism*. London 1980.

Nagarjuna. *Mulamadhyamakakarika*, translated with an introductory essay by K. K. Inanda. New York 1970.

————. *Vigrahavyavartani: Dialectical Method of Nagarjuna*, translated by K. Bhattacharya. Delhi 1978.

Nakamura, H. *Ways of Thinking of Eastern Peoples: India, China, Tibet, Japan*. Honolulu 1964.

————. *A Comparative History of Ideas*. Tokyo 1975.

Nandy, A. *The Intimate Enemy: The Loss and Recovery of Self Under Colonialism*. Delhi 1983.

Naravane, V. S. *Modern Indian Thought: A Philosophical Survey*. New York 1964.

Nassauer, K., and K. Huber. *Denker der Hellenischen Frühzeit*. Frankfurt 1948.

Needham, J. *Science and Civilisation in China*. London 1956.

————. *History and Human Value: A Chinese Perspective for World Science and Technology*. Cambridge 1961.

Nestle, W. *Vom Mythos zum Logos*. Berlin 1941.

————. *Griechische Geistesgeschichte*. Stuttgart 1956.

Neugebauer, C. *Einführung in die afrikanische Philosophie*. Munich 1989.

Neumann, K. *Der Wahrheitspfad (Dhammapadam)*. Munich 1921.

————. *Die Reden Gotamo Buddhos aus der Mittleren Sammlung Majjhimanikayo*, 3 vols. Munich 1922.

————. *Die Reden Gotamo Buddhos aus der längeren Sammlung Dighanikayo*, 4 vols. Munich 1927–1928.

Nitta, Y. (ed.). *Japanische Beiträge zur Phänomenologie*. Munich 1984.

Northrop, F. S. C. *The Meeting of East and West: An Inquiry Concerning World Understanding*. New York 1946–1947.

Nordhofen, E. "Die Farbe Bunt." *Die Zeit*, no. 29 (11 July 1997).

Ohashi, R. (ed.). *Die Philosophie der Kyoto-Schule*. Freiburg 1990.

Olela, H. "The African Foundation of Greek Philosophy." *African Philosophy: An Introduction*, edited by R. A. Wright. Washington, D.C. 1977.

Oruka, H. O. "The Fundamental Principles in the Question of African Philosophy." *Second Order* 4, no. 1 (1975).

———. "Four Trends in Current African Philosophy." In *Philosophy in the Present Situation of Africa*. Wiesbaden 1981.

———. *African Philosophy*. Nairobi 1986.

———. "Grundlegende Fragen der afrikanischen Sage-Philosophy." *Vier Fragen zur Philosophie in Afrika, Asien und Lateinamerika*, edited by F. von Wimmer. Vienna 1988.

Otto, R. *Mysticism East and West*. New York 1932.

Palmer, R. *Hermeneutics: Interpretation Theory in Schleiermacher, Dilthey, Heidegger, Gadamer*. Evanston 1969.

Pandurang, V. K. *History of Dharmashâstra: Ancient and Medieval Religious and Civil Law in India*, 4 vols. Bombay 1930–1953.

Panikkar, K. M. *Asien und die Herrschaft des Westens*. Zürich 1955.

Panikkar, R. "What Is Comparative Philosophy Comparing?" In *Interpreting Across Boundaries,* edited by G. J. Larson and E. Deutsch. Princeton 1988.

Pannwitz, R. *Die Krisis der europäischen Kultur,* vol. 2. Nuremburg 1917.

Patanjali. "The Yoga Shutras and Vyâsas' yoga-bhâsya." In *Sacred Books of the Hindus IV*, edited by R. Prasada. Allahabad 1924.

Pesala, B. *The Debate of King Milinda*. Delhi 1991.

Plessner, H. *Die Stufen des Organischen und der Mensch*. Berlin 1975.

———. *Die Frage nach der conditio humana*. Frankfurt 1976.

———. *Zwischen Philosophie und Gesellschaft*. Frankfurt 1979.

———. *Mit anderen Augen: Aspekte einer philosophischen Anthropologie*. Stuttgart 1982.

Popper, K. *Die offene Gesellschaft und ihre Feinde*, 2 vols. Bern 1957.

Post, L. A. *Thirteen Epistles of Plato*. Oxford 1925.

Potter, K. H. *Presuppositions of India's Philosophies*. Connecticut 1963.

——— (ed.). *The Encyclopedia of Indian Philosophies*. Delhi 1970.

Prabhu, J. (ed.) "The Intercultural Challange of R. Panikkar." In *Maryknoll:* New York 1996.

Prabhu, P. H. *Hindu Social Organization*. Bombay 1963.

Prasad, G. *Rig Veda*, 3 vols. Mathura 1969.

Prasad, H. S. (ed.). *Time in Indian Philosophy*. Delhi 1992.

Pusalker, A. D. *Studies in the Epics and Puranas*. Bombay 1951.

Pye, M., and R. Morgan (eds.). *The Cardinal Meaning: Essays in Comparative Hermeneutics: Buddhism and Christianity*. The Hague 1975.

Radhakrishnan, S., and C. A. Moore (eds.). *Indian Philosophy,* 2 vols. London (vol. 1) 1923, (vol. 2) 1927.

———. *A Source Book in Indian Philosophy*. Princeton 1957.

Radhakrishnan, S., and J. H. Muirhead. *The Philosophy of the Unpanisads*. London 1935.

———. *Contemporary Indian Philosophy*. London 1936, 1952.

Radhakrishnan, S. *The Philosophy of Rabindranath Tagore*. London 1918.

——— (ed.). *History of Philosophy Eastern and Western,* 2 vols. London 1952–1953.

———. *Die Gemeinschaft des Geistes.* Darmstadt 1953.

———. *East and West: Some Reflections.* London 1955.

———. *Die Bhagavadgîtâ.* Baden-Baden 1958.

——— (trans.). *The Brahma Sutra: The Philosophy of Spiritual Life.* London 1960.

Radhakrishnan, S., and P. T. Raju (eds.). *The Concept of Man: A Study in Comparative Philosophy.* London 1960.

Raju, P. T. *Idealistic Thought of India.* Cambridge 1953.

———. *Lectures on Comparative Philosophy.* Poona 1969.

———. *Introduction to Comparative Philosophy.* Carbondale 1970.

———. *The Philosophical Traditions of India.* London 1971.

———. *Spirit, Being and Self: Studies in Indian and Western Philosophy.* New Delhi 1982.

Raman, K. V. *Nagarjuna's Philosophy as Presented in the Maha- Prajnaparmita-Sastra.* New Delhi 1978.

Randle, H. N. *Indian Logic in Early Schools.* London 1930.

Rangacarya, M. R. B. (ed.). *The Sarva-Siddhanta-Sangraha of Sankaracarya.* Madras 1909.

Ranke-Graves, R. *Griechische Mythologie,* 2 vols. Reinbek bei Hamburg 1955.

Rawls, J. *A Theory of Justice.* Cambridge 1971.

———. "The Idea of an Overlapping Consensus." *Oxford Journal of Legal Studies* 7 (1987): 1–25.

Rescher, N. *Pluralism: Against the Demand of Consensus.* Oxford 1993.

Richard, H. *Platonica.* London 1911.

Richardson, J., and J. Lambert. *The Sociology of Race.* Lancashire 1985.

Ricoeur, P. *History and Truth,* edited by C. A. Kelbley. Evanston 1965.

———. *The Conflict of Interpretations: Essays in Hermeneutics,* edited by Don Ihde, translated by Willis Domingo. Evanston 1974.

———. *Geschichte und Wahrheit.* Munich 1974.

———. "Philosophical Hermeneutics and Theological Hermeneutics." In *Philosophy of Religion and Theology: The American Academy of Religion* (1975).

Riepe, D. *The Naturalistic Tradition in Indian Thought.* Washington 1961.

———. *The Philosophy of India and Its Impact on America's Thought.* Springfield 1970.

Ritter, J. (ed.). *Historisches Wörterbuch,* vols. 4 and 7. Basel/Stuttgart 1971.

Rorty, R. *Philosophy as the Mirror of Nature.* Oxford 1980.

———. *Beyond Objectivism and Relativism.* Philadelphia 1983.

———. "Habermas and Lyotard on Postmodernity." *Praxis International* 4, no. 1 (1984).

Rossmann, K. (ed.). *Deutsche Geschichtsphilosophie von Lessing bis Jaspers.* Basel 1959.

Rostovzeff, M. *Geschichte der antiken Welt,* 2 vols. Wiesbaden 1941.

Roy, K. *Hermeneutics: East and West.* Calcutta 1993.

Rüb, M. "Konsens, Dissens und Individualität." *Merkur* (1989).

Ruben, W. *Indische und griechische Metaphysik.* Leipzig 1931.

Rudolph, E. "Mit Blick auf Europa selbst." *Dialektik,* no. 2 (1997): 11–31.

Russell, B. *A History of Western Philosophy.* London 1946.

Saher, P. J. *Indische Weisheit und das Abendland.* Meisenheim 1965.

Said, E. W. *Orientalism.* London 1978.

———. *Culture and Imperialism.* London 1994.

Samkara. *Sarvasiddhanta-samgraha,* translated by P. S. Bose. Calcutta 1929.

Sandvoss, R. E. *Geschichte der Philosophie,* 2 vols. Munich 1989.

Sarkar, B. K. *The Political Institutions and Theories of the Hindus.* Calcutta 1939.

Scheler, M. *Gesammeize Werke,* vol. 5, Bern 1954.

———. *Schriften aus dem Nachlaß I: Zur Ethik und Erkenntnislehre.* Bern 1957.

———. *Philosophische Weltanschauung.* Munich 1968.

———. *Die Idee des Friedens und der Pazifismus,* edited by M. S. Frings. Munich 1974.

———. *Späte Schriften,* vol. 9. Bern 1976.

Schilling, K. *Weltgeschichte der Philosophie.* Berlin 1964.

Schilpp, P. A. (ed.). *The Philosophy of Sarvepalli Radhakrishnan.* New York 1952.

Schlegel, F. *Über die Sprache und Weisheit der Indier.* Heidelberg 1808.

Schleiermacher, F. (ed.). "Platon, Des Sokrates Verteidigung." In *Platon, Xenophon, Memorabilien.* Munich 1960.

Schopenhauer, A. *Werke in 5 Bdn.* Zürich 1988.

Schott, R. "Das Geschichtsbewußtsein schriftloser Völker." *Archiv für Begriffsgeschichte* 12 (1968): 166–201.

Schroeder, L. V. *Pythagoras und die Inder.* Leipzig 1984.

Schuhmann, K. *Husserl-Chronik.* The Hague 1977.

———. "Malvine Husserls Skizze eines Lebensbildes von E. Husserl." *Husserl Studies,* no. 5 (1988): 106–28.

Schwab, R. *La Renaissance orientale.* Paris 1950.

Schweitzer, A. *Die Weltanschauung der indischen Denker.* Berlin 1971.

Seal, B. N. *The Positive Sciences of the Ancient Hindus.* London 1915.

Seebohm, T. *Zur Kritik der hermeneutischen Vernunft.* Bonn 1972.

Shankara. *Das Kleinod der Unterscheidung (Viveka-chudamani), Die Erkenntnis der Wahrheit (Tattva-Bodha),* edited by K. von Friedrichs, Munich 1981.

Sharma, C. *A Critical Survey of Indian Philosophy.* Delhi 1976.

Sharma, D. *The Differentiation Theory of Meaning in Indian Logic.* The Hague 1969.

———. *The Negative Dialectics of India.* East Lansing 1970.

Sharma, D. S. *Dialectic in Buddhism and Vedanta.* Benares 1928.

Sharma, I. C. *Ethical Philosophy of India.* New York 1970.

Sharma, Y. (ed.). *Caraka-Samhitâ.* Bombay 1933.

Shastra, P. D. *The Essentials of Eastern Philosophy.* New York 1928.

Shastri, D. *A Short History of Indian Materialism: Sensationalism and Hedonism.* Calcutta 1930.

Shastri, P. *Introduction to Purva Mimamsa.* Calcutta 1923.

Shastri, P. D. *The Doctrine of Maya in the Philosophy of the Vedanta.* London 1911.

Simmel. G. *Die Probleme der Geschichtsphilosophie.* Leipzig 1893.

Sinari, R. A. *The Structure of Indian Thought.* Springfield 1970.

Smart, J. J. C. "The River of Time." *Mind* 58 (1949).

Smart, N. *Doctrine and Argument in Indian Philosophy.* London 1964.

———. *World Philosophies.* London/New York 1999.

Smith, A. G. (ed.). *Communication and Culture.* New York 1966.

Snell, B. *Die Entwicklung des Geistes.* Hamburg 1946.

———. *Leben und Meinungen der Sieben Weisen.* Munich 1952.

Sokolowski, R. *Moral Action: A Phenomenological Study.* Bloomington 1985.

Soyinka, W. *Diese Vergangenheit muß sich ihrer Gegenwart stellen.* Zürich 1988.

Spinner, H. F. "Theoretical Pluralism." *Kommunikation* 4 (1968): 181–201

Sprung, M. (ed.). *The Question of Being: East-West Perspectives.* London 1978.

Srinivas, M. N. *Caste in Modern India and other Essays.* Bombay 1962.

Srinivasachari, P. N. *The Philosophy of Bhedabheda.* Adyar 1950.

Srivastava, R. S. *Contemporary Indian Philosophy.* Delhi 1965.

Staal, J. F. *Advaita and Neo-Platonism: A Critical Study in Comparative Philosophy.* Madras 1961.

Stagenhagen, K. *Absolute Stellungnahme: Eine ontologische Untersuchung über das Wesen der Religion.* Erlangen 1925.

Stcherbatsky, T. *Buddhist Logic,* 2 vols. New York 1962.

Steinbach, K. *Die informierte Gesellschaft.* Stuttgart 1966.

Stenzel, J. *Platon der Erzieher.* Leipzig 1928.

———. "Der Begriff der Erleuchtung bei Platou." In *Kleine Schriften zur griechischen Philosophie.* Darmstadt 1956.

Steuchus, A. *De perenni philosophia.* London 1974.

Stocker, M. *Plural and Conflicting Values.* Oxford 1990.

Störig, H. J. *Kleine Weltgeschichte der Philosophie,* 2 vols. Stuttgart 1961.

Strasser, S. "Das Gottesproblem in der Spätphilosophie E. Husserls." *Philos. Jahrbuch der Görres-Gesellschaft* 67 (1959): 130–32.

Strauß, V. (ed.). *Tao Te King.* Zürich 1959.

Strawson, P. F. *Individuals: An Essay in Descriptive Metaphysics.* London 1959.

Sumner, C. I. *African Philosophy.* Adis Abeba 1980.

———. *Sources of African Philosophy.* Stuttgart 1986.

———. *The Source of African Philosophy: The Ethiopian Philosophy of Man.* Stuttgart 1986.

Tagore, R. *Sadhana*. Munich 1921.

———. *Boundless Sky: An Anthology*, edited by R. S. Das. Calcutta 1964.

Takakusu, J., Wing-tsit C., and C. A. Moore (ed.). *The Essentials of Buddhist Philosophy*. Honolulu 1974.

Thibaut, G. (ed.). *Sacred Books of the East, XXXIV and XXXVIII* Oxford 1986.

Thompson, J. B. *Critical Hermeneutics*. Cambridge 1983.

Thyssen, J. *Geschichte der Geschichtsphilosophie*. Berlin 1936.

Tillich, P. *The Protestant Era*. Chicago 1948.

Topitsch, E. *Die Sozialphilosophie Hegels als Heilslehre und Herrschaftsideologie*. Berlin 1967.

Totok, W. *Handbuch der Geschichte der Philosophie*, 4 vols. Frankfurt 1964.

Toynbee, A. *A Study of History*, 10 vols. Oxford 1933–1954.

———. *A Study of History: Abridgement of Volumes I–VI*, edited by D. C. Somervell. Oxford 1947.

———. *Der Gang der Weltgeschichte*. Stuttgart 1950.

———. *A Study of History*, edited by A. Toynbee and J. Caplan. New York 1972.

Troeltsch, E. *Der Historismus und seine Probleme*. Tübingen 1922.

Tymieniecka, A.-T. (ed.). *Phenomenology of Life in a Dialogue Between Chinese and Occidental Philosophy*. Belmont 1984.

Überweg, F. *Grundriß der Geschichte der Philosophie*, 5 vols. Berlin 1923–1928.

Ulenbrook, J. (ed.). *Tao Te King*. Frankfurt 1980.

Unger, U. "Die Namen des Tao-Lao Tsi XXV." *Sinologische Rundbriefe*, no. 18. Münster 1982.

van der Leeuw, G. *Phänomenologie der Religion*. Tübingen 1956.

Vattimo, G. *The End of Modernity: Nihilism and Hermeneutics of Postmodern Culture*. Baltimore 1988.

Venkateswara, S. V. *Indian Culture through the Ages*. London 1928.

Verges, F. G. " Rorty and the New Hermeneutics." *Philosophy* 62, no. 241 (1987): 307–23.

Vidyabhusana, S. C. *A History of Indian Logic*. Calcutta 1921.

Vireswarananda, S. *Brahmasutras*. Calcutta 1936.

von Samosata, L. *Sämtliche Werke*, edited by T. M. von Übersetzung. Leipzig 1788–1789.

Vorländer, K. *Geschichte der Philosophie*, edited by E. von Metzke and A. Hamburg 1949.

Vyas, K. C. *Social Renaissance in India*. Bombay 1957.

Waldenfels, B. *Der Stachel des Fremden*. Frankfurt 1990.

Waley, A. (trans.). *The Analects of Confucius*. London 1938.

Waligora, M. "Albert Schweitzer über Indien." *Conceptus* 25, no. 65 (1991): S. 47–55.

Weber, A. "Die Griechen in Indien." *Sitzungsberichte der Preußischen Akademie der Wissenschaften*. Berlin 1890.

Weinmayr, E. "Denken im Übergang—Kitarô Nishida und Martin Heidegger." *Japan und Martin Heidegger,* edited by H. von Buchner. Sigmaringen 1989.

Welleser, M. (ed.). *Die mittlere Lehre des Nagarjuna nach der chinesischen Version übertragen.* Heidelberg 1904.

Welsch, W. *Wege aus der Moderne: Schlüsseltexte der Postmoderne-Diskussion.* Weinheim 1988.

West, M. L. *Early Greek Philosophy and the Orient.* Oxford 1971.

Wierlacher, A. (ed.). *Das Fremde und das Eigene: Prolegomena zu einer interkulturellen Germanistik.* Munich 1985.

Wilamowitz-Moellendorf, U. V. *Platon: Sein Leben und seine Werke,* vol. 2. Frankfurt 1969.

Wilhelm, R. *Lao-Tse und der Taoismus.* Stuttgart 1948.

———. *Dschung Dsi, Das wahre Buch vom südlichen Blütenland.* Düsseldorf 1969.

———. *Laotse, Tao te King.* Cologne 1979.

——— (ed.). *Kungfutse, Gespräche, Lun Yü.* Cologne 1967.

Willmer, A. *Zur Dialektik von Moderne und Postmoderne.* Frankfurt 1985.

Willson, A. L. *A Mythical Image: The Ideal of India in German Romanticism.* Durham 1964.

Wimmer, F. *Interkulturelle Philosophie: Geschichte und Theorie,* 2 vols. Vienna 1990.

——— (ed.). *Vier Fragen zur Philosophie in Afrika, Asien und Lateinamerika.* Vienna 1988.

——— (ed.). *Postkoloniale Philosophie: Afrika.* Vienna 1992.

Winch, P. *The Idea of Social Science and Its Relation to Philosophy.* London 1958.

Windelband, W. *Lehrbuch der Geschichte der Philosophie,* edited by H. von Heimsoeth. Tübingen 1957.

Wiredu, K. *Philosophy and an African Culture.* Cambridge 1980.

———. "On an African Orientation in Philosophy." *Second Order* 1, no. 2 (1972).

———. "Some Contemporary Issues in Philosophy in Africa." *Teaching and Research in Philosophy: Africa,* edited by UNESCO. Paris 1984.

Wittfogel, K. A. "Hegel über China." *Unter dem Banner des Marxismus* 5 (1931): 346–62.

Wright, E. (ed.). *Studies in Chinese Thought.* Chicago 1953.

Wright, R. A. *African Philosophy: An Introduction.* Washington, D.C. 1977.

Yu-Lan, F. *A Short History of Chinese Philosophy.* New York 1958.

———. *A History of Chines Philosophy,* 2 vols., translated by D. Bodde. Princeton 1973.

——— (trans.). *Chung-Tzu: A New Selected Translation with an Exposition of the Philosophy of Kuo Hsiang.* Shanghai 1933.

Yutang, L. *The Wisdom of Confucius.* New York 1938.

——— (ed.). *The Wisdom of Laotse.* New York 1948.

———. *The Wisdom of China and India.* New York 1942.

Zea, L. *La Filosofia Latinoamericana.* Mexico 1978.

—————. *Signale aus dem Abseits—Eine lateinamerikanische Philosophie der Geschichte.* Munich 1989.

Zeller, E. *Grundriß der Geschichte der griechischen Philosophie.* Leipzig 1920.

Zimmer, H. *Philosophies of India.* New York 1957.

Zücher, E. *The Buddhist Conquest of China.* Leiden 1959.

Index

Absolute of Consciousness, 84
absolutism, 8, 99–107; analogous
hermeneutics vs., 18, 101;
"Cartesian anxiety" and, 100;
Chinese perception of, 100;
Christianity and, 100, 105–106;
descriptive metaphysics and, 99;
fundamentalism vs., 107; Indian
perception of, 102–104;
interreligiosity in, 100–102; Islam
and, 100; metaphysics and, 99;
overlapping structures and, 100–101;
pluralism vs., 102, 105, 106;
postmodernism and, 38, 40–41;
relativism vs., 99–100; revisionary
metaphysics, 99; tolerance and,
104–107; Truth and, 100, 103–104;
unity vs. uniformity, 47, 50, 51, 53, 54,
55; values, philosophy of, 102–104
Adorno, Theodor, 9
Africa, 35, 110
agathon, Supreme Reality and, 74–80
Alexander the Great, 7, 35, 109
analogous hermeneutics, xiii, 3, 13–23,
28; absolutism vs., 18, 101;
"analogy" defined for, 15–16;
anthropocentrism in, 19–20, 21–22;
Asia vs. Europe in, 19; centrism vs., 18;
commensurability vs.
incommensurability in, 16–17;
comparative philosophy and, 17;
"compossibility " in, 15; cultural
traditions and, 16–17; defining
analogous hermeneutics, 16; diversity
in, 15; East–West dichotomy in, 19;
Eurocentrism in, 13, 14; Indian
culture and philosophy in, 15, 17–18;

Indian vs. Aristotelian logic in, 20–21;
"interculturality" defined in, 14–15,
17–19; logic and, 20–21; non-
European philosophy and, 13;
overlapping structures in, 14, 16;
pluralism in, 15, 16; relativism and,
18–19; religious traditions and, 16–18,
22, 28, 101; second renaissance and,
17; theocentrism and, 20, 21–22;
third renaissance and, 18; translating
cultures in, 14, 16; understanding
and, 13; univerism in, 19–22;
universalism and, 14, 16, 19–22;
Western philosophy in, 15
analogy defined in analogous
hermeneutics, 15–16
anarchism, postmodernism and, 40
animism, 22
anthropocentrism, analogous
hermeneutics in, 19–20, 21–22
anthropomorphism, 27
apocalyptic belief and perception of time,
linear vs. cyclical, 61–62
Aquinas, Thomas; analogous
hermeneutics and, 28; on God,
perception of, 92
Aristotelian syndrome, Eurocentricism,
116
Aristotle, analogous hermeneutics and,
21
artha, 103
Aryan culture and philosophy (*See also*
Indian culture and philosophy; Hindu
culture and philosophy; Vedic culture
and philosophy),
7, 17
Asia, 35, 110

145

Bello, Angela Alles, on God, perception of, 88
Bernstein, Richard, on Absolutism, 100
Betti, on unity vs. uniformity, 56–57
Boidi, Christina, on Eurocentricism, 118
Brahmanic concept of Supreme Reality, 69–74, 79–80
British imperialism, 7, 49
Buber, on tolerance, 107
Buddha; on tolerance, 107; on unity vs. uniformity, 49
Buddhism, 8, 17, 21, 110; Absolutism and, 101; on God, perception of, 88–89; unity vs. uniformity and, 49

"Cartesian anxiety" and Absolutism, 100
Cartesian way in perception of God, 86
Central American perception of time, linear vs. cyclical, 61
centrism, analogous hermeneutics vs., 18
charity, principle of, 8
Chinese culture and philosophy 8, 19, 21, 30; Absolutism and, perception of, 100, 105; time, linear vs. cyclical in, 61, 63; unity vs. uniformity in, 49, 50
Christianity, 17, 28, 38, 109; Absolutism and, 100, 101, 105–106; Eurocentricism and, 112–113, 115, 119–120; God, perception of, 88; intolerance and, 106; time, perception of, linear vs. cyclical, 61–62; unity vs. uniformity and, 49, 50, 51–52
Clash of Civilization, The, 14, 115, 118
Collingwood, on unity vs. uniformity, 56–57
colonialism, 5, 8, 17, 22, 35, 38, 110
Columbus, Christopher, 35
commensurability vs. incommensurability in analogous hermeneutics, 16–17
communication (*See also* understanding; reciprocity), 25
communism, intolerance and, 106
comparative philosophy; analogous hermeneutics, 17; postmodernism and, 41–42

"compossibility" in analogous hermeneutics in, 15
"concrete universal" of Hegel, 36
Confucianism, 8; God, perception of, 87, 88; unity vs. uniformity and, 49
Confucius; analogous hermeneutics and, 21; time view of, linear vs. cyclical, 63
continua of humans and nature, 19
contradiction, law of, 21, 26
Council of Nicaea, 117
creative hermeneutics, 58
Critique of Pure Reason, 17
cultural influence on philosophy, 1–2, 4–5, 26; analogous hermeneutics, 16; defining culture, 4; multiculturality, 8–9
culturalism, 2
Cusanus, on Eurocentricism, 112
cyclical conception of time, 59–67

Davidson, Donald, 8; analogous hermeneutics and, 16
Dayananda, analogous hermeneutics and, 28
de Groot, J.J.M., analogous hermeneutics and, 19
deconstructivism, postmodernism and, 40
democracy, postmodernism and, 38
Derrida; analogous hermeneutics and, 14; on Eurocentricism, 111; postmodernism and, 41, 42; on Supreme Reality, 78
descriptive metaphysics, in Absolutism, 99
Deussen, on *philosophia perennis*, 29–30
dharma, 103
Dialogues of Plato, 75–76, 77, 78, 80
Dilthey, Wilhelm, on unity vs. uniformity, 52, 53, 56–57
Diogenes Laertius, on Eurocentricism, 111
Dion, 74
Dionysii, 74
diversity, 31; analogous hermeneutics in, 15; postmodernism and, 39, 40
Dravidian culture and philosophy (*See also* Vedic culture and philosophy), 7

Dumery, H., on God, perception of, 88
Duroselle, Jean–Baptiste, on
  Eurocentricism, 117

Eastern philosophy (*See* non-European
  philosophy; also *See* specific cultures)
East–West dichotomy; analogous
  hermeneutics and, 19;
  postmodernism and, 36–37, 42
ekam sad, 25, 30, 32, 105
Eliade, Mircea, 2, 13; on Eurocentricism,
  110–111; on unity vs. uniformity, 58
epistemologically oriented hermeneutics,
  3
ethos, unity vs. uniformity, 56–57
Eurocentrism, 5, 9, 10, 119–120;
  analogous hermeneutics vs., 13, 14;
  postmodernism and, 37, 42; unity vs.
  uniformity in, 50
Europe and European thought,
  109–123; Aristotelian syndrome
  and, 116; Christianity in, 112–113,
  115, 119–120; colonialism and,
  110; culture of, 113–116; defining
  "European" identity, 109–111;
  emergence of Europe, 111–112;
  Eurocentrism, 119–120;
  European philosophy and, 112;
  Europeanization of the world and,
  113, 119–120; God as perceived in,
  114; history of, 120–122; imperialism
  and, 110; non-European philosophy,
  110; non-European view of, 121;
  reason or *logos* in, 112–113;
  Renaissance in, 110–111; second
  Renaissance in, 110–111; Truth as
  perceived by, 115; unity and, 116–117;
  veracity of, 117–118
European philosophy, 3, 30, 112; unity
  vs. uniformity in, 49
Europeanization of world, 37, 113,
  119–120

foreign cultures, reaction to, 4, 7, 35, 49
French revolution, intolerance and, 106
Fuentes, Carl, on Eurocentricism, 122
fundamentalism vs. Absolutism, 107

Gadamer; analogous hermeneutics and,
  15, 16, 18, 19, 22; on unity vs.
  uniformity, 50, 52, 53, 56–57
Gandhi; Absolutism and, 106; analogous
  hermeneutics and, 28; tolerance and,
  107
Gandhi, Mahatma, 8
Gazni, Mahmud, 7
God (*See also* Supreme Reality), 83–97;
  Absolute of Consciousness as, 84;
  belief vs. philosophy and, 92–93;
  Buddhist perception of, 88–89;
  Cartesian way and, 86; Christian
  perception of, 88; Confucian
  perception of, 87, 88; on
  Eurocentricism, 114; Hegel's
  perception of, 89–90; historical vs.
  philosophical paths to, 85; Hume's
  perception of, 89–90; Huserl's
  perception of, 83–97; monistic God,
  88; noematic God, 92–93;
  phenomenological concept of, 83–97;
  phenomenological vs. teleological vs.
  theological, 85–87; phenomenology
  and, 90–91; phenomenology of
  religion and, 87–89; Scheler's
  perception of, 90–91; search for,
  86–87; Taoist perception of, 88–89;
  teleology and, 84–85; theological God,
  85–87; time, linear vs. cyclical, 60;
  transcendent God, 83, 86, 87, 90–91
Goethe, on Eurocentricism, 112–113
Gould, Stephen Jay, 62
Granet, Marcel, on analogous
  hermeneutics, 21
Greek culture, unity vs. uniformity, 49

Habermas, 7; analogous hermeneutics
  and, 16; on postmodernism, 38
Halbfass, Wilhelm, on Eurocentricism,
  110
harmony, law of, 21
Hegel, 5, 10; analogous hermeneutics
  and, 17, 22, 31; on Eurocentricism,
  111, 113–116, 119; on God, perception
  of, 89–90; *philosophia perennis* of,
  29–30; postmodernism and, 36, 37, 38,

39, 42; on unity vs. uniformity, 45, 47, 49–52
Heidegger, 10; analogous hermeneutics and, 19; on Eurocentrism, 111–112, 118, 119; *philosophia perennis* of, 29–30; on unity vs. uniformity, 50, 52, 53, 56–57
hen, Supreme Reality and, 74–80
Henningsen, on Eurocentrism, 116
henotheism, 27
"hermeneutic circle"; postmodernism and, 42; unity vs. uniformity and, 54
hermeneutics (*See also* analogous hermeneutics), 2–3; absolutism and, 54, 55; analogous (*See* analogous hermeneutics); creative hermeneutics, 58; epistemologically oriented, 3; ethos of, 56–57; four-fold system of, 3; hermeneutic circle in, 42, 54; insight and, 56; interreligiosity in, 100–102; nonreductive, open, normative, 52–58; pluralism and, 56; Truth and, 54; understanding in, 52–58; unity vs. uniformity and, 52–58; *Weltanschauungen* and, 55
Herodotus, analogous hermeneutics and, 19
Herra, Rafael Angel, on Eurocentrism, 116
Hindu culture and philosophy (*See also* Aryan culture and philosophy; Indian culture and philosophy; Vedic culture and philosophy), 7, 28–29; Absolutism and, 101; time, perception of, linear vs. cyclical, 61, 62–63; Trinity of, 28
historical perspective of philosophy, 8
historicity and time, linear vs. cyclical, 65–66
history; Eurocentric view of, 120–122; time, cyclical vs. linear perception of, 59–67; unity vs. uniformity, 48, 51
Horizontverschmelzung, 15
Hulsmann, on Eurocentrism, 120
human rights, postmodernism and, 38
Hume, on God, perception of, 83, 89–90

Huntington, Samuel P.; analogous hermeneutics and, 14; on Eurocentrism, 115, 118
Husserl, 10; on Eurocentrism, 111, 113–114, 119; God, perception of, 83–97; *philosophia perennis*, 29–30; postmodernism and, 37, 42; on time, linear vs. cyclical, 64
Huxley, Aldous, analogous hermeneutics and, 30

imperialism, 5, 22, 35, 38, 110
Indian culture and philosophy (*See also* Hindu culture and philosophy; Vedic philosophy), 7, 17, 27–29, 30, 35, 37, 109; Absolutism and, 102–104; *artha, kama, moska, dharma* in, 103; hermeneutic tradition of, 15; karma in, 63; knowledge in, 102–104; rebirth/reincarnation in, 63; time perception of, linear vs. cyclical, 62–63; unity vs. uniformity and, 49, 50; values, philosophy of, 102–104
insight, unity vs. uniformity, 56
intercultural philosophy defined, xi–xiii, 5–7
interculturality, 9–11, 14–15; analogous hermeneutics and, 17–19; postmodernism and, 36–37, 41–42
interreligiosity and Absolutism, 100–102
Islamic culture and philosophy, 7–8; Absolutism and, 100, 101; unity vs. uniformity and, 49

Jaina philosophy, 21, 31
James, on time, linear vs. cyclical, 64
Japsers, Karl; analogous hermeneutics and, 19, 30; Absolutism and, 106; on Eurocentrism, 115, 118; *philosophia perennis* of, 29–30; postmodernism and, 37; tolerance and, 107; on unity vs. uniformity, 46, 47, 50, 56–57
Jesus, tolerance and, 107

kama, 103
Kant, Emanuel; Absolutism and, 103; analogous hermeneutics and, 17
karma, 63
King Milinda's debate, 7
Kluckhohn, C., on understanding other cultures, 4
knowledge, in Indian philosophy, 102–104
Koran, 102
Kroeber, A., on understanding other cultures, 4
Kulturkampf, intolerance and, 106

Lao Tzu, 21, 112
Latin America, 110, 118
liberalism, postmodernism and, 38
Lichtenberg, Georg, 8; on Eurocentricism, 110
Liebnitz, analogous hermeneutics and, 15
linear conception of time, 59–67
logic, 20–21, 26, 31; analogous hermeneutics and, 20–21; contradiction, law of, 21; Eurocentric, 112–113; harmony, law of, 21; Indian vs. Aristotelian, 20–21; Supreme Reality and, 76–77
logos, 10, 22
logos qua logos , 5
Lowith, Karl; analogous hermeneutics and, 19; on Eurocentricism, 115; on time, linear vs. cyclical, 66
Lyotard, postmodernism and, 38, 39–40

Marx, Karl; postmodernism and, 38; on unity vs. uniformity, 47
Meier, Christian, on Eurocentricism, 120–121
Mensching, Gustav, on Absolutism, 105–106
metaphysics and Absolutism, 99
metaphysics of unity (Hegel), 45
metonymic theory of Truth, 31–32
metoynymy, 113

minorities, 9
Misch, on unity vs. uniformity, 56–57
missionarism, 5, 17, 22, 35, 38
Mohanty, Jitendra Nath, on time, linear vs. cyclical, 65
monism, 88
monoculturalism and postmodernism, 36
monotheism, 27, 40, 104
moska, 103
Muller, F. Max, analogous hermeneutics and, 17, 27
multiculturality, 8–9
Muslim (*See* Islam)

Nagasena, 7
Native American culture and philosophy, 8
negativism, Supreme Reality vs., 70, 78–79
Neumann, on God, perception of, 88–89
Nicholas of Cusa, on Absolutism, 100, 105
Nietzche; postmodernism and, 38; on time, linear vs. cyclical, 63
nihilism; postmodernism and, 40; Supreme Reality vs., 70
noematic God, 92–93
non-European philosophy, 5, 10, 13, 36, 110
Nordhofen, Eckhard, on Eurocentricism, 109

One (*See* Supreme Reality)
Orientalism, 115
overlapping structures; Absolutism, 100–101; analogous hermeneutics and, 14, 16; intercultural philosophy and, 6

panactivism/panpessimism, unity vs. uniformity, 57
Panikkar, Raimon, on Eurocentricism, 109
Pannwitz, Rudolf, postmodernism and, 38

particularity, 25–26
perennial philosophy (*See also philosophia perennis*), 30
perspective differences in understanding, 3
phenomenology, God, perception of, 83–97
philosophia perennis, 28, 29–31, 37
philosophy defined, xi–xiii, 1–2
Plato, Supreme Reality and, Seventh Epistle of, 74–80
Platonic dialectic, 76
pluralism, 2, 4, 6, 9; Absolutism vs., 102, 105, 106; analogous hermeneutics and, 15, 16; postmodernism and, 39, 42; Supreme Reality vs., 76; unity vs. uniformity vs., 46, 56
political influence on philosophy, 2, 6, 26
polytheism, 27, 40, 104
postmodernity, 35–44; absolutism and, 38, 40–41; anarchism and, 40; colonialism in, 38; comparative philosophy in, 41–42; deconstructivism and, 40; democracy and, 38; diversity in, 39, 40; East–West dichotomy in, 36–37, 42; Eurocentrism and, 37, 42; Europeanization and, 37; foreign cultures in, 35; Habermas and, 38; Hegel in, 39; "hermeneutic circle" in, 42; human rights in, 38; imperialism in, 38; interculturality and, 36–37, 41–42; liberalism and, 38; Lyotard and, 38, 39–40; missionarism in, 38; monoculturalism and, 36; nihilism and, 40; *philosophia perennis* in, 37; plurality in, 39, 42; postmodernity defined, 38–41; relativism and, 40; religion and, 40; solipsism and, 40; strong version of, 40; Toynbee's coining of term, 38; Truth in, 36, 41, 43; understanding in, 43; unified subject theory of, 36; universalism and, 41, 42; weak version of, 40; Westernization of the world and, 37; world language and, 35, 41

reason; Eurocentric, 112–113; Supreme Reality and, 76–77
rebirth/reincarnation, 63
reciprocity of understanding, 3, 4, 6, 8, 26, 36, 110
Reformation and unity vs. uniformity, 51
relativism; Absolutism vs., 99–100; analogous hermeneutics and, 18–19; postmodernism and, 40; unity vs. uniformity and, 50
religio perennis, 28–29
religion, 6–8, 26–29; analogous hermeneutics and 16, 18, 22, 28, 101; God of phenomenology vs. theology in, 83–97; interreligiosity vs., 100–102; monisim in, 88; phenomenology of, 87–89; postmodernism and, 40; *religio perennis*, 28–29; time perception of, cyclical vs. linear, 59–67; tolerance in, 104–107; unity vs. uniformity in, 47, 50, 51–52
Renaissance, 110–111
Republic, The, 76
revisionary metaphysics, Absolutism and, 99
Ricoeur, analogous hermeneutics and, 14
rigvedas, 105, 112–113
Roman culture, unity vs. uniformity in, 49
Roy, Ram Mohan, analogous hermeneutics and, 28

Said, Edward, on Eurocentricism, 115
sanatana dharma, 28–29
Sanskrit, 17, 110
Scheler, Max, 2; analogous hermeneutics and, 22; on God, perception of, 90–91; *philosophia perennis* of, 29–30; on unity vs. uniformity, 45, 50–51, 56–57
Schopenhauer; *philosophia perennis* of, 29–30; on unity vs. uniformity, 56–57
second Renaissance, Eurocentricism and, 110–111
secularism, intolerance and, 106

Shamkara's concept of Supreme Reality, 69–74, 79–80

Sharma, C., analogous hermeneutics and, 27

solipsism, postmodernism and, 40

Steuchus, Augustinus; analogous hermeneutics and, 30; *philosophia perennis* of, 29

Strasser, Stephan, on God, perception of, 87

Strawson, Peter Frederick, on Absolutism, 99

Sufi culture and philosophy, 8

Supreme Reality (*See also* absolutism; God), 26–27, 69–80; Brahman concept of, 69–74, 79–80; logic and, 76–77; negativism vs., 70, 78–79; nihilism vs., 70; Plato's Seventh Epistle and, 74–80; plurality vs., 76; reason and, 76–77; Shamkara's concept of, 69–74, 79–80; unity and, 76

syllogisms, 20–21

Tagore, Rabindra Nath, 122; on Absolutism, 102; analogous hermeneutics and, 28; postmodernism and, 43

Taoism, 8; God, perception of, 88–89; unity vs. uniformity in, 49

teleology, God, perception of, 84–85

temporality and time, linear vs. cyclical, 65–66

theocentrism, analogous hermeneutics and, 20, 21–22

theology (*See also* God; religion), 85–87

third renaissance and analogous hermeneutics, 18

Tilak, analogous hermeneutics and, 28

Tillich, on time, linear vs. cyclical, 63

Timaeus, 76–77, 79

time, cyclical vs. linear perception of, 59–67; anthropocentric bias in, 62; apocalyptic belief and, 61–62; Central American perception of, 61; Chinese perception of, 61, 63;

Christianity's perception of, 61–62; empirico-phenomenological approach to, 60–61; "eternal recurrence of same," 63; factors in time-consciousness, 64; God and, 60; Hindu perception of, 61, 62–63; historicity, 65–66; Indian perception of, 62–63; intercultural perspective of, 65; *karma* and, 63; rebirth/reincarnation, 63; temporality, 65–66; time-arrow concept, 61–62; time-cycle concept, 61–62

Time's Arrow, Time's Cycle, 62

tolerance, 8, 48–49, 104–107

Toynbee, Arnold; on Eurocentrism, 121; postmodernism and, 38; on time, linear vs. cyclical, 63

transcendental attitude, 26

transcendent God, 83, 86, 87, 90–91

translating cultures, 14, 16, 30

Trinity, Hindu, 28

Truth, 4–5, 26–27, 30–31; Absolutism vs., 100, 103–104; Eurocentric, 115; metonymic theory of, 31–32; postmodernism and, 36, 41, 43; tolerance and, 104–107; unity vs. uniformity and, 46, 54

Tzu, Chuang, 20, 22, 118

understanding, 3, 4, 6, 8, 10, 25, 26, 110; analogous hermeneutics and, 13; postmodernism and, 43; unity vs. uniformity and, 52–58

"unforced dialogue," 7

unified subject theory of postmodernism, 36

uniformity (*See* unity vs. uniformity)

unity vs. uniformity, 45–58; *Weltanschauungen* in, 46, 55; absolutism and, 47, 50, 51, 53, 54, 55; Christianity and, 50, 51–52; creative hermeneutics in, 58; ethos of, 56–57; Eurocentrism and, 50, 116–117; foreign cultures and, reaction to, 49; Hegel's philosophy of unity in, 49–52; hermeneutic circle in,

54; history and, 48, 51; insight and, 56; intolerance from misconception of, 48–49; metaphysics of unity (Hegel) in, 45; nonreductive, open, normative hermeneutics and, 52–58; panactivism/panpessimism in, 57; plurality vs., 46, 56; principle of unity in, 46–49; Reformation and, 51; relativism, 50; religion, and 47, 50, 51–52; Supreme Reality and, 76; Truth and, 46, 54; understanding in, 52–58; world era (*Weltalter*) and, 45

universalism, 2, 4; analogous hermeneutics and, 14, 16, 19–22; postmodernism and, 41, 42

universality, 25–26

Upanishads, 17, 110

Valery, on Eurocentricism, 111

values, philosophy of, 102–104

van der Leeuw, Gerardus, on God, perception of, 88

Vedic culture and philosophy (*See also* Hindu culture and philosophy; Indian culture and philosophy), 7, 17, 25, 26–31, 105

Vedic Dictum, 26–31; metonymic theory of Truth and, 31–32; *philosophia perennis* and, 29–31

Vico, on unity vs. uniformity, 56–57

von Samosata, Lukian, on Eurocentricism, 111

Weltalter, 2, 45

Weltanschauungen, 8, 19, 22, 31, 38; unity vs. uniformity, 46, 55

Western philosophy (*See* European philosophy)

Westernization of the world, postmodernism and, 37

Wimmer, Franz Martin, on Eurocentricism, 114

Wittgenstein; analogous hermeneutics and, 18; postmodernism and, 35, 41

world age (*Weltalter*), 2, 45

world language, postmodernism and, 35, 41

Zea, Leopoldo, on Eurocentrism, 10, 112

About the Author

Ram Adhar Mall is professor of philosophy at Bremen University, Germany. He received his M.A. in philosophy from Calcutta University and did further studies in philosophy in Calcutta, Göttingen, and Cologne, where he earned his Ph.D. in 1963. Returning to India, Mall joined the Philosophy Department of Jadavpur University, Calcutta. At the end of 1967, he came to Germany, worked at the Husserl-Archive, University of Cologne, with Professor Ludwig Landgrebe and did his "Habilitation" at the University of Trier, Germany, in 1981. Mall is the founding president of the International Society for Intercultural Philosophy and co-editor of the series "Studies in Intercultural Philosophy." He has taught at different Indian and German Universities. His main fields of interest are empiricism, phenomenology, hermeneutics, intercultural philosophy, and comparative religious studies.

Mall's publications include *Hume's Concept of Man: An Essay in Philosophical Anthropology* (1967), *Experience and Reason: The Phenomenology of Husserl and Its Relation to Hume's Philosophy* (1973), *Naturalism and Criticism* (1975), and many German-language works.